SECOND EDITION

STEP FORWARD

STANDARDS-BASED LANGUAGE LEARNING FOR WORK AND ACADEMIC READINESS

SERIES DIRECTOR
Jayme Adelson-Goldstein

Lesson Plans

Kristin Donnalley Sherman

OXFORD
UNIVERSITY PRESS

198 Madison Avenue
New York, NY 10016 USA

Great Clarendon Street, Oxford, OX2 6DP, United Kingdom

Oxford University Press is a department of the University of Oxford.
It furthers the University's objective of excellence in research, scholarship,
and education by publishing worldwide. Oxford is a registered trade
mark of Oxford University Press in the UK and in certain other countries

ISBN: 978 0 19 449287 4

Printed in China

This book is printed on paper from certified and well-managed sources

ACKNOWLEDGMENTS

Back cover photograph: Oxford University Press building/David Fisher

CONTENTS

1 Creativity

Unit Overview

This unit explores creativity, ways to increase it, and how it is stimulated by the brain with a range of employability skills and contextualizes multiple meanings and adverbials for writing. By the end of this unit, you will be able to conduct and present research on creativity.

KEY OBJECTIVES

Lesson 1	Identify aspects of creativity
Lesson 2	Identify ways to increase creativity
Lesson 3	Use context to select from multiple meanings of a word; employ formal adverbials in summary writing
Lesson 4	Read about creative people and discuss how the brain stimulates creativity
Lesson 5	Use the writing process to summarize an article
Lesson 6	Conduct and present research related to creativity

UNIT FEATURES

Academic Vocabulary	*alternative, approach, attitude, creative, cultivate, curiosity, encourage, inspire, spark, wonder*
Employability Skills	• Invent creative uses for everyday objects • Interpret an infographic • Synthesize ideas across readings, a lecture, and an infographic • Find solutions for bringing creativity into people's lives • Actively incorporate others into a discussion • Collaborate to research a topic • Clarify roles for delivering a group presentation

Resources	**Class Audio** CD1, Tracks 02–04
	Teacher Resource Center
	    Multilevel Activities 5 Unit 1
	    Multilevel Grammar Activities 5 Unit 1
	    Unit 1 Test
	Oxford Picture Dictionary Studying, Succeeding in School, Jobs and Occupations, Job Skills, Soft Skills, English Composition, Internet Research, Hobbies and Games, Electronics and Photography, Entertainment, Music

Lesson Overview

MULTILEVEL OBJECTIVES

On-level: Describe and talk about aspects of creativity
Pre-level: Identify aspects of creativity
Higher-level: Explain aspects of creativity

LANGUAGE FOCUS

Grammar: Simple present to describe self
Vocabulary: *creative, approach*, synonyms for *creativity*

For vocabulary support, see these **Oxford Picture Dictionary** topics: Hobbies and Games, pages 238–239; Electronics and Photography, pages 240–241; Entertainment, pages 242–243; Music, page 244

STRATEGY FOCUS

To match vocabulary and definitions, look for words that are related to the new words you want to learn.

READINESS CONNECTION

In this lesson, students learn about teamwork by conducting research together.

PACING

To compress this lesson: Conduct 1C as a whole-class activity.

To extend this lesson: Have students work in pairs to role-play approaches to creatively solving a problem (see page 5).

And/or have students complete **Multilevel Activities 5 Unit 1, Lesson 1**.

Lesson Notes

CORRELATIONS

CCRS: SL.8.1.a. Come to discussions prepared, having read or researched material under study; explicitly draw on that preparation by referring to evidence on the topic, text, or issue to probe and reflect on ideas under discussion.

SL.8.1.c. Pose questions that connect the ideas of several speakers and respond to others' questions and comments with relevant evidence, observations, and ideas.

SL.8.1.d. Acknowledge new information expressed by others, and, when warranted, qualify or justify their own views in light of the evidence presented.

L.6.4.c. Consult reference materials (e.g., dictionaries, glossaries, thesauruses), both print and digital, to find the pronunciation of a word or determine or clarify its precise meaning or its part of speech.

ELPS: ELP Standard 2

• participate in conversations, extended discussions, and written exchanges about a range of substantive topics, texts, and issues

• build on the ideas of others

• express his or her own ideas clearly and persuasively

• ask and answer questions that probe reasoning and claim

ELP Standard 8

using context, questioning, and consistent knowledge of English morphology,

• determine the meaning of general academic and content-specific words and phrases, figurative and connotative language, and idiomatic expressions in spoken and written texts about a variety of topics, experiences, or events

Warm-up and Review
10–15 minutes (books closed)

Show examples of different kinds of creative work: someone painting, playing music, performing in a play, reading aloud, etc. Ask: *What do these activities have in common? What qualities do you need to do these things?*

Introduction
5 minutes

1. Tell students creative activities you enjoy, whether you do them yourself or appreciate the work of others. Ask questions to elicit creative activities students enjoy.

2. State the objective: *Today we're going to think about and discuss aspects of creativity.*

1 Discuss creativity

Presentation I
20–25 minutes

 1. Group students and assign roles: manager, fact checker, recorder, and reporter. Explain that students will work with their group to brainstorm sources of information and categorize their list.

2. Check comprehension of the activity. Ask: *Who looks up the words in a dictionary?* [fact checker] *Who sorts words into categories?* [recorder] *Who tells the class your answers?* [reporter] *Who keeps everyone on track and manages time?* [manager]

3. Set a time limit (three minutes) and have students work together to complete the task.

4. Call time and have the reporters from each group take turns calling out their categories. Then elicit words for each category. Record students' answers on the board. If groups disagree, write each group's choice next to the word.

For 1A, use mixed-level groups.

• **On-level** Assign these students the roles of fact checker and reporter.

• **Pre-level** Assign these students the role of recorder.

• **Higher-level** Assign these students the role of manager.

When setting up task-based activities, verify that students understand their roles using physical commands. For example: *If you report on your team's work, stand up.* [reporter] *If you keep the team on task, point to the clock.* [manager] *If you write the words into categories, raise your hand.* [recorder] *If you look up words in the dictionary, hold up your dictionary/smartphone/tablet.* [fact checker]

B 1. Direct students to look at the definition. Ask: *To have creativity, what do you also need to have?* [skill and imagination] *What do you need to do?* [produce something new or produce art]

2. Write *creativity* on the board, and elicit synonyms and other word forms from the whole class. Write their ideas. Point out the connection between students' ideas and their responses in 1A.

Possible Answers

synonyms: *ingenuity, inventiveness, originality, imagination*
other forms of the word: *create, creative, creatively, creativeness*

C Direct students to look at the quiz. Call on students to read each statement aloud. Ask: *Which of the sentences does Linh strongly or somewhat agree with?* [1, 2, 4, 5] *Which does she strongly disagree with?* [3] Ask: *Do you think she is creative? Why? What shows Linh is creative in each statement?* Elicit answers from the whole class. Point out the connection between their ideas and the definition in 1B.

Guided Practice I
10–20 minutes

D 1. Direct students to look at the underlined words. Point to these forms of the word that you wrote in 1B. Elicit the parts of speech.

2. Tell students to look at the first question. Ask: *What is a synonym for* creative? [*imaginative*]

3. Set a time limit (five minutes). Direct students to work with their partners to complete the activity. Have a volunteer from each pair give their responses. Check answers as a class.

Possible Answers

1. Creative problem solving is finding new ways to solve a problem.
2. Question 3 is about creating things.
3. Question 1 is related to creativity because you have to be comfortable with new situations to be creative. Question 4 is related because you must have imagination to try to understand different points of view. Question 5 is related because it takes creativity to think of ideas to contribute when working with a team.

Presentation II
20–25 minutes

 1. Group students and assign roles: manager, recorder, reporter, and editor. Explain that students will work with their group to follow the steps. Verify students' understanding of the roles: the manager keeps track of time, the recorder writes the statement, the reporter reports back to the class, and the editor checks grammar and spelling.

2. Set a time limit (ten minutes) for students to complete the task. Write a sentence frame on the board: *We think that _____ is a way of being creative because it _____.*

3. Call time and have the reporters from each group take turns calling out their statements. If groups disagree, ask groups to explain their objections.

EXTENSION ACTIVITY

Creative Problem Solving

1. Ask students to work with a partner and role-play creative problem solving. Ask each pair to think of a problem they face at work or at home. Each partner should role-play a different approach to the problem.

2. Set a time limit (three minutes). Have students act out their role plays for the class.

3. Ask the class to discuss ways in which the students did or did not show their abilities to solve problems creatively with others.

Evaluation
10–15 minutes

SELF-ASSESSMENT

1. Ask students to spend some time reflecting on what they have learned.

2. Set a time limit (three minutes). Ask for volunteers to share their thoughts.

Lesson Overview	**Lesson Notes**

MULTILEVEL OBJECTIVES

On- and Higher-level: Read about, practice, and analyze alternative uses tasks (AUTs); listen and take and edit notes on boosting creativity

Pre-level: Read about the alternative uses task; listen and take notes on boosting creativity

LANGUAGE FOCUS

Grammar: Simple present

Vocabulary: *alternative*, expressions to introduce a lecture

For vocabulary support, see this **Oxford Picture Dictionary** topic: Job Skills, pages 176–178

STRATEGY FOCUS

When taking notes, use short phrases and abbreviations.

READINESS CONNECTION

In this lesson, students invent creative uses for everyday objects

PACING

To compress this lesson: Assign 1C and D for homework.

To extend this lesson: Have students complete an AUT for another common object (see page 8); Have students role-play a conversation about creativity in different jobs (see page 9).

And/or have students complete **Multilevel Activities 5 Unit 1, Lesson 2**.

CORRELATIONS

CCRS: RI/RL.7.1 Cite several pieces of textual evidence to support analysis of what the text says explicitly as well as inferences drawn from the text.

SL.8.1.a. Come to discussions prepared, having read or researched material under study; explicitly draw on that preparation by referring to evidence on the topic, text, or issue to probe and reflect on ideas under discussion.

SL.8.1.c. Pose questions that connect the ideas of several speakers and respond to others' questions and comments with relevant evidence, observations, and ideas.

SL.8.1.d. Acknowledge new information expressed by others, and, when warranted, qualify or justify their own views in light of the evidence presented.

ELPS: ELP Standard 1

use a wide range of strategies to:

- determine central ideas or themes in oral presentations and spoken and written texts
- analyze the development of the themes/ideas
- cite specific details and evidence from texts to support the analysis

ELP Standard 2

- participate in conversations, extended discussions, and written exchanges about a range of substantive topics, texts, and issues
- build on the ideas of others
- express his or her own ideas clearly and persuasively
- ask and answer questions that probe reasoning and claim

<table>
<tr><td>

ELP Standard 8

using context, questioning, and consistent knowledge of English morphology,

• determine the meaning of general academic and content-specific words and phrases, figurative and connotative language, and idiomatic expressions in spoken and written texts about a variety of topics, experiences, or events

</td><td></td></tr>
</table>

Warm-up and Review
10–15 minutes (books closed)

Bring in an unusual kitchen tool or show an image of one. Write: *What can you do with this?* Pair or group students to brainstorm as many uses for the tool as possible.

Introduction
5 minutes

1. Elicit students' ideas and write them on the board. Have students vote on the most creative idea.

2. State the objective: *Today we're going to identify ways to increase creativity.*

1 Read about the alternative uses task

Presentation
20–25 minutes

 1. Write *alternative* on the board. Ask: *What does* alternative *mean?* [another way to do something]

2. Call on a student to read the information.

3. Group students and assign roles: manager, fact checker, recorder, and reporter. Explain that students will work with their group to brainstorm uses for a sock.

4. Check comprehension of the activity. Ask: *Who will lead the group?* [manager] *Who will take notes on uses?* [recorder] *Who will report our ideas to the class?* [reporter] *Who will look up the spelling of words?* [fact checker]

5. Set a time limit (two minutes) and have students work together to complete the task.

6. Call time and have the reporters from each group take turns calling out alternative uses. Record students' answers on the board. With a show of hands, have the class vote on the three most creative ideas.

For 1A, use mixed-level groups.

• **On-level** Assign these students the roles of fact checker and reporter.

• **Pre-level** Assign these students the role of recorder.

• **Higher-level** Assign these students the role of manager.

Guided Practice I
15–20 minutes

B 1. Read the directions aloud. Check comprehension. Ask: *What do you do when you skim?* [read quickly] *What are you going to skim for?* [the sentences that explain what the AUT is]

2. Set a time limit (three minutes). Direct students to skim the text and underline what the AUT is.

3. Elicit the answer from the class.

Answer
Underlined in text: *This technique involves looking at a simple object, such as a brick or a sock. After looking at the item for two minutes, the subject thinks of as many uses for it as possible.*

C 1. Read the directions aloud. Check comprehension. Ask: *What should you pay attention to as you read?* [the ways we can use an AUT]

2. Set a time limit (five minutes). Direct students to work independently to reread and answer the question.

3. Ask students to compare their answer with a partner. Then check the answer as a class.

Possible Answer
It can be useful for evaluating a person's ability to be creative and also for developing creativity.

 **D** 1. Have students work independently to reread the article and answer the questions. Remind them to mark the text where they find answers.

2. Set a time limit (five minutes) for students to discuss their answers with a partner.

3. Invite pairs to share their responses. Check answers as a class. Ask students to say where in the article they found the answers.

> **Possible Answers**
>
> 1. Underlined in text: *a paperweight, a step, a doorstop. It could also be used to break a window.*
> 2. Underlined in text: *The AUT was developed in the 1960s as a means of evaluating creativity and a person's ability to see a problem from different angles; as a way to*
> 3. Underlined in text: *improved performance on a problem-solving task*
> 4. Answers will vary. The writer used *however* to show that Wen, Butler, and Koutstaal's results were different from the original purpose of the AUT.
> 5. Answers will vary. The author used *this suggests* to show that this information isn't 100 percent certain.

Presentation II
20–25 minutes

E 1. Have students rejoin their teams from 1A. Explain that students will work with their group to try the AUT again.

2. Check comprehension of the activity. Ask: *Who looks up words?* [fact checker] *Who takes notes?* [recorder] *Who reports to the class?* [reporter] *Who leads the discussion?* [manager]

3. Set a time limit (five minutes) and have students work together to complete the task.

4. Call time and have the reporters from each group take turns saying whether their team was more creative the second time. Then elicit reasons. Record students' answers on the board. If members of the team disagree, ask them to explain further.

> **EXTENSION ACTIVITY**
>
> **Team Practice**
>
> To extend 2E, draw a large blank chart on the board. As each reporter shares with the class, the recorder from that group fills in the chart. If other teams came up with the same answers, they should not enter the information again.

2 Listen and take notes

Guided Practice II
20–25 minutes

 **A** 1. Say: *Now we're going to listen to a lecture about boosting creativity.*

2. Set a time limit (five minutes). Direct students to brainstorm predictions about what the speaker might say.

3. Elicit ideas from the whole class. Write their ideas on the board.

 **B** **1.02** 1. Play the beginning of the audio. Direct students to listen without writing.

2. Go over the Listening Note and the question.

3. Replay the audio. Ask students to complete the statement of the main idea.

4. Elicit the answer.

> **Answer**
>
> how you can become a more creative person

Communicative Practice
10–20 minutes

 **C** **1.03** 1. Copy the first three rows of the chart onto the board.

2. Model the task. Tell students to look at the first column of item 1. Ask: *What does* cultivate *mean?* [to develop] Point to the middle column. Ask: *What can you write instead of the word* question *when you take notes?* [a question mark] Ask: *How many ideas does the speaker talk about?* [three]

3. Review words and phrases that signal a number of steps, examples, or reasons (*first, one, second, two, next, another, finally, third, last*). Tell students to listen for these words and phrases.

4. Play the whole audio. Direct students to take notes as they listen.

> **MULTILEVEL STRATEGIES**
>
> Replay the audio for 2B to allow pre-level students to catch up while you challenge on- and higher-level students.
>
> • **Pre-level** Have these students listen again to complete the chart.
>
> • **On- and Higher-level** Have these students add more details and examples. Encourage them to note the signal words they hear.

<table>
<tr><td colspan="3">Possible Answers</td></tr>
<tr><td colspan="3">Employability Skills Lecture Series: Boosting Creativity</td></tr>
<tr><td>Main Idea</td><td>How?</td><td>How does this increase creativity?</td></tr>
<tr><td>1. Cultivate your <u>curiosity</u>.</td><td>ask?s</td><td>expose self to a variety of answers</td></tr>
<tr><td>2. Don't be afraid of <u>failure</u>.</td><td><u>take risks/try</u></td><td><u>fear of failure prevents it</u></td></tr>
<tr><td>3. It's important to maintain a <u>positive attitude</u>.</td><td>take care of self <u>rest/sleep/ exercise/diet</u></td><td>not creative when <u>stressed/ bored/angry</u></td></tr>
<tr><td colspan="3">Conclusion:
Developing your creativity can help you <u>be successful in the job market</u> and enjoy work + life.</td></tr>
</table>

 **1.03** 1. Set a time limit (five minutes) for students to discuss their answers with a partner.

2. Replay the audio. Ask students to check the information and make additions as needed.

Presentation II
20–25 minutes

 1. Read the questions aloud. Call on a student to read the expressions of agreement and disagreement.

2. Pair students to discuss the questions and practice using the expressions.

3. Elicit responses from the class. Encourage students to use the expressions provided.

Answers
1. The speaker says any job can be creative and that creativity improves any job. 2. Answers will vary.

TIP

Write key words from the lecture: *comfortable, organize, curiosity, expose, failure, succeed, maintain, fulfilling.* Elicit other forms of these words. Tell students to notice how speakers use different words from the same word family to restate ideas without repeating the words exactly. This variety makes the text more interesting.

Evaluation
10–15 minutes

SELF-ASSESSMENT

1. Ask students to complete the checkboxes individually.

2. Tell students that you are going to read each of the items in the checklist aloud. If they are not at all confident with that skill, they should hold up a closed fist. If they are not very confident, they should hold up one finger. If they are somewhat confident, two fingers; confident, three fingers; very confident, four fingers. If they think they could teach the skill, they should hold up five fingers. Read each item in the checklist aloud and identify students who may need further support.

TIP

For homework, you could ask students to write a sentence or two about what reading and listening skills they still need to work on or, if they are confident in all of the skills, what skill they are most proud of.

Lesson Overview

MULTILEVEL OBJECTIVES

On-level and Higher-level: Recognize and use words with multiple meanings and adverbials for writing

Pre-level: Recognize multiple meanings of words and adverbials for writing

LANGUAGE FOCUS

Grammar: Adverbials for writing

Vocabulary: *attitude, cultivate, wonder, curiosity,* words with multiple meanings

For vocabulary support, see this **Oxford Picture Dictionary** topic: Soft Skills, page 178

STRATEGY FOCUS

Use linking and degree adverbials in writing.

READINESS CONNECTION

In this lesson, students collaborate to distinguish meanings and parts of speech of words with multiple meanings.

PACING

To compress this lesson: Have students do 2C for homework.

To extend this lesson: Have students write sentences to expand their vocabulary (see page 11); Have students rewrite their summaries to use different forms of key words (see page 12).

And/or have students complete **Multilevel Activities 5 Unit 1, Lesson 3**.

Lesson Notes

CORRELATIONS

CCRS: SL.8.1.a. Come to discussions prepared, having read or researched material under study; explicitly draw on that preparation by referring to evidence on the topic, text, or issue to probe and reflect on ideas under discussion.

SL.8.1.d. Acknowledge new information expressed by others, and, when warranted, qualify or justify their own views in light of the evidence presented.

L.6.4.c. Consult reference materials (e.g., dictionaries, glossaries, thesauruses), both print and digital, to find the pronunciation of a word or determine or clarify its precise meaning or its part of speech.

L.8.6 Acquire and use accurately level-appropriate general academic and domain-specific words and phrases; gather vocabulary knowledge when considering a word or phrase important to comprehension or expression.

ELPS: ELP Standard 2

• participate in conversations, extended discussions, and written exchanges about a range of substantive topics, texts, and issues

• build on the ideas of others

• express his or her own ideas clearly and persuasively

ELP Standard 8

using context, questioning, and consistent knowledge of English morphology,

• determine the meaning of general academic and content-specific words and phrases, figurative and connotative language, and idiomatic expressions in spoken and written texts about a variety of topics, experiences, or events

Warm-up and Review
10–15 minutes (books closed)

1. Ask: *What have you learned about creativity so far?*
As students call out ideas, write them on the board.
[*making things, solving problems, working with others,
alternative uses, being curious, not being afraid of
failure, positive attitude*]

2. Circle the words that you know have more than
one meaning. [*make, use, curious, positive, attitude*]
Choose one of the words and elicit different
meanings.

Introduction
5 minutes

State the objective: *Today we are going to use context
to select from multiple meanings of a word and employ
formal adverbials in summary writing.*

1 Vocabulary: Multiple meanings

Presentation and Guided Practice I
20–25 minutes

 1. Write *multiple meanings* on the board. Ask:
What are some meanings for the word move?
Elicit ideas (for example, to change homes/
locations, to change your body position, a
turn in a game like chess).

2. Read the directions aloud. Explain that
the activity has two parts: completing the
sentences and checking the correct definitions.
Ask: *How many words are there?* [four] *How
many definitions are given for each word?* [two]

3. Direct students to complete the task
independently. Set a time limit (five minutes).

4. Have students compare answers in pairs.

5. Elicit the answers.

Answers
1. attitude ✓ the way that you think and feel about somebody or something 2. cultivate ✓ to develop a way of behaving 3. angle ✓ a particular way of thinking about something 4. wonder ✓ to think about something and try to decide what is true

• **Pre-level** Have students work in pairs to complete the task. • **Higher-level** Have students write a sentence for each word that uses the other definition.

Suggest that students look for common
collocations of the words in the chart. This can
help them recognize the meaning of the words
more quickly. For example, the collocation
a right angle means the space between two
lines, whereas *consider from this angle* means a
particular way of thinking about something.

Communicative Practice
15–20 minutes

 1. Read the directions aloud.

2. Set a time limit (five minutes) for students
to discuss the meaning of the words with a
partner.

3. Invite pairs to share their responses. Check
answers as a class.

Answers
develop (v) to start to have a skill that becomes better and stronger means (n) a way of doing something might (modal v) used to show that something is possible

EXTENSION ACTIVITY
Vocabulary 1. Have students work independently to write sentences using different meanings of the words *develop, means,* and *might* than those used in the article in Lesson 2. 2. Pair students to share their sentences. 3. Call on students to read their sentences to the class.

 **2 Grammar: Adverbials for writing**

Presentation and Guided Practice II
20–25 minutes

A 1. Demonstrate how to read the grammar chart. Read each sentence aloud and have students repeat after you.

2. Direct students to circle the examples of adverbials. Write the sentences on the board.

3. Ask questions to check meaning: *What linking adverbials do we use to show a result?* [*as a result, therefore*] *What linking adverbials introduce examples?* [*for example, for instance*] *What can we use to add information?* [*in addition*] *What are examples of degree adverbials?* [*slightly, somewhat, extremely, absolutely*] *Which one refers to only a little bit?* [*slightly*] *Which one is the strongest?* [*absolutely*]

4. Ask questions to check comprehension: *What kind of adverbial is often a phrase?* [*linking*] *Where are the linking adverbials in a sentence?* [*at the beginning of a sentence or clause*] *Where do you usually see degree adverbials?* [*before adjectives*]

5. Tell students that they will collaborate to complete the Language Connection paragraph. Model collaboration by working with the class to complete the first sentence.

6. Pair students and have them work together to complete the paragraph.

7. Project or write the completed paragraph on the board and have pairs verify the accuracy of their responses. Ask volunteers which sentences confused them and discuss.

Answers
Linking adverbials, degree adverbials, Linking adverbials, degree adverbials, linking adverbials

TIP

When you write the sentences from the chart on the board, label the parts of the sentence above the words and phrases. This will help students, especially pre-level students, understand the structure and use of adverbials.

Guided Practice III
20–25 minutes

 1. Point out that students will need to write two sentences or clauses for each of the first three adverbials.

2. Pair students to complete the task. Set a time limit (five minutes).

3. Ask volunteers to write examples on the board.

MULTILEVEL STRATEGIES

• **Cross-ability** Pair a pre-level student with a higher-level student to complete the task.

 1. Explain that the adverbials in the chart in 2A are examples of more formal language that we use in most writing. Point out that we use informal language in speaking and often when we write to family and friends.

2. Write the underlined words on the board. Model their use in sentences; for example, *You often have totally creative ideas.* Elicit other examples from students.

3. Ask students to work individually to replace the underlined words with adverbials from the chart. Remind students to pay attention to both meaning and placement in the sentence.

Possible Answers
a totally: an absolutely Like: For example, / For instance, That's why: As a result, / Therefore, Besides that: In addition, you know: for instance, / for example, kind of: somewhat / slightly really: extremely

 1. Set a time limit (five minutes) for students to discuss their answers with a partner.

2. Elicit answers from the class.

EXTENSION ACTIVITY

Summary Practice

1. Tell students to write a summary of the article in Lesson 2 using at least three adverbials from the chart.

2. Pair students to share their summaries.

3. Call on students to read their summaries to the class.

Evaluation

10–15 minutes

SELF-ASSESSMENT

1. If students need more help with identifying the correct definition of a word, provide more examples of words with multiple meanings in sentences.

2. If students need more practice with adverbials, suggest that they write sentences and share them in pairs.

Lesson Overview

| Lesson Notes |

MULTILEVEL OBJECTIVES

On-level: Read about creative people and discuss how the brain stimulates creativity

Pre-level: Read about creative people and respond to questions about creativity in discussion

Higher-level: Read about creative people and lead and summarize discussion on how the brain stimulates creativity

LANGUAGE FOCUS

Grammar: Simple present

Vocabulary: *inspire, encourage, capacity, spur, carve out, spark*

For vocabulary support, see these **Oxford Picture Dictionary** topics: Succeeding in School, page 10; Jobs and Occupations, pages 170–173; Electronics and Photography, pages 240–241; Music, page 244

STRATEGY FOCUS

Use phrases to invite others to speak.

READINESS CONNECTION

In this lesson, students actively incorporate others into a discussion.

PACING

To compress this lesson: Assign 2B and 2C for homework.

To extend this lesson: Have students role-play an interview with one of the MacArthur fellows (see page 16); Have students summarize their research on creative people (see page 17).

And/or have students complete **Multilevel Activities 5 Unit 1, Lesson 4.**

CORRELATIONS

CCRS: RI/RL.7.1 Cite several pieces of textual evidence to support analysis of what the text says explicitly as well as inferences drawn from the text.

RI/RL.6.4 Determine the meaning of words and phrases as they are used in a text, including figurative, connotative, and technical meanings; analyze the impact of a specific word choice on meaning and tone.

RI.6.7 Integrate information presented in different media or formats (e.g., in charts, graphs, photographs, videos, or maps) as well as in words to develop a coherent understanding of a topic or issue.

W.7.7 Conduct short research projects to answer a question, drawing on several sources and generating additional related, focused questions for further research and investigation.

SL.8.1.a. Come to discussions prepared, having read or researched material under study; explicitly draw on that preparation by referring to evidence on the topic, text, or issue to probe and reflect on ideas under discussion.

SL.8.1.d. Acknowledge new information expressed by others, and, when warranted, qualify or justify their own views in light of the evidence presented.

L.6.4.c. Consult reference materials (e.g., dictionaries, glossaries, thesauruses), both print and digital, to find the pronunciation of a word or determine or clarify its precise meaning or its part of speech.

ELPS: ELP Standard 1

use a wide range of strategies to:

• cite specific details and evidence from texts to support the analysis

ELP Standard 2

• participate in conversations, extended discussions, and written exchanges about a range of substantive topics, texts, and issues

• build on the ideas of others

• express his or her own ideas clearly and persuasively

<table>
<tr><td>

ELP Standard 7

- adapt language choices and style according to purpose, task, and audience with ease in various social and academic contexts
- use a wide variety of complex general academic and content specific words and phrases
- employ both formal and more informal styles and tones effectively in spoken and written texts, as appropriate

</td><td>

ELP Standard 8

using context, questioning, and consistent knowledge of English morphology,

- determine the meaning of general academic and content-specific words and phrases, figurative and connotative language, and idiomatic expressions in spoken and written texts about a variety of topics, experiences, or events

</td></tr>
</table>

Warm-up and Review
10–15 minutes (books closed)

1. Bring in or find online at least five examples of creative inspiration—a photo, a piece of art, something from nature, a poem, an interesting design, a quote, someone running or hiking. Show students the examples for one minute and have them write all the ideas the work inspires. After repeating the process with each example, discuss which prompt inspired the most ideas in students.

2. List the following on the board: *an argument with a friend, a writing assignment, a housing problem, a work project.* Elicit the ways students get inspiration to deal with each situation and write them on the board.

Introduction
5 minutes

1. Describe for students how you get inspiration.

2. State the objective: *Today we are going to read about creative people and discuss how the brain stimulates creativity.*

1 Get ready to read

Presentation I
20–25 minutes

A (1.04) 1. Say: *Now we're going to listen to students talk about how they get inspired.* Read the question aloud. Check comprehension.

2. Play the audio.

3. Elicit the ideas they heard. Check any that are on the board from the warm-up.

B (1.04) 1. Replay the audio. Ask students to check the ways the students in the audio invite each other to speak.

2. Check answers as a class.

> **Answers**
>
> Does someone want to start?
> Would you like to jump in here?
> What do you think?
> Do you have any thoughts about this?
> How about you?

 1. Write *most effective methods* on the board.

2. Group students and assign roles: manager, fact checker, recorder, and reporter. Explain that students will work with their group to discuss methods for generating ideas and solving problems.

3. Check comprehension of the activity. Ask: *Who will check vocabulary?* [fact checker] *Who takes notes?* [recorder] *Who will report back to the class?* [reporter] *Who will make sure everyone speaks?* [manager]

4. Set a time limit (three minutes) and have students work together to complete the task.

5. Call time and have the reporters from each group take turns reporting their most effective methods for generating ideas or solving problems. Record students' answers on the board. After hearing from each group, invite the next group to speak with one of the expressions in 1B.

2 Preview and read

Guided Practice I
20–25 minutes

 1. Read the directions aloud. Ask: *What do you do when you scan?* [look for specific information, such as names, dates, or specific words]

2. Have students answer the question individually, and then check answers as a class. If any students answer incorrectly, ask them to support their answer. Establish the correct answer.

<table>
<tr><td>Answer</td></tr>
<tr><td>the MacArthur Fellowship, which comes with a large cash prize</td></tr>
</table>

 **B** 1. Ask students to read the article silently, answer the question, and then compare answers with a partner.

2. Check answers as a class.

<table>
<tr><td>Answers</td></tr>
<tr><td>psychologist, activist, painter, journalist, scientist</td></tr>
</table>

Presentation II
20–25 minutes

C 1. Group students and assign roles: manager, fact checker, recorder, and reporter. Explain that students will work with their group to answer the questions.

2. Check comprehension of the activity. Ask: *How many questions will you answer?* [three] *What should you do when you find the answers?* [underline or bracket the text]

3. Set a time limit (three minutes) and have students work together to complete the task.

4. Call time and have the reporters from each group take turns calling out the answers. Then elicit the location in the text. Record students' answers on the board. If groups disagree, have them reread the text to confirm.

<table>
<tr><td>Answers</td></tr>
<tr><td>1. Underlined (or bracketed) in text: extraordinary originality and dedication in their creative pursuits and a marked capacity for self-direction. Answers may vary. In this quotation, marked means "strong."
2. Answers will vary. Sample answer: Nashashibi and Hannah-Jones both like to be alone to think. He says he rides his bike to "think and process," which is similar to what she says about using her time on the train to "think things through."
3. Underlined (or bracketed) in text: the MacArthur Foundation avoids that language because the grant, they say, is not given for intellectual ability, but for a variety of important qualities. Restatements will vary.</td></tr>
</table>

WORD STUDY

 **D** 1. Ask students to stay in their groups from 2C.

2. Set a time limit (three minutes) and have students work together to complete the task.

3. Call time and have the reporters from each group take turns calling out the meanings of the words. Then elicit reasons for their answers. Record students' answers on the board.

<table>
<tr><td colspan="3">Answers</td></tr>
<tr><td>Word</td><td>Part of Speech</td><td>Definition</td></tr>
<tr><td>capacity</td><td>noun</td><td>the ability to understand or do something</td></tr>
<tr><td>spur</td><td>verb</td><td>a fact or an event that makes you want to do something better or more quickly</td></tr>
<tr><td>carve out</td><td>verb</td><td>to take something out of a larger whole</td></tr>
<tr><td>spark</td><td>verb</td><td>to cause something to start to develop, especially suddenly</td></tr>
</table>

E 1. Have students remain in their groups from 2C and 2D.

2. Write the question on the board. Set a time limit (five minutes) for groups to answer the question.

3. Call on reporters to share the group's ideas. Elicit examples from the text to support their answers.

<table>
<tr><td>Possible Answers</td></tr>
<tr><td>Levy Paluck, Nashashibi, and Hannah-Jones follow the lecturer's advice about maintaining a positive attitude. They take time to relax, have fun, listen to music, exercise, and think. Both Akunyili and Victora follow the speaker's advice regarding cultivating curiosity. They both seek out ideas by exposing themselves to different people or writers.</td></tr>
</table>

<table>
<tr><td>EXTENSION ACTIVITY
Interview Role Play</td></tr>
<tr><td>1. Pair students to take turns role-playing an interview with one of the MacArthur Fellows.
2. Call on pairs to perform their role plays for the class.</td></tr>
</table>

3 Build on it

Presentation I
20–25 minutes

 **1.** Have students look at the infographic. Ask: *What is the main focus of the infographic?* [creativity] *How do you know?* [It's in the center.] *How many aspects or parts of creativity does the infographic show?* [three]

2. Set a time limit (ten minutes). Have students work individually to complete the task and then compare answers with a partner. Ask volunteers to share their answers with the class.

TIP

Write unfamiliar terms on the board: *network, default, salience, executive control.* Tell students to research the terms. Set a time limit (three minutes). Elicit definitions. Point out that the words have a specific meaning in the context of the infographic.

Possible Answers

1. three different networks in the brain
2. because the three networks work together in creative thinking

B **1.** Ask students to return to their groups and assign roles: manager, fact checker, recorder, and reporter. Explain that students will work with their group to discuss the questions.

2. Read the questions aloud.

3. Direct students' attention to the example conversation. Ask: *What phrase does A use to express an opinion?* [I think] *Does B agree or disagree?* [disagree] *How do you know? What expressions tell you that?* [*That might be true. But...*] Point out that speakers can use words and phrases, like *might*, to soften disagreement. Point out that both speakers give reasons to support their answers.

4. Set a time limit (three minutes) and have students work together to complete the task. Remind students to invite others to speak.

5. Call time and have the reporters from each group take turns calling out the answers.

Possible Answers

1. Maybe the connection between the three networks gets stronger.
2. When Hannah-Jones works on the train, she may be activating her executive control network because she is very focused on the problem.

PROBLEM SOLVING

 **1.** Direct students to look at the photos. Call on students to describe what they see.

2. Read the questions aloud. Write *Problem* and *Solutions* on the board.

3. Set a time limit (three minutes) and have students discuss the questions in their groups.

4. Call time and elicit ideas for the problems shown in the pictures. Then elicit solutions from each team. Record students' answers on the board.

Possible Answers

1. The family is just watching TV and not interacting. This isn't very creative.
2. They could play a game together to stimulate their creativity; they could cook something together; they could get inspiration by visiting a library or a museum.

APPLY YOUR KNOWLEDGE

 **1.** If students will use the Internet for this task, establish what device(s) they'll use: a class computer, tablets, or smartphones. Alternatively, print information from the Internet before class and distribute it to groups of students. If they are searching online, suggest that they enter the person's name and "inspiration."

2. Set a time limit (five minutes) for students to find information.

3. Call on students to share what they found out. Write the ideas on the board.

4. With the class, identify the ideas that have already been mentioned in the unit.

EXTENSION ACTIVITY

Apply Your Knowledge

1. Tell students to write a paragraph about the creative person they researched, similar to the paragraphs in the article in 2B. (Pre-level students can work together to create an infographic about the creative person.)
2. Pair students to read their paragraphs aloud.
3. Call on students to tell the class about their partner's person.

Evaluation

10–15 minutes

SELF-ASSESSMENT

1. Have students check the boxes individually.

2. Ask students to identify the objective they had the most difficulty with. Then pair or group students accordingly.

3. Ask students to come up with two solutions to address the problem they are having.

Lesson Overview

Lesson Notes

MULTILEVEL OBJECTIVES

On-level: Use the writing process to summarize an article

Pre-level: Write sentences

Higher-level: Summarize an article using adverbials

LANGUAGE FOCUS

Grammar: Adverbials

Vocabulary: For vocabulary support, see this **Oxford Picture Dictionary** topic: English Composition, pages 202–203

STRATEGY FOCUS

Use adverbials for writing to maintain a formal style.

READINESS CONNECTION

In this lesson, students work together to identify and summarize important ideas in an article.

PACING

To compress this lesson: Complete the chart in 1C as a class.

To extend this lesson: Have students work with others to develop summaries (see page 21).

And/or have students complete **Multilevel Activities 5 Unit 1, Lesson 5**.

CORRELATIONS

CCRS: W/WHST.6-8.2.a. Introduce a topic clearly, previewing what is to follow; organize ideas, concepts, and information, using strategies such as definition, classification, comparison /contrast, and cause/effect; include formatting (e.g., headings), graphics (e.g., charts, tables), and multimedia when useful to aiding comprehension.

W/WHST.6-8.2.b. Develop the topic with relevant facts, definitions, concrete details, quotations, or other information and examples.

W/WHST.6-8.2.c. Use appropriate transitions to create cohesion and clarify the relationships among ideas and concepts.

W/WHST.6-8.2.d. Use precise language and domain-specific vocabulary to inform about or explain the topic.

W/WHST.6-8.2.f. Provide a concluding statement or section that follows from and supports the information or explanation presented.

W/WHST.6-8.4 Produce clear and coherent writing in which the development and organization and style are appropriate to task, purpose, and audience.

W/WHST.6-8.5 With some guidance and support from peers and others, develop and strengthen writing as needed by planning, revising, editing, rewriting, or trying a new approach, focusing on how well purpose and audience have been addressed.

L.6.3/7.3.c. Choose language that expresses ideas precisely and concisely, recognizing and eliminating wordiness and redundancy.

L.8.6 Acquire and use accurately level-appropriate general academic and domain-specific words and phrases; gather vocabulary knowledge when considering a word or phrase important to comprehension or expression.

ELPS: ELP Standard 7

- adapt language choices and style according to purpose, task, and audience with ease in various social and academic contexts
- use a wide variety of complex general academic and content specific words and phrases
- employ both formal and more informal styles and tones effectively in spoken and written texts, as appropriate

ELP Standard 9

- recount a complex and detailed sequence of events or steps in a process, with an effective sequential or chronological order
- introduce and effectively develop an informational topic with facts, details, and evidence

<table>
<tr>
<td>

- use complex and varied transitions to link the major sections of speech and text and to clarify relationships among events and ideas
- provide a concluding section or statement

</td>
<td>

ELP Standard 10

- produce and expand simple, compound, and complex sentences

</td>
</tr>
</table>

Warm-up and Review
10–15 minutes (books closed)

1. Tell the class about a movie you have seen or book you have read recently. Give a summary of the plot. Then ask questions to review *summary*: *How does the length of a summary compare to the entire story or article?* [It's much shorter.] *What do you include in a summary?* [only the important/main ideas, not the details]

2. Pair students to give a summary of something they have read or watched recently.

Introduction
5 minutes

1. Say: *A summary is a short description of a longer text.*

2. State the objective: *Today we will use the writing process to summarize an article.*

1 Write a summary

Presentation I
10–15 minutes

A 1. Have students revisit the article on pages 6–7. Check comprehension. Ask: *What were the most important ideas?*

2. Elicit students' answers and write them on the board.

Guided Practice I
15–20 minutes

B 1. Direct students to look at the article. Point out that a writer often talks about the main idea in the introduction and the conclusion.

2. Check comprehension of the activity. Ask: *What do you have to write?* [a statement introducing the main idea of the article]

3. Have students work individually to write their statement.

C 1. Read the directions aloud. Check comprehension. Ask: *What do you write in the top box of the chart?* [examples of professions] *What do you write next to each number in the second box?* [the ways each person stimulates his or her creativity]

2. Remind students that they can just write words and phrases in the chart.

3. Have students work individually to complete the chart.

Possible Answers
psychologist, activist, painter, journalist, scientist
1. talking and relaxing with colleagues 2. long bike rides 3. reading literature 4. listening to music on the train 5. talking to colleagues

D 1. Check comprehension. Ask: *Which paragraph is the conclusion?* [the last one] *What are some strategies you can use to write something in different words?* Elicit or provide these ideas: use synonyms, use different word forms, use a different sentence structure.

2. Model the task. Choose a sentence from the text to rewrite in different words. For example, *She believes that having frequent group celebrations helps spur creativity.* Rewrite using one or more of the strategies: *According to Levy Paluck, celebrating frequently with a group of colleagues helps her be more creative.*

3. Write the following sentence frame on the board: *According to the writer, creative people _____.*

4. Have students work individually to write their conclusion/concluding sentence.

E 1. Read the directions aloud. Check comprehension. Ask: *How many sentences do you think your summary will have?* [at least four]

2. Draw students' attention to the Writer's Note. Elicit linking adverbials and their use. Then elicit degree adverbials.

3. Write a paragraph frame on the board

4. Have students work individually to write their summaries.

MULTILEVEL STRATEGIES

Adapt 1E to the level of your students.

• **Pre-level** Work with these students to write a group summary. Write a template on the board: *In "How the 'Geniuses' Get Their Ideas," the writer explains... The article features... The geniuses get their inspiration by...because...* At each ellipsis, stop and elicit completions. Have these learners copy the paragraph into their notebooks.

• **Higher-level** Encourage these students to write their summaries in two ways, using different adverbials and different synonyms, word forms, or sentence structures.

---

2 Get feedback and revise

Guided Practice II
10–15 minutes

A Direct students to check their writing using the editing checklist. Tell them to read each item in the list and check their papers before moving on to the next item. Explain that students should not edit their writing at this stage. They should just use the checklist to check their work and mark any areas they want to revise.

Communicative Practice
10–15 minutes

B 1. Read the directions aloud. Emphasize to students that they are responding to their partners' work, not correcting it.

2. Use the paragraph in 2C in Lesson 3 to model the activity. Say: *I think the summary is clear in general, but I think the first sentence of the last paragraph is not extremely clear. I'm not sure what "the last one" refers to because the writer gives several suggestions.*

3. Direct students to exchange papers with a partner and follow the instructions.

 **C** Allow students time to edit and revise their writing using the editing checklist and their partner's feedback. If necessary, students could complete this task as homework.

TIP

After students complete 2C, ask them to find new partners. Have them take turns reading their paragraphs aloud. Their partners should raise their hands when they hear something that is unclear.

EXTENSION ACTIVITY

Summary Practice

1. Tell students to write three sentences to summarize the text in Lesson 1. Students can work individually or in cross-ability pairs.

2. Have students find partners and compare summaries.

3. Ask volunteers to write two or three summaries on the board. Correct as needed.

Evaluation
10–15 minutes

SELF-ASSESSMENT

1. Read the directions aloud. Assign a time limit (five minutes) and have students work independently.

2. Before collecting student work, invite two or three volunteers to share their sentences. Ask students to raise their hands if they wrote similar answers.

Lesson Overview

MULTILEVEL OBJECTIVES

On-level: Conduct, evaluate, organize and present research related to creativity

Pre-level: Collaborate to conduct and present research related to creativity

Higher-level: Conduct, evaluate, organize and present research related to creativity. Additionally, they could describe one or two people who have exceptional creativity.

LANGUAGE FOCUS

Grammar: Simple present, adverbials

Vocabulary: For vocabulary support, see this **Oxford Picture Dictionary** topic: Internet Research, pages 212–213

STRATEGY FOCUS

Speak up and make eye contact to hold your audience's attention.

READINESS CONNECTION

In this lesson, students clarify roles for delivering a group presentation.

PACING

To compress this lesson: Assign teams to conduct research (1B) and rehearse (2C) their presentations outside class.

To extend this lesson: Have students debrief in pairs on techniques for developing creativity (see page 25).

And/or have students complete **Multilevel Activities 5 Unit 1, Lesson 6**.

Lesson Notes

CORRELATIONS

CCRS: W.7.7 Conduct short research projects to answer a question, drawing on several sources and generating additional related, focused questions for further research and investigation.

W.7.8 Gather relevant information from multiple print and digital sources, using search terms effectively; assess the credibility and accuracy of each source; and quote or paraphrase the data and conclusions of others while avoiding plagiarism and following a standard format for citation.

SL.8.4 Present claims and findings, emphasizing salient points in a focused, coherent manner with relevant evidence, sound valid reasoning, and well-chosen details; use appropriate eye contact, adequate volume, and clear pronunciation.

SL.8.5 Integrate multimedia and visual displays into presentations to clarify information, strengthen claims and evidence, and add interest.

SL.8.6 Adapt speech to a variety of contexts and tasks, demonstrating command of formal English when indicated or appropriate.

L.8.6 Acquire and use accurately level-appropriate general academic and domain-specific words and phrases; gather vocabulary knowledge when considering a word or phrase important to comprehension or expression.

ELPS: ELP Standard 2

- participate in conversations, extended discussions, and written exchanges about a range of substantive topics, texts, and issues
- build on the ideas of others
- express his or her own ideas clearly and persuasively

ELP Standard 3

- deliver oral presentations
- compose written informational texts
- fully develop the topic with relevant details, concepts, examples, and information
- integrate graphics or multimedia when useful about a variety of texts, topics, or events

Warm-up and Review
10–15 minutes (books closed)

1. Write a problem on the board (for example, not enough options in the cafeteria/vending machines). Put students in teams arranged in a circle. Give each student a stack of sticky notes or index cards. Tell students to write one idea on each card and put the card next to the person on their right. They should continue filling out cards with as many ideas as they can. When anyone runs out of ideas or wants inspiration, he or she takes a card/note from the pile on their left.

2. Set a time limit (ten minutes). Have teams sort the cards into similar groups.

3. Call on students to share their ideas.

Introduction
5 minutes

1. Explain that the warm-up activity was a technique for developing creativity called the pin card technique.

2. State the objective: *Today we will conduct and present research related to creativity.*

1 Research a technique for developing creativity

Communicative Practice
40–45 minutes

A 1. Group students, but do not assign roles yet. Explain that students will work with their team to narrow their choices of topics to research.

2. Set a time limit (five minutes) and have students work together to complete the task.

3. Call on a volunteer from each team to identify the team's top choice and write them on the board. Encourage teams to choose different topics.

MULTILEVEL STRATEGIES

To adapt 1A:

- **On-level** and **Higher-level** Tell students to divide up the topics and write one-sentence descriptions of each.

- **Pre-level** Pass out information with a very brief description of each technique.

mind-mapping: using a diagram to connect ideas

Six Thinking Hats: looking at a problem six different ways

random word stimulation: using a random word to jump-start ideas

lateral thinking: looking at a problem from a different view

meditation for creativity: a way of thinking, slowing down your brain

daydreaming for creativity: letting your thoughts wander/go anywhere

creative circles practice: turning blank circles into recognizable objects

B 1. Check comprehension of the task. Ask: *How many sources do you need?* [at least three]

2. Draw students' attention to the Research Tip. Elicit the multi-word terms each team will use. Provide suggestions as needed. Point out that students will get more helpful information if they choose good multi-search terms.

3. Have students work in their teams to find multiple sources on their topics. Then have team members identify who is responsible for researching each source.

C 1. Check comprehension of the task. Ask: *Will you work in teams or individually?* [individually] *How many questions are you trying to answer?* [five]

2. Model the task by telling students about the pin card technique. Say: *Work groups sometimes use this technique. It works best with teams. It's easy to do. It works because it keeps ideas moving through the group. You can use it to identify solutions to a group problem where you want input from everyone.*

3. Have students work individually to take notes on their topic from their assigned source.

D 1. Check comprehension of the task. Ask: *How many steps do you need to follow?* [four]

2. Have students report on their research in their teams.

3. Assign roles: manager, fact checker, reporter, and IT specialist. Explain that students will work with their group to collect, evaluate, and organize the team's research.

4. Check comprehension of the activity. Ask: *Who will double-check the sources and make sure the information is correct?* [fact checker] *Who will take notes on the information we will include as well as how we will demonstrate the technique and the examples we will create?* [recorder] *Who will download and/or print any images or materials?* [IT specialist] *Who will facilitate the discussion?* [manager]

5. Set a time limit (20 minutes). Remind students that the questions in 1C can help them decide what information to include. Point out that questions 2 and 4 could be connected in their presentation. For example, in the warm-up, you demonstrated the technique and gave an example of how it could be used.

2 Present your research

Presentation
40–45 minutes

A 1. Have students stay in their teams from 1D. Check comprehension of the task. Ask: *What is an oral report?* [a presentation] *What do you need to do in the introduction?* [tell the name of the technique, who uses it, and when it works best] *When do you demonstrate the technique?* [in the body of the presentation] *What do you tell the audience in the conclusion?* [why the technique is useful or interesting]

2. Set a time limit (five minutes) and have students work as a team to create an outline.

B 1. Explain that students will work with their group to present their research to the class. Have students assign roles for the presentation. Suggest that one student introduce the technique, another demonstrate it, and a third present the conclusion. Remind them that every team member should speak.

2. Check comprehension of the activity. Ask: *How many team members will speak?* [all of them] *What technical support does your presentation need?* [for example, advancing the slides or playing video] *Who will provide technical assistance in your group?*

3. Draw students' attention to the Presentation Strategy. Demonstrate speaking in a quiet, mumbling voice and looking down at notes. Ask: *Is this how you should speak?* [no] *Why not?* [Listeners can't hear you or understand you.] Emphasize that students need to speak in a loud, clear voice. Ask: *Why should you focus on people at the back of the room?* [so you project your voice to them] *Why should you make eye contact?* [It engages the audience, and you look more confident.]

4. Set a time limit (five minutes) and have students work as a team to divide the work.

MULTILEVEL STRATEGIES

To adapt 2B:
- **Pre-level** Create sentence frames for the introduction: *Our presentation is about a technique called _____. _____ use it. It works best when _____.*
- **Higher-level** Have students show how the technique works using a demonstration or pictures. They can also field questions from the audience at the end of the presentation.

C 1. Check comprehension of the activity. Ask: *What should you focus on in your presentation?* [speaking up, or talking in a loud/clear voice, and making eye contact]

2. Set a time limit (ten minutes) and have students rehearse their parts. Remind students to use linking adverbials if appropriate.

D 1. Draw a chart on the board, listing the teams in the first column. In the other columns, list the note-taking prompts or shortened forms of them: *Technique, Transitions, Strengths, Advice.* Check comprehension of the activity. Ask: *Should you focus on the negative parts of the presentation?* [no]

2. Set a time limit (three minutes) for each presentation and invite each team to present in turn.

3. Ask each team to nominate a reporter to give feedback on the other teams' presentations.

4. Beginning with the first team to present, collect feedback from the reporters. Write feedback in the chart on the board.

> **EXTENSION ACTIVITY**
>
> **Pair Debrief**
>
> 1. Have each student find a partner on another team.
>
> 2. Tell students to share their opinions about each of the techniques for developing creativity.

Evaluation
10–15 minutes

SELF-ASSESSMENT

1. Pair students to share their self-assessments.

2. Elicit suggestions from the class for developing more confidence in each of the three assessment areas.

2 Time

Unit Overview

This unit explores time, how it is viewed in different cultures, and how it has been measured over time with a range of employability skills and contextualizes suffixes used in noun formation and subordinate clauses. By the end of this unit, you will be able to conduct and present results of a survey on time management.

KEY OBJECTIVES

Lesson 1	Identify and discuss aspects of time management
Lesson 2	Evaluate different cultural views of time
Lesson 3	Identify word families and suffixes used in noun formation; learn to combine ideas with subordinating clauses
Lesson 4	Read about timekeeping throughout history and discuss historical events
Lesson 5	Use the writing process to summarize an article
Lesson 6	Conduct a survey on time management and present the survey results to the class

UNIT FEATURES

Academic Vocabulary	*accomplishment, devise, distraction, emerge, interruption, management, perception, precise, priority, procrastination*
Employability Skills	• Evaluate differing values • Analyze similarities and differences across times and cultures • Interpret information in a timeline • Analyze and draw conclusions based on survey results • Resolve conflicts resulting from different cultural attitudes toward time • Clarify and challenge ideas in a discussion • Collaborate to develop quantifiable survey questions • Present survey results and suggestions based on those results

Resources	**Class Audio** CD1, Tracks 05-07
	Teacher Resource Center
	    Multilevel Activities 5 Unit 2
	    Multilevel Grammar Activities 5 Unit 2
	    Unit 2 Test
	Oxford Picture Dictionary Time, The Calendar, Soft Skills, U.S. History, World History, English Composition, Internet Research

Lesson Overview

MULTILEVEL OBJECTIVES

On-level and Pre-level: Identify and discuss aspects of time management

Higher-level: Identify, discuss, and analyze aspects of time management

LANGUAGE FOCUS

Grammar: Gerunds

Vocabulary: *management*, words and phrases related to time

For vocabulary support, see this **Oxford Picture Dictionary** topic: Time, pages 18–19

READINESS CONNECTION

In this lesson, students interpret information in a chart.

PACING

To compress this lesson: Do 1D as a class.

To extend this lesson: Have students analyze other groups' presentations (see page 29).

And/or have students complete **Multilevel Activities 5 Unit 2, Lesson 1**.

Lesson Notes

CORRELATIONS

CCRS: RI.6.7 Integrate information presented in different media or formats (e.g., in charts, graphs, photographs, videos, or maps) as well as in words to develop a coherent understanding of a topic or issue.

RST.6-8.7 Integrate quantitative or technical information expressed in words in a text with a version of that information expressed visually (e.g., in a flowchart, diagram, model, graph, or table).

SL.8.1.a. Come to discussions prepared, having read or researched material under study; explicitly draw on that preparation by referring to evidence on the topic, text, or issue to probe and reflect on ideas under discussion.

SL.8.1.c. Pose questions that connect the ideas of several speakers and respond to others' questions and comments with relevant evidence, observations, and ideas.

SL.8.1.d. Acknowledge new information expressed by others, and, when warranted, qualify or justify their own views in light of the evidence presented.

ELPS: ELP Standard 2

- participate in conversations, extended discussions, and written exchanges about a range of substantive topics, texts, and issues
- build on the ideas of others
- express his or her own ideas clearly and persuasively
- refer to specific and relevant evidence from texts or research to support his or her ideas
- ask and answer questions that probe reasoning and claim

ELP Standard 8

using context, questioning, and consistent knowledge of English morphology,

- determine the meaning of general academic and content-specific words and phrases, figurative and connotative language, and idiomatic expressions in spoken and written texts about a variety of topics, experiences, or events

Warm-up and Review
10–15 minutes (books closed)

Draw a pie chart on the board. Divide it into the approximate amount of time you spend on different activities during the day (for example, teaching: 25 percent, sleeping: 30 percent, entertainment: 15 percent, eating: 5 percent, social media: 5 percent, other: 12 percent, with 8 percent remaining). Explain or elicit what wasted time is. [time spent with nothing accomplished] Tell the class about your pie chart, including the percentage you noted for wasted time. Direct students to list all the activities they do during the day and then create a pie chart to show their results. Have students share their pie charts with a partner.

Introduction
5 minutes

1. Say: *Sometimes we can be surprised when we analyze how we spend our time.*

2. State the objective: *Today we're going to identify and discuss aspects of time management.*

1 Discuss time management

Presentation I
20–25 minutes

A 1. Read the directions aloud. Put students in teams to share their examples.

2. Elicit ideas and write them on the board.

B 1. Direct students to look at the definition. Ask: *Do you always think of time as something that you measure? Are there other ways to think about time?*

2. Write *time* on the board. Elicit related words and phrases from the whole class and write them on the board. Point out the connections between their ideas and their responses in 1A.

> **Possible Answers**
>
> to manage time well/poorly, to waste time, to be on time, to finish on time, to spend time

C 1. Direct students to look at the chart. Ask: *What kind of chart is it?* [bar graph] *What does it show?* [time management mistakes]

2. Direct students to look at the photo. Ask: *What do you see in the photo?* [a man looking at his phone thinking they can't finish the project by tomorrow] Point out any connections between the items and students' ideas in 1A.

> **MULTILEVEL STRATEGIES**
>
> To adapt 1C:
>
> • **Mixed-ability** Pair pre-level students with on- or higher-level students. Have pairs confirm definitions of the words in the chart and then list possible synonyms or other word forms. Call on students to explain the terms.

Guided Practice
10–20 minutes

D 1. Direct students to look at the first question. Check comprehension of the collocation. Ask: *What does it mean to manage time poorly?* [not use time well]

2. Set a time limit (five minutes). Direct students to work in pairs to complete the activity. Have a volunteer from each pair give their responses. Check answers as a class.

> **Possible Answers**
>
> 1. He looks stressed about finishing on time, but he's on his phone instead of working.
> 2. not eliminating distractions, procrastinating, multitasking
> 3. yesterday or a few days ago

Presentation II
20–25 minutes

E 1. Read the directions and steps aloud. Tell students to look at the chart again. Ask: *What are the four things people should do to eliminate most time management mistakes?* [prioritize, plan, eliminate distractions, estimate effort required better]

2. Group students and assign roles: manager, recorder, actor A, and actor B. Explain that students will work with their group to analyze the information. Verify students' understanding of the roles: the manager keeps the team on task and on time and edits the conversation, the recorder writes down the conversation the team creates, and the two actors play the roles of the two workers for the class.

3. Check comprehension of the task: *Which step does the entire team complete together?* [step 1]

4. Set a time limit (ten minutes) for the task.

5. Call time and have the actors from each group take turns performing their conversations.

Answers

mistakes made most often: not prioritizing and not planning; less of a problem: multitasking and not doing any time management; ways to manage time well: prioritize, plan, eliminate distractions, estimate effort required well, don't procrastinate, don't multitask, do time management

MULTILEVEL STRATEGIES

To adapt 1E:

• **On-level** Assign students the role of recorder.

• **Pre-level** Assign students the roles of actors.

• **Higher-level** Assign students the role of manager.

EXTENSION ACTIVITY

Analysis

1. Write a chart on the board with the headings *Team*, *Mistake*, and *Solution*.

2. Direct students to copy the chart into their notebooks.

3. Tell students to take notes in the chart as teams present their conversations.

4. Ask: *What did the conversations have in common? What solutions do you think will work best?*

Evaluation
10–15 minutes

SELF-ASSESSMENT

1. Ask students to spend some time reflecting on what they have learned. Set a time limit (three minutes).

2. Ask for volunteers to share their thoughts.

Lesson Overview

Lesson Notes

MULTILEVEL OBJECTIVES

On-level and Higher-level: Read about, listen to, and evaluate different cultural views of time

Pre-level: Read and listen to information about cultural views of time

LANGUAGE FOCUS

Grammar: Simple present, subordinating and coordinating clauses

Vocabulary: *distraction, interruption, perception,* transition words

For vocabulary support, see these **Oxford Picture Dictionary** topics: Time, pages 18–19; Soft Skills, page 178

STRATEGY FOCUS

Listen for how a speaker signals topics and transitions.

READINESS CONNECTION

In this lesson, students analyze similarities and differences across times and cultures.

PACING

To compress this lesson: Do 1C and 1D as an out-of-class assignment.

To extend this lesson: Have students work with others to create summaries (see page 32); Have students research and share time management tips (see page 33).

And/or have students complete **Multilevel Activities 5 Unit 2, Lesson 2.**

CORRELATIONS

CCRS: RI/RL.7.1 Cite several pieces of textual evidence to support analysis of what the text says explicitly as well as inferences drawn from the text.

SL.8.1.a. Come to discussions prepared, having read or researched material under study; explicitly draw on that preparation by referring to evidence on the topic, text, or issue to probe and reflect on ideas under discussion.

SL.8.1.c. Pose questions that connect the ideas of several speakers and respond to others' questions and comments with relevant evidence, observations, and ideas.

SL.8.1.d. Acknowledge new information expressed by others, and, when warranted, qualify or justify their own views in light of the evidence presented.

SL.8.2 Analyze the purpose of information presented in diverse media and formats (e.g., visually, quantitatively, orally) and evaluate the motives (e.g., social, commercial, political) behind its presentation.

ELPS: ELP Standard 1

use a wide range of strategies to:

- determine central ideas or themes in oral presentations and spoken and written texts
- analyze the development of the themes/ideas
- cite specific details and evidence from texts to support the analysis

ELP Standard 2

- participate in conversations, extended discussions, and written exchanges about a range of substantive topics, texts, and issues
- build on the ideas of others
- express his or her own ideas clearly and persuasively
- ask and answer questions that probe reasoning and claim

Warm-up and Review
10–15 minutes (books closed)

Write *Agree* and *Disagree* on opposite sides of the board. Call a group of students to the board. Say: *I am almost never late to an appointment.* Direct students to array themselves along the continuum between *Agree* and *Disagree* to indicate their position. Call on students to explain. Say: *I am often late to social events* and repeat the process with the same students. Continue with other students and other statements about time—for example, *As long as I get everything done, I'm not too worried about specific deadlines. I think it's rude to interrupt a conversation to say I have to go somewhere. When I have an appointment, I usually arrive early. I look at my watch or phone to check the time frequently.*

Introduction
5 minutes

1. Say: *As you can see, people view time differently.*

2. State the objective: *Today we will evaluate different cultural views of time.*

1 Read about how cultures view time differently

Presentation I
10–15 minutes

A   1. Put students in teams. Assign roles: manager, fact checker, recorder, and reporter.

2. Read the directions aloud.

3. Assign a time limit (three minutes). Call on reporters to share their ideas.

Guided Practice I
15–20 minutes

B   1. Read the directions aloud. Check comprehension. Ask: *What are you going to read?* [the first paragraph] *What does the article categorize?* [perceptions of time]

2. Set a time limit (five minutes). Direct students to underline the information that answers the question when they find it.

3. Elicit the answer.

Answer
two categories: *monochronic view of time* and *polychronic view of time*

TIP

Direct students' attention to the organization of the article. Ask: *How many paragraphs are there?* [four] *Where can you often find the main idea?* [in the introduction, often in the last sentence] *What is the topic of paragraph 2?* [monochronic culture] *Which sentence is the topic sentence?* [the first one] *What is the topic of paragraph 3?* [polychronic culture] *Which sentence is the topic sentence?* [the first one] *What does the conclusion do?* [describes a problem and solution] Point out that understanding the structure of an article can help students understand the main points and where to find them.

C   1. Read the directions aloud. Check comprehension. Ask: *How many example characteristics do you need to identify?* [one for each category]

2. Set a time limit (five minutes). Direct students to answer the question.

3. Elicit ideas from the whole class.

Answer
monochronic: time as "precious commodity"; emphasis on schedules, deadlines, and getting things done; focus on one task at a time; may not like distractions or interruptions
polychronic: view time in a more flexible way; value relationships as much as deadlines; comfortable working on multiple tasks at one; less likely to see interruptions as a problem

To adapt 1C:

- **Mixed-ability:** Pair pre-level students with on- or higher-level students. Have pre-level students follow along while partners read the text aloud and explain any unfamiliar vocabulary.

Communicative Practice
10–20 minutes

D 1. Read the questions aloud.

2. Ask students to think about and mark their answers in the text.

3. Set a time limit (five minutes) for students to discuss their answers with a partner.

4. Invite pairs to share their responses. Check answers as a class.

Answers
1. because people don't view time in exactly the same way everywhere in the world

2. Possible answer:
monochronic: People with this view see time as something that is in limited supply, so they focus more on schedules and deadlines. They may be less flexible about time.
polychronic: People with this view see time in a more flexible way. They give equal value to relationships and deadlines, so they may focus on socializing and building relationships even if it means being late to start a meeting. They may also be more comfortable with multiple tasks and interruptions when working.
3. starting a meeting late because people were socializing
4. Possible answer:
monochronic: Every day, I make a schedule for my day.
"…there is an emphasis on schedules"
There's no reason to ever miss a deadline.
"In a monochronic culture, people tend to view time as a precious commodity that is in limited supply. As a result, there is an emphasis on schedules, deadlines, and 'getting things done.'"

polychronic: It's important to finish a conversation, even if I'm late for an appointment. "…they value relationships as much as meeting deadlines."
I don't mind distractions like texts or phone calls when I'm working. "…less likely to see interruptions as problematic."

Presentation II
20–25 minutes

E 1. Read the directions aloud. Then read each statement from question 4 in 1D aloud and have students raise their hands if the statement expresses their view of time. Call on students to explain further.

2. Pair students to describe someone they know with a different view of time. Call on students to share their descriptions.

EXTENSION ACTIVITY
Summary Practice
1. Tell students to write a summary of the article.
2. Pair students to compare summaries.

2 Listen and take notes

Guided Practice II
20–25 minutes

A 1. Say: *Now we're going to listen to a lecture about time management strategies.*

2. Read the directions aloud.

3. Pair students. Set a time limit (three minutes). Direct students to complete the task.

4. Elicit ideas from the whole class. Write their ideas on the board.

B  **1.05** 1. Play the beginning of the audio. Direct students to listen without writing.

2. Replay the audio. Ask students to write what the speaker asks.

3. Pair students to discuss how they would answer the question. Elicit ideas from the class.

Answers
Question: How many of you feel that you could improve your time management?
Responses will vary.

C  **1.06** 1. Direct students' attention to the Listening Note. Point out that these phrases signal that the speaker is introducing topics or making transitions.

2. Direct students to look at the chart. Ask: *What are the three parts in the chart?* [*Time management issue, Why is it a problem?, Suggestions*] *How many issues are there?* [four]

3. Play the whole audio. Direct students to write notes in the chart as they listen.

<table>
<tr><td colspan="3">Answers</td></tr>
<tr><td colspan="3">Employability Skills Lecture Series
Lecture Topic: <u>Time management</u></td></tr>
<tr><td>Time management issue</td><td>Why is it a problem?</td><td>Suggestions</td></tr>
<tr><td>Not prioritizing</td><td>Need to know what's most important to manage time well</td><td>Do most important task 1st</td></tr>
<tr><td><u>interruptions</u> and <u>distractions</u></td><td><u>waste too much time</u></td><td>Some apps help
<u>Turn off ringer</u>
<u>Close email</u></td></tr>
<tr><td>multitasking</td><td>switching without knowing
<u>brain can't do</u>
↓ <u>productivity</u></td><td>Don't do it</td></tr>
<tr><td><u>procrastination</u></td><td>Don't get things done</td><td>Break task down
<u>Ask for help</u></td></tr>
</table>

MULTILEVEL STRATEGIES

- **On-level** Have students complete the activity as described.
- **Pre-level** Provide students with the answers in random order so they can choose the correct one.
- **Higher-level** Tell students to take notes on additional examples or explanations.

Communicative Practice
10–20 minutes

 **1.06** 1. Set a time limit (five minutes) for students to compare and discuss their answers with a partner.

2. Replay the audio. Ask students to confirm or add to their notes.

Presentation II
20–25 minutes

E  **1.16** 1. Read the directions aloud.

2. Play the audio.

3. Elicit answers from the class.

Answers
1. Our topic today is...
2. First (of all)
3. My next point is
4. Additionally,
5. Another (important) issue is...

F  1. Read the directions aloud. Direct students' attention to the expressions.

2. Pair students to discuss their answers using the expressions.

3. Call on students to share their ideas with the class.

Answer
more monochronic viewpoint

EXTENSION ACTIVITY

Research Other Tips

1. Tell students to go online and search for "time management tips." Have them find two new ones.

2. Call on students to share what they found.

Evaluation
10–15 minutes

SELF-ASSESSMENT

1. Read each item. Have students raise their hands if they had difficulty.

2. Pair students who had difficulty with those who did not to review ways to achieve each objective.

Lesson Overview	Lesson Notes

MULTILEVEL OBJECTIVES

On-level: Identify word families and suffixes used in noun formation; learn to combine ideas with subordinating clauses

Pre-level: Identify word families and suffixes used in noun formation; understand how to combine ideas with subordinating clauses

Higher-level: Identify word families and suffixes used in noun formation; combine ideas with subordinating clauses

LANGUAGE FOCUS

Grammar: Subordinate clauses

Vocabulary: *accomplishment, precise, priority, procrastination,* noun endings

For vocabulary support, see these **Oxford Picture Dictionary** topics: Time, pages 18–19; The Calendar, pages 20–21

STRATEGY FOCUS

Use subordinate clauses to combine ideas.

READINESS CONNECTION

In this lesson, students work with others to write questions about time management.

PACING

To compress this lesson: Students do 1A and 1B for homework.

To extend this lesson: Have students rephrase information (see page 36); Have students find and write sentences with subordinate clauses (see page 37).

And/or have students complete **Multilevel Activities 5 Unit 2, Lesson 3**.

CORRELATIONS

CCRS: SL.8.1.a. Come to discussions prepared, having read or researched material under study; explicitly draw on that preparation by referring to evidence on the topic, text, or issue to probe and reflect on ideas under discussion.

SL.8.1.c. Pose questions that connect the ideas of several speakers and respond to others' questions and comments with relevant evidence, observations, and ideas.

SL.8.1.d. Acknowledge new information expressed by others, and, when warranted, qualify or justify their own views in light of the evidence presented.

L.6.1/8.1.j. Explain the function of phrases and clauses in general and their function in specific sentences.

L.6.1/8.1.l. Place phrases and clauses within a sentence, recognizing and correcting misplaced and dangling modifiers.

L.6.4.b. Use common, grade-appropriate Greek or Latin affixes and roots as clues to the meaning of a word (e.g., *audience, auditory, audible*).

L.6.4.c. Consult reference materials (e.g., dictionaries, glossaries, thesauruses), both print and digital, to find the pronunciation of a word or determine or clarify its precise meaning or its part of speech.

ELPS: ELP Standard 2

- participate in conversations, extended discussions, and written exchanges about a range of substantive topics, texts, and issues
- build on the ideas of others
- express his or her own ideas clearly and persuasively

<table>
<tr><td>

ELP Standard 8

using context, questioning, and consistent knowledge of English morphology,

- determine the meaning of general academic and content-specific words and phrases, figurative and connotative language, and idiomatic expressions in spoken and written texts about a variety of topics, experiences, or events

</td><td>

ELP Standard 10

- use complex phrases and clauses
- produce and expand simple, compound, and complex sentences

</td></tr>
</table>

Warm-up and Review
10–15 minutes (books closed)

As a review of the terms *monochronic* and *polychronic*, say examples of each view of time in random order. Direct students to raise their right hands if the detail describes a monochronic viewpoint and their left hands if it describes a polychronic viewpoint.

Introduction
5 minutes

1. Say: *One way to restate or rephrase ideas is to use different word forms. Another way can be to change the sentence from the active to passive voice.*

2. State the objective: *Today we are going to identify word families and suffixes used in noun formation and learn to combine ideas with subordinating clauses.*

1 Vocabulary: Noun endings

Presentation and Guided Practice I
20–25 minutes

 1. Write *manage* and *management* on the board. Ask: *Which is a noun?* [*management*] *How do you know?* [It ends in *-ment*.]

2. Copy the chart on the board.

3. Read the directions aloud.

4. Direct students to complete the task independently.

5. Call on students to add words to the chart on the board.

Answers
1. manage; management
2. distract; <u>distraction</u>
3. <u>procrastinate</u>; procrastination
4. interrupt; <u>interruption</u>
5. accomplish; <u>accomplishment</u>
6. <u>prioritize</u>; priority
7. perceive; <u>perception</u>

- **On-level** Have students complete activity as directed and then check their answers in a dictionary.
- **Pre-level** Have students use dictionaries.
- **Higher-level** Have students add definitions to their charts.

Communicative Practice
15–20 minutes

 1. Read the directions aloud.

2. Pair students. Set a time limit (five minutes) for students to complete the activity.

3. Elicit and underline the suffix in each noun (*-ment, -ion, -ity*).

4. Call on students to share their lists and write the words.

5. Elicit other common noun endings (*-er / -or, -ness, -ism, -ship, -ance / -ence, -is*).

Answers
endings: *-ment, -ion* or *-tion, -ity*
possible other words: *development, employment, appointment; demonstration, admission, decision; ability, activity, similarity, responsibility*

 1. Read the directions aloud.

2. Set a time limit (five minutes) for students to complete the activity individually.

3. Call on volunteers to read the completed sentences aloud.

Answers
1. perceive or manage
2. accomplish
3. priority
4. interrupt
5. distraction

Presentation II
20–25 minutes

D 1. Read the directions aloud.

2. Put students in teams and assign roles: manager, fact checker, recorder, and reporter.

3. Set a time limit (five minutes).

4. Have each team join another team to ask and answer their questions.

5. Call on reporters to share their questions.

To adapt 1D:

• **Higher-level** Direct students to write three additional questions.

EXTENSION ACTIVITY

Rephrasing Practice

1. Tell students to write three time management tips using words from the chart.

2. Pair students to exchange tips and rewrite them using different word forms.

3. Call on students to read their tips to the class.

2 Grammar: Subordinate clauses

Presentation and Guided Practice II
20–25 minutes

A 1. Demonstrate how to read the first two charts. Read each sentence aloud and have students repeat after you. Ask: *Can a subordinate clause come before the main clause?* [yes] *Can it come after?* [yes] *How can you recognize the subordinate clause?* [It begins with a word like *although, since, unless,* or *when.*]

2. Direct students' attention to the third chart. Say: *Subordinate clauses express relationships between ideas. They often answer questions like* When? Why? *and* Under what condition? Elicit the relationship between the ideas in the first two charts. [contrast, cause/effect, condition, time]

3. Have students complete the Language Connection about subordinate clauses. Go over the answers with the class.

Answers
combine, is not, use, do not use

To adapt 2A:

• **On-level** Have students work independently.

• **Pre-level** Have students work with higher-level classmates.

• **Higher-level** Have students work with pre-level classmates.

TIP

Write additional sentences with subordinate clauses in different positions on the board. Don't add commas even if necessary. Then work with the class to identify the subordinators, the subordinate clauses, the main clauses, the meaning, and whether a comma is needed. Point out that if students identify the subordinators first, understanding the structure of the sentence is easier.

Guided Practice III
20–25 minutes

B 1. Ask students to work individually to complete the task and then compare answers with a partner.

2. Ask volunteers to write the sentences on the board.

Answers
1. SC
2. SC
3. MC
4. MC
5. SC

To adapt 2B:

• **On-level** Have students work independently.

• **Pre-level** Group pre-level students. Ask them to identify and circle the subordinators first.

• **Higher-level** Direct students to rewrite the sentences using different clause order and/or subordinators.

C 1. Read the directions aloud.

2. Call on a student to read the sentences in item 1. Ask: *What relationship between ideas do you need to express?* [contrast] *What subordinators can you use?* [although, even though, though, while]

3. Ask students to work individually to combine the sentences using subordinate clauses.

4. Call on volunteers to write their sentences on the board. Correct as necessary.

Possible Answers
1. While people with a monochronic view consider time a precious commodity, people with a polychronic view tend not to.   2. Because people with a monochronic view of time tend to focus on one thing at a time, they may not like interruptions.   3. There can be misunderstandings in the workplace if people do not understand different perceptions of time.

D 1. Set a time limit (five minutes) for students to share their sentences in 2C with a partner.

2. Ask volunteers to write sentences on the board.

3. If students disagree, ask them to look at the chart and explain their answers.

EXTENSION ACTIVITY
Examples from the News
1. Have students work in pairs to find articles or other texts online.
2. Ask them to locate four to eight sentences using subordinate clauses. They should find one expressing each relationship.
3. Tell students to rewrite their examples as two separate sentences without subordinators.
4. Pair students to exchange their sentences and combine them with subordinate clauses.
5. Call on students to write their sentences on the board.

Evaluation
10–15 minutes

SELF-ASSESSMENT

1. Have students complete the self-assessment.

2. Provide additional practice as needed.

Lesson Overview

Lesson Notes

MULTILEVEL OBJECTIVES

On-level and Pre-level: Read about timekeeping throughout history and discuss historical events

Higher-level: Read about timekeeping throughout history and discuss and analyze historical events

LANGUAGE FOCUS

Grammar: Simple past active and passive forms

Vocabulary: *devise, migration, measure, emerge, precedence*

For vocabulary support, see these **Oxford Picture Dictionary** topics: The Calendar, pages 20–21; U.S. History, page 208; World History, page 209

STRATEGY FOCUS

Use phrases to clarify and challenge conclusions.

READINESS CONNECTION

In this lesson, students interpret information in a timeline.

PACING

To compress this lesson: Assign 2B and/or 2C for homework.

To extend this lesson: Have students create conversations in which they clarify or challenge conclusions (see page 40); Have students make timelines of their lives (see page 42).

And/or have students complete **Multilevel Activities 5 Unit 2, Lesson 4**.

CORRELATIONS

CCRS: RI/RL.7.1 Cite several pieces of textual evidence to support analysis of what the text says explicitly as well as inferences drawn from the text.

RI/RL.6.4 Determine the meaning of words and phrases as they are used in a text, including figurative, connotative, and technical meanings; analyze the impact of a specific word choice on meaning and tone.

RI.6.5 Analyze how a particular sentence, paragraph, chapter, or section fits into the overall structure of a text and contributes to the development of the ideas.

RI.7.5 Analyze the structure an author uses to organize a text, including how the major sections contribute to the whole and to the development of the ideas.

RI.8.6 Determine an author's point of view or purpose in a text and analyze how the author acknowledges and responds to conflicting evidence or viewpoints.

RI.6.7 Integrate information presented in different media or formats (e.g., in charts, graphs, photographs, videos, or maps) as well as in words to develop a coherent understanding of a topic or issue.

RST.6-8.7 Integrate quantitative or technical information expressed in words in a text with a version of that information expressed visually (e.g., in a flowchart, diagram, model, graph, or table).

RI.8.9 Analyze a case in which two or more texts provide conflicting information on the same topic and identify where the texts disagree on matters of fact or interpretation.

W.7.7 Conduct short research projects to answer a question, drawing on several sources and generating additional related, focused questions for further research and investigation.

SL.8.1.a. Come to discussions prepared, having read or researched material under study; explicitly draw on that preparation by referring to evidence on the topic, text, or issue to probe and reflect on ideas under discussion.

SL.8.1.c. Pose questions that connect the ideas of several speakers and respond to others' questions and comments with relevant evidence, observations, and ideas.

SL.8.1.d. Acknowledge new information expressed by others, and, when warranted, qualify or justify their own views in light of the evidence presented.

SL.8.2 Analyze the purpose of information presented in diverse media and formats (e.g., visually, quantitatively, orally) and evaluate the motives (e.g., social, commercial, political) behind its presentation.

L.6.4.c. Consult reference materials (e.g., dictionaries, glossaries, thesauruses), both print and digital, to find the pronunciation of a word or determine or clarify its precise meaning or its part of speech.

ELPS: ELP Standard 1

use a wide range of strategies to:

- cite specific details and evidence from texts to support the analysis
- summarize a text

ELP Standard 2

- participate in conversations, extended discussions, and written exchanges about a range of substantive topics, texts, and issues
- build on the ideas of others
- express his or her own ideas clearly and persuasively
- refer to specific and relevant evidence from texts or research to support his or her ideas
- ask and answer questions that probe reasoning and claims
- summarize the key points and evidence discussed

ELP Standard 7

- adapt language choices and style according to purpose, task, and audience with ease in various social and academic contexts
- use a wide variety of complex general academic and content specific words and phrases
- employ both formal and more informal styles and tones effectively in spoken and written texts, as appropriate

ELP Standard 8

using context, questioning, and consistent knowledge of English morphology,

- determine the meaning of general academic and content-specific words and phrases, figurative and connotative language, and idiomatic expressions in spoken and written texts about a variety of topics, experiences, or events

Warm-up and Review
10–15 minutes (books closed)

On slips of paper, write events from the timeline on pages 20–21 but omit the dates: the wheel invented, papyrus/early paper invented, first Olympics, explorers from Greenland reach North America, first printing press, telephone invented, first gas-powered car, first airplane, first personal computers, etc. Call students to the front of the class and give each student a slip. Direct them to stand in a line to show the time order of the events. Explain that they may not know the dates, but they should take their best guesses. When they are standing in place, have students reread the events so the rest of the class can discuss/confirm their order. After the class reaches a consensus, have them check their order against the timeline on pages 20–21.

Introduction
5 minutes

State the objective: *Today we will read about timekeeping throughout history and discuss historical events.*

1 Get ready to read

Presentation I
20–25 minutes

A 🔊 **1.07** 1. Say: *Now we're going to listen to a conversation.*

2. Play the audio. Direct students to answer the question.

Answer
They're discussing whether people need or buy clocks and watches anymore.

B 🔊 **1.07** 1. Replay the audio. Ask students to check the expressions.

2. Check answers as a class.

Answers
Why do you say that? What do you mean? Can/Could you back that up? How about this?

TIP

Check comprehension of the expressions in 1B. Ask: *What does it mean to* back something up*?* [provide evidence] Explain or elicit that speakers say *How about this?* before they present contradictory information or evidence.

C 1. Read the directions aloud. Call on students to read the statements aloud.

2. Group students and assign roles: manager, recorder, reporter, and editor. Check comprehension of tasks: *Who keeps the team on task and on time?* [manager] *Who takes notes and writes any new statements?* [recorder] *Who checks grammar and spelling?* [editor] *Who reports to the class?* [reporter]

3. Set a time limit (three minutes) and have students work together to complete the task.

4. Call time and have the reporters from each group take turns calling out their ideas. Ask editors to write any original statements on the board.

Answers
Answers will vary.

MULTILEVEL STRATEGIES

To adapt 1C:

• **On-level** Assign these students the roles of recorder and manager.

• **Pre-level** Assign these students the role of reporter.

• **Higher-level** Assign these students role of editor.

EXTENSION ACTIVITY
Partner Debates

1. Pair students who chose opposite statements (for example, *We don't need clocks nowadays.* and *We still need clocks.*).

2. Have pairs create conversations in which they debate the issue using the expressions from 1B.

3. Call on volunteers to perform their conversations for the class.

2 Preview and read

Guided Practice I
20–25 minutes

A 1. Read the directions aloud. Ask: *What should you do when you preview an article?* [read the title and headings, look at visuals, skim the first and last paragraphs, skim first lines of other paragraphs]

2. Have students answer the question individually, and then check answers as a class.

Answers
chronologically or historically over time

TIP

Guide students in the preview process. Ask: *What is the title?* [A History of Time-keeping] *What do you see in the pictures?* [a sundial and an old clock] *What will the article be about?* [measuring or keeping time over the course of history]

B 1. Ask students to read the article silently and answer the question and then compare answers with a partner.

2. Check answers as a class. Say: *The first time you read an article, you should focus on the main idea or ideas.*

Possible Answer
because society became larger and more complex

MULTILEVEL STRATEGIES

To adapt 2B:

• **Pre-level** Work with pre-level students to have them read the article aloud. Stop after each paragraph and check comprehension.

• **On-level** Have students complete the activity as directed.

• **Higher-level** Direct students to write the main idea of the article in their own words.

Presentation II
20–25 minutes

C 1. Read the directions aloud. Call on students to read the questions aloud.

2. Set a time limit (ten minutes) and have students work individually to complete the task.

3. Call time. Have students compare answers in pairs.

4. Go over the answers with the class.

Possible Answers
1. the rhythms of nature: sunrise and sunset, changing of the seasons, position of the stars 2. because society was smaller and less complex and time-keeping was more linked to the rhythms of nature 3. 1. sundials: only work when sun is shining; 2. Egyptian division into 24 hours: length of one hour varied between summer and winter because of difference in daylight 4. water clock; water will drip at a fairly constant rate from a container with a hole at the bottom. 5. Schedules were more linked and manufacturers and merchants needed more precise time-keeping. 6. It divided the day into 24 equal units. 7. The growth of manufacturing and trade and denser urban communities made more precise time-keeping more important and necessary. 8. The author believes there are possible advantages and disadvantages as a result of this development.

TIP

Tell students to read the questions first and underline important or key words. This will help students know what information to pay attention to as they read. For example, *nature* and *information* are key words they can scan for to find the answer to the first question.

WORD STUDY

1. Read the directions and the prompts aloud.

2. Write the chart on the board.

3. Set a time limit (five minutes). Have students work in pairs to answer the questions.

4. Ask volunteers to write words in the chart.

5. Elicit definitions.

Answers
migration: movement of large numbers of people or animals from one place to another measure: to find the size, quantity etc. of something in standard units emerge: to start to exist, appear or become known precedence: the condition of being more important than somebody or something else

Verb	Noun
migrate	migration
measure	measurement
emerge	emergence
precede	precedence

1. Direct students' attention to the Speaking Note. Read the directions and questions aloud.

2. Have students work with their teams from 1C. Assign roles: manager (keep team on time and on task), fact checker (check facts and look up words), recorder (take notes), and reporter (report to the class).

3. Set a time limit (five minutes).

4. Call time. Ask reporters from each team to share their ideas.

Answers
Answers will vary.

3 Build on it

Presentation I
20–25 minutes

A 1. Have students stay in their teams from 2E and look at the timeline. Remind students that some of these events were used in the warm-up activity.

2. Read the directions and questions aloud, or call on students to read them aloud.

3. Set a time limit (ten minutes). Have students work in teams to complete the task. Suggest that fact checkers use their phones to check math.

Answers
1. 2,492 2. longest: the time span between the first two events; shortest: the time span between the last two events 3. Answers will vary. 4. Answers will vary.

 1. Have students stay in their teams with the same roles.

2. Read the directions and questions aloud.

3. Elicit answers. Use expressions to clarify or challenge conclusions.

Answers
Answers will vary.

PROBLEM SOLVING

 1. Ask students to stay in their teams with the same roles. Explain that students will work with their group to discuss the questions. Remind students to use expressions to clarify or challenge conclusions if appropriate.

2. Set a time limit (five minutes) and have students work together to complete the task.

3. Call time and have the reporters from each group take turns calling out their answers.

Answers
Answers will vary.

APPLY YOUR KNOWLEDGE

1. Ask students to complete the research task individually.

2. Have students work in their teams from 2E with the same roles to share their research.

3. Call on reporters to share their teams' ideas with the class.

EXTENSION ACTIVITY

Personal Timelines

1. Tell students to make timelines that cover the span of their lives so far. Direct them to add the world events that had the greatest impact on them personally.

2. Pair students to share their timelines.

Evaluation
10–15 minutes

SELF-ASSESSMENT

1. Direct students to complete the self-assessment individually.

2. Have students choose the one objective they have the most difficulty with.

3. Group students according to their weakest skill. Provide each group with suggestions or feedback.

<table>
<tr><td>

Lesson Overview

</td><td>

Lesson Notes

</td></tr>
</table>

MULTILEVEL OBJECTIVES

On-level: Use the writing process to summarize an article

Pre-level: Write sentences

Higher-level: Summarize an article using subordinate clauses

LANGUAGE FOCUS

Grammar: Subordinate clauses

Vocabulary: For vocabulary support, see this **Oxford Picture Dictionary** topic: English Composition, pages 202–203

STRATEGY FOCUS

Use time expressions to show the order of events.

READINESS CONNECTION

In this lesson, students synthesize information to write a summary.

PACING

To compress this lesson: Do 1B as a class.

To extend this lesson: Have students use a discussion board to post summaries and give feedback (see page 45). And/or have students complete **Multilevel Activities 5 Unit 2, Lesson 5.**

CORRELATIONS

CCRS: W/WHST.6-8.2.a. Introduce a topic clearly, previewing what is to follow; organize ideas, concepts, and information, using strategies such as definition, classification, comparison /contrast, and cause/effect; include formatting (e.g., headings), graphics (e.g., charts, tables), and multimedia when useful to aiding comprehension.

W/WHST.6-8.2.b. Develop the topic with relevant facts, definitions, concrete details, quotations, or other information and examples.

W/WHST.6-8.2.c. Use appropriate transitions to create cohesion and clarify the relationships among ideas and concepts.

W/WHST.6-8.2.d. Use precise language and domain-specific vocabulary to inform about or explain the topic.

W/WHST.6-8.2.f. Provide a concluding statement or section that follows from and supports the information or explanation presented.

W/WHST.6-8.4 Produce clear and coherent writing in which the development and organization and style are appropriate to task, purpose, and audience.

W/WHST.6-8.5 With some guidance and support from peers and others, develop and strengthen writing as needed by planning, revising, editing, rewriting, or trying a new approach, focusing on how well purpose and audience have been addressed.

L.6.3/7.3.c. Choose language that expresses ideas precisely and concisely, recognizing and eliminating wordiness and redundancy.

L.8.6 Acquire and use accurately level-appropriate general academic and domain-specific words and phrases; gather vocabulary knowledge when considering a word or phrase important to comprehension or expression.

ELPS: ELP Standard 7

- adapt language choices and style according to purpose, task, and audience with ease in various social and academic contexts
- use a wide variety of complex general academic and content specific words and phrases
- employ both formal and more informal styles and tones effectively in spoken and written texts, as appropriate

<table>
<tr><td>

ELP Standard 9

- recount a complex and detailed sequence of events or steps in a process, with an effective sequential or chronological order
- introduce and effectively develop an informational topic with facts, details, and evidence
- use complex and varied transitions to link the major sections of speech and text and to clarify relationships among events and ideas
- provide a concluding section or statement

</td><td>

ELP Standard 10

- produce and expand simple, compound, and complex sentences

</td></tr>
</table>

Warm-up and Review
10–15 minutes (books closed)

Go around the room and call on each student to say one thing he or she remembers from the article on time-keeping in Lesson 4. Jot notes on the board.

Introduction
5 minutes

State the objective: *Today we will use the writing process to summarize an article.*

1 Write a summary

Presentation I
20–25 minutes

 1. Have students revisit the article on pages 18–19. Check comprehension. Ask: *What is the article about? What are the most important ideas?*

2. Elicit responses. Record any new information not mentioned in the warm-up on the board.

Guided Practice I
15–20 minutes

 1. Direct students to look at the chart. Ask about the article's organization: *What paragraph is the introduction?* [the first] *The conclusion?* [the last]

2. Check comprehension of the activity. Ask: *Do you need to write complete sentences in the chart?* [no]

3. Have students work individually to complete their charts.

Answers

Introduction:
Thousands of years ago, people relied on the rhythms of nature to keep track of time.

Early examples of devices, problems/issues:
sundials: dependent on sun shining
ancient Egyptians: divided day into 24 units (hours) based on daylight and darkness, but length of hour varied in summer and winter
water clock: most precise but could freeze in cold places

Reasons better timekeeping devices needed:
needed something not based on nature
society became more urban and complex →
needed more precise time-keeping

Timekeeping solution:
mechanical clock: divided day into 24 equal units and didn't depend on nature

Conclusion:
mechanical clock = revolution because made measurement of time consistent and separated human events from nature

---

C 1. Read the directions aloud. Check comprehension. Ask: *What do you need to include in a statement of the main idea?* [the topic, or what the article is about, and the controlling idea, or the writer's main focus/point]

2. Have students work individually to write their statements. Encourage students to use the sentence frame. Then ask students to compare statements in pairs.

Write the sentence frame from 1C on the board: *In [title of article], the writer describes...* Tell students that sometimes they can find a statement of the main idea in the text and copy it. Other times they may need to make a new sentence. One way to do this is to put the topic in the subject position of the sentence. Elicit the topic and write it in the ellipses. [the ways people keep or measure time] Then elicit the most important point the writer makes. [that they have changed over time]

D 1. Check comprehension. Ask: *What paragraph do you need to reread?* [the last]

2. Have students work individually to write their conclusions.

Direct students' attention to the last paragraph. Elicit synonyms and other word forms for key words in the conclusion. [*mechanical clock, time daily activities, gain precedence, change, rhythm of human life*] Remind students that they can use synonyms and different word forms to rephrase ideas.

E 1. Read the directions aloud. Check comprehension. Ask: *What will you include in your summary?* [introduction, notes from the chart, conclusion]

2. Draw students' attention to the Writer's Note. Ask: *What do all these connecting words show?* [the order of events] *Which words or phrases can we use for the earliest events?* [*in the beginning, at first, first, at the start*] *Which words or phrases can we use to signal a new event somewhere in the middle?* [*next, then, after that*] *Which words or phrases introduce the last event?* [*finally, lastly the last*]

3. Have students work individually to write their summaries.

MULTILEVEL STRATEGIES

To adapt 1E:

• **On-level** Have students write summaries as directed.

• **Pre-level** Work with students in a group to write the summary together.

• **Higher-level** Have students add examples and details to their summaries.

2 Get feedback and revise

Guided Practice II
10–15 minutes

A Direct students to check their writing using the editing checklist. Tell them to read each item in the list and check their papers before moving on to the next item. Explain that students should not edit their writing at this stage. They should just use the checklist to check their work and mark any areas they want to revise.

Communicative Practice
10–15 minutes

B 1. Read the directions aloud. Emphasize to students that they are responding to their partners' work, not correcting it.

2. Direct students to exchange papers with a partner and follow the instructions.

C Allow students time to edit and revise their writing using the editing checklist and their partner's feedback. If necessary, students could complete this task as homework.

MULTILEVEL STRATEGIES

To adapt 2C:

• **Mixed-ability** Pair pre-level students with on- and higher-level students. Have all students point out ideas that are not clear. Instruct on- and higher-level partners to give feedback on spelling and grammar if helpful.

EXTENSION ACTIVITY

Discussion Board

1. Tell students to post their summaries to a discussion board.

2. Direct students to give feedback on two of their classmates' summaries.

Evaluation
10–15 minutes

SELF-ASSESSMENT

1. Call on students to read their completed sentences aloud.

2. Use the responses to the second statement to plan follow-up activities.

Lesson Overview

MULTILEVEL OBJECTIVES

On-level: Students conduct a survey on time management and present the results to the class

Pre-level: Students help conduct a survey and time management and present results to the class

Higher-level: Students conduct a survey, analyze results, and present them to the class

LANGUAGE FOCUS

Grammar: Simple present, adverbs of frequency

Vocabulary: Time management

For vocabulary support, see these **Oxford Picture Dictionary** topics: Time, pages 18–19; Internet Research, pages 212–213

STRATEGY FOCUS

Signal transitions between speakers to help your audience follow the flow of information.

READINESS CONNECTION

In this lesson, students collaborate to develop quantifiable survey questions.

PACING

To compress this lesson: Assign 1A for homework, or provide students with topics to expedite 1A.

To extend this lesson: Have students work in pairs to debrief about their presentations (see page 49).

And/or have students complete **Multilevel Activities 5 Unit 2, Lesson 6**.

Lesson Notes

CORRELATIONS

CCRS: W.7.7 Conduct short research projects to answer a question, drawing on several sources and generating additional related, focused questions for further research and investigation.

W.7.8 Gather relevant information from multiple print and digital sources, using search terms effectively; assess the credibility and accuracy of each source; and quote or paraphrase the data and conclusions of others while avoiding plagiarism and following a standard format for citation.

SL.8.4 Present claims and findings, emphasizing salient points in a focused, coherent manner with relevant evidence, sound valid reasoning, and well-chosen details; use appropriate eye contact, adequate volume, and clear pronunciation.

SL.8.6 Adapt speech to a variety of contexts and tasks, demonstrating command of formal English when indicated or appropriate.

L.6.3/7.3.b. Maintain consistency in style and tone.

L.6.3/7.3.c. Choose language that expresses ideas precisely and concisely, recognizing and eliminating wordiness and redundancy.

L.8.6 Acquire and use accurately level-appropriate general academic and domain-specific words and phrases; gather vocabulary knowledge when considering a word or phrase important to comprehension or expression.

ELPS: ELP Standard 2

- participate in conversations, extended discussions, and written exchanges about a range of substantive topics, texts, and issues
- build on the ideas of others
- express his or her own ideas clearly and persuasively

ELP Standard 3

- deliver oral presentations
- compose written informational texts
- fully develop the topic with relevant details, concepts, examples, and information

ELP Standard 5	ELP Standard 7
• carry out both short and more sustained research projects to answer a question or solve a problem • gather information from multiple print and digital sources • use advanced search terms effectively • synthesize information from multiple print and digital sources • analyze and integrate information into clearly organized spoken and written texts	• adapt language choices and style according to purpose, task, and audience with ease in various social and academic contexts • use a wide variety of complex general academic and content specific words and phrases • employ both formal and more informal styles and tones effectively in spoken and written texts, as appropriate

Warm-up and Review
10–15 minutes (books closed)

Write a mind map on the board with *Time management* in a circle in the center. With the class, elicit ideas related to time management and add them to the mind map with radiating lines and circles.

Introduction
5 minutes

1. Say: *Time management has many aspects.*

2. State the objective: *Today we will conduct a survey on time management and present the survey results to the class.*

1 Create a survey on time management

Communicative Practice
40–45 minutes

A 1. Group students but do not assign roles yet. Explain that students will work with their team to identify survey topics.

2. Read the directions aloud.

3. Direct students' attention to the Research Tip. Ask: *Why might it be helpful to look at examples of surveys?* [to get ideas about the types of questions to include, to see how questions are written]

4. Check comprehension of the task. Ask: *How many topics should you include?* [several]

5. Set a time limit (ten minutes) and have students work together to complete the task. Alternatively, assign this as an out-of-class assignment.

B 1. Read the directions aloud.

2. Call on students to read the questions aloud.

3. Ask: *Why are these good question types to use?* [they have limited answers, yes/no, only four frequency adverbs]

4. Draw students' attention to the Research Tip. Check comprehension. Ask: *What is a quantifiable answer?* [one that helps you count results] Ask: *Can you quantify the answers to the example questions?* [yes]

5. Set a time limit (five minutes). Direct students to complete the task individually or in pairs.

MULTILEVEL STRATEGIES

To adapt 1B:

• **On-level and pre-level** Direct students to write five questions.

• **Higher-level** Direct students to write eight to ten questions.

TIP

Write some open-ended questions on the board (for example, *How do you procrastinate?*). Elicit answers from the class. Point out or elicit that when a question has many answers, it is hard to talk about the results.

C 1. Have students rejoin their teams to choose the eight to ten best questions.

2. Set a time limit (five minutes).

3. Call time. Tell students to write the questions so they each have a copy.

Provide students with a model chart that they can use to capture their results. Write the example questions in the chart. Ask the questions of the class, and note their answers (by name or by tally of number of responses). Encourage students to do the same with their questions. Point out that they can use the same kind of chart to assemble their data in 1E.

QUESTION	ANSWER CHOICES			
Do you ever procrastinate?	Yes 16		No 9	
How often do you procrastinate?	Often 7	Sometimes 6	Rarely 3	Never 9
How many tasks do you usually do at one time?	1 7	2 10	3 8	

D 1. Check comprehension of the task. Ask: *How many people will you each survey?* [four or five]

2. Set a time limit (for example, two days or before the next class).

E 1. Have students analyze their results in their teams.

2. Assign roles: manager, IT/number cruncher, recorder, and editor. Explain that students will work with their team to complete the task.

3. Check comprehension of the activity. Ask: *Who compiles the information from all sources?* [recorder] *Who checks that the numbers are accurate?* [IT/number cruncher] *Who keeps the team on time and on task?* [manager] *Who checks that grammar and spelling are correct?* [editor]

4. Set a time limit (ten minutes) and have students work together.

MULTILEVEL STRATEGIES

To adapt 1E:

- **On-level** Assign these students the roles of IT/number cruncher and manager.
- **Pre-level** Assign these students the role of recorder.
- **Higher-level** Assign these students the role of editor.

2 Present your survey results

Presentation
40–45 minutes

A 1. Have students stay in their teams. Check comprehension of the task. Ask: *What does the outline include?* [introduction, body, and conclusion] *What should you do in the introduction?* [tell the audience how you structured the survey and why] *What will the survey results help you do in the conclusion?* [offer suggestions for time management]

2. Read the phrases to summarize survey results aloud. Point out that editor and number cruncher on each team should work together to use these phrases.

3. Draw students' attention to the Presentation Strategy. Read it aloud.

4. Set a time limit (five to ten minutes) and have students work as a team to outline their oral report and choose a way to signal transitions between speakers.

B 1. Explain that students will work with their team to present their survey results.

2. Check comprehension of the activity. Ask: *Who will speak?* [everyone]

3. Set a time limit (five minutes) and have students work as a team to divide the roles and the sections of the presentation (for example, introduction, questions 1–2, questions 3–4, conclusion).

C 1. Read the bulleted items aloud.

2. Check comprehension of the activity. Ask: *Should you rehearse the presentation in exactly the way you will present to the class?* [yes]

3. Set a time limit (ten minutes) and have students rehearse their presentations in teams.

D 1. Draw a chart on the board, listing the teams in the first column. In the other columns, list the note-taking prompts or shortened forms of them: *Clear presentation, Transitions, Strengths, Advice.* Check comprehension of the activity. Ask: *What will you write under Clear presentation?* [how clearly each team presented its survey results] Remind students to just use words and phrases in the chart.

2. Set a time limit (five minutes) for each presentation, and ask each team to present in turn.

E 1. Have teams discuss their feedback for the other teams.

2. Ask each team to nominate a reporter to give feedback on the other teams' presentations.

3. Beginning with the first team to present, collect feedback from the reporters. Write feedback in the table you drew on the board in 2D.

EXTENSION ACTIVITY

Pair Debrief

1. Pair students from different presentation groups.

2. Write *gender, age, job,* and *other* on the board.

3. Have pairs discuss the people they surveyed. Ask: *How might the factors on the board affect answers?*

4. Elicit responses from the class.

Evaluation
10–15 minutes

SELF-ASSESSMENT

1. Pair students to share their self-assessments.

2. Elicit suggestions from the class for developing more confidence in each of the assessment areas.

3 Information

Unit Overview

This unit explores sources of information, ways to evaluate them, and how statistics can reflect bias with a range of employability skills and language to identify bias and adjective clauses. By the end of this unit, you will be able to conduct and present research related to interpreting information.

KEY OBJECTIVES

Lesson 1	Identify and evaluate sources of news and information
Lesson 2	Evaluate sources of information
Lesson 3	Identify bias; combine ideas with adjective clauses to create complex sentences
Lesson 4	Interpret statistics in a text; identify and discuss bias in a text that cites statistics
Lesson 5	Use the writing process to summarize an article
Lesson 6	Conduct and present research related to information

UNIT FEATURES

Academic Vocabulary	*authoritative, biased, coerce, conspiracy, confirmation, convincing, manipulate, scheme, source, statistics*
Employability Skills	• Interpret statistics in texts and visuals • Analyze different forms of bias • Advise on how to research and present full, accurate, and reliable information • Collaborate to synthesize and evaluate sources • Work with a team to research and report on an example of bad information
Resources	**Class Audio** CD1, Tracks 08–10 **Teacher Resource Center** Multilevel Activities 5 Unit 3 Multilevel Grammar Activities 5 Unit 3 Unit 3 Test **Oxford Picture Dictionary** Feelings, The Library, English Composition, Mathematics, Internet Research, Entertainment

Lesson Overview

Lesson Notes

MULTILEVEL OBJECTIVES

On-level: Identify and evaluate sources of news and information

Pre-level: Identify and discuss sources of news and information

Higher-level: Identify and discuss sources of news and information; lead discussion

LANGUAGE FOCUS

Grammar: Present, present continuous, present perfect

Vocabulary: *Information, inform, informative* and synonyms, *source, statistic*

For vocabulary support, see these **Oxford Picture Dictionary** topics: The Library, page 135; Internet Research, pages 212–213; Entertainment, pages 242–243

READINESS CONNECTION

In this lesson, students interpret statistics in texts and visuals.

PACING

To compress this lesson: Do 1D as a class.

To extend this lesson: Have students role-play reporting information they have gathered (see page 53).

And/or have students complete **Multilevel Activities 5 Unit 3, Lesson 1**.

CORRELATIONS

CCRS: RI.6.7 Integrate information presented in different media or formats (e.g., in charts, graphs, photographs, videos, or maps) as well as in words to develop a coherent understanding of a topic or issue.

RST.6-8.7 Integrate quantitative or technical information expressed in words in a text with a version of that information expressed visually (e.g., in a flowchart, diagram, model, graph, or table).

SL.8.1.a. Come to discussions prepared, having read or researched material under study; explicitly draw on that preparation by referring to evidence on the topic, text, or issue to probe and reflect on ideas under discussion.

SL.8.1.c. Pose questions that connect the ideas of several speakers and respond to others' questions and comments with relevant evidence, observations, and ideas.

SL.8.1.d. Acknowledge new information expressed by others, and, when warranted, qualify or justify their own views in light of the evidence presented.

L.6.4.c. Consult reference materials (e.g., dictionaries, glossaries, thesauruses), both print and digital, to find the pronunciation of a word or determine or clarify its precise meaning or its part of speech.

SL.8.4 Present claims and findings, emphasizing salient points in a focused, coherent manner with relevant evidence, sound valid reasoning, and well-chosen details; use appropriate eye contact, adequate volume, and clear pronunciation.

ELPS: ELP Standard 2

- participate in conversations, extended discussions, and written exchanges about a range of substantive topics, texts, and issues
- build on the ideas of others
- express his or her own ideas clearly and persuasively
- refer to specific and relevant evidence from texts or research to support his or her ideas
- ask and answer questions that probe reasoning and claim
- summarize the key points and evidence discussed

ELP Standard 8

using context, questioning, and consistent knowledge of English morphology,

- determine the meaning of general academic and content-specific words and phrases, figurative and connotative language, and idiomatic expressions in spoken and written texts about a variety of topics, experiences, or events

Warm-up and Review
10–15 minutes (books closed)

Pass out different sources of news and information, such as newspapers, magazines, flyers, menus, bus/train schedules. Give students a couple of minutes to look through them. Ask students what these things have in common. Elicit answers.

Introduction
5 minutes

1. Tell students where you usually get news and information and why.

2. State the objective: *Today we're going to think about and discuss sources of news and information.*

1 Discuss sources of news and information

Presentation I
20–25 minutes

1. Group students and assign roles: manager, fact checker, recorder, and reporter. Explain that students will work with their group to brainstorm sources of information and categorize the words in their list.

2. Read the directions aloud. Ask: *What category do you think* television *might belong to?* [broadcast or media] *What category might* flyers *belong to?* [print or low-tech] Point out that they will decide how to categorize the sources of information.

3. Check comprehension of the activity. Ask: *Who looks up the words in a dictionary?* [fact checker] *Who writes the words in the categories?* [recorder] *Who tells the class your answers?* [reporter] *Who keeps everyone on track and manages time?* [manager]

4. Set a time limit (three minutes) and have students work together to complete the task.

5. Call time and have the reporters from each group take turns calling out their categories. Help the class combine categories as needed. Then elicit words for each category. Record students' answers on the board. If groups disagree, write each group's choice next to the word.

MULTILEVEL STRATEGIES

For 1A, use mixed-level groups.

• **On-level** Assign these students the roles of fact checker and reporter.

• **Pre-level** Assign these students the role of recorder.

• **Higher-level** Assign these students the role of leader.

TIP

When setting up task-based activities, verify that students understand their roles using physical commands. For example, say: *If you report on your team's work, stand up.* [reporter] *If you keep the team on task, point to the clock.* [manager] *If you sort the words into categories, raise your hand.* [recorder] *If you look up words in the dictionary, hold up your dictionary/ smartphone/tablet.*

1. Direct students to look at the definition. Ask: *According to the definition, is information about facts or opinions?* [facts]

2. Write *information* on the board. Elicit examples from the whole class, and write their ideas on the board. Point out the connection between their ideas and their responses in 1A.

Answers

synonyms: *fact, details, data, statistics*
forms: *inform, informative, informational*

Direct students to look at graph and photo. Ask: *What is the source where most people get their news?* [television] *Is the number going up or down?* [down] *What sources were people using more in 2017 than in 2016?* [news websites, radio, social media] *What sources do you use the most?* Elicit examples from the whole class. Write their ideas. Point out the connection between their ideas and the definition in 1B.

Guided Practice
10–20 minutes

 **1.** Direct students to look at the first question. Check comprehension of the collocation. Ask: *What is a source?*

2. Set a time limit (five minutes). Direct students to work with their partners to complete the activity. Have a volunteer from each pair give their responses. Check answers as a class.

Answers
1. The source of information is a survey conducted July 30–August 12, 2018. 2. They gathered the information by surveying people. 3. Answers will vary.

Presentation II
20–25 minutes

 **1.** Group students and assign roles: manager, recorder, reporter, and editor. Explain that students will work with their team to analyze the information. Verify students' understanding of the roles: the manager keeps track of time, the recorder writes the statement, the reporter presents the work to the class, and the editor checks grammar and spelling.

2. Set a time limit (ten minutes) for the discussion. Write the following sentence frame on the board: *We think that ____ are the most/ least reliable sources of information because ____.*

3. Call time and have the reporters from each group take turns calling out their statements. If groups disagree, ask groups to explain their objections.

EXTENSION ACTIVITY
Different Sources of News
1. Ask students to work with a partner and role-play reporting the information in the graph in 1C. Ask each student to role-play in the style of a different news source they have discussed (for example, partner A role-plays a radio news program and partner B role-plays a social media post).
2. Set a time limit (three minutes). Have students act out their role plays for the class.
3. Ask the class to find similarities and differences in the news sources. Ask: *Which method of reporting was most reliable? Why?*

Evaluation
10–15 minutes

SELF-ASSESSMENT

1. Ask students to spend some time reflecting on what they have learned.

2. Set a time limit (three minutes). Ask for volunteers to share their thoughts.

Lesson Overview

MULTILEVEL OBJECTIVES

On-level and Higher-level: Evaluate sources of information

Pre-level: Identify ways to evaluate sources of information

LANGUAGE FOCUS

Grammar: Simple present

Vocabulary: *authoritative, confirmation, bias, conspiracy*

For vocabulary support, see this **Oxford Picture Dictionary** topic: Internet Research, pages 212–213

STRATEGY FOCUS

Listen for questions and expressions used to introduce main ideas.

READINESS CONNECTION

In this lesson, students work together to evaluate sources of information.

PACING

To compress this lesson: Assign 1C and 1D for homework.

To extend this lesson: Have students discuss how someone's worldview may be connected to confirmation bias (see page 56).

And/or have students complete **Multilevel Activities 5 Unit 3, Lesson 2**.

Lesson Notes

CORRELATIONS

CCRS: RI/RL.7.1 Cite several pieces of textual evidence to support analysis of what the text says explicitly as well as inferences drawn from the text.

RI/RL.6.4 Determine the meaning of words and phrases as they are used in a text, including figurative, connotative, and technical meanings; analyze the impact of a specific word choice on meaning and tone.

SL.8.1.a. Come to discussions prepared, having read or researched material under study; explicitly draw on that preparation by referring to evidence on the topic, text, or issue to probe and reflect on ideas under discussion.

SL.8.1.c. Pose questions that connect the ideas of several speakers and respond to others' questions and comments with relevant evidence, observations, and ideas.

SL.8.1.d. Acknowledge new information expressed by others, and, when warranted, qualify or justify their own views in light of the evidence presented.

SL.8.2 Analyze the purpose of information presented in diverse media and formats (e.g., visually, quantitatively, orally) and evaluate the motives (e.g., social, commercial, political) behind its presentation.

L.6.4.a. Use context (e.g., the overall meaning of a sentence or paragraph; a word's position or function in a sentence) as a clue to the meaning of a word or phrase.

ELPS: ELP Standard 1

use a wide range of strategies to:

- determine central ideas or themes in oral presentations and spoken and written texts
- analyze the development of the themes/ideas
- cite specific details and evidence from texts to support the analysis

ELP Standard 2

- participate in conversations, extended discussions, and written exchanges about a range of substantive topics, texts, and issues
- build on the ideas of others
- express his or her own ideas clearly and persuasively
- ask and answer questions that probe reasoning and claim

ELP Standard 8

using context, questioning, and consistent knowledge of English morphology,

- determine the meaning of general academic and content-specific words and phrases, figurative and connotative language, and idiomatic expressions in spoken and written texts about a variety of topics, experiences, or events

Warm-up and Review
10–15 minutes (books closed)

Write some conspiracy theories on the board, such as *The Earth is flat, Aliens are living among us, Elvis Presley is still alive.* Point at each in turn and ask students: *Do you believe this?* Call on students to answer and explain why they do or do not believe it.

Introduction
5 minutes

1. Say: *Many people believe in conspiracy theories.*

2. State the objective: *Today we will evaluate sources of information.*

1 Read about conspiracy theories and confirmation bias

Presentation I
20–25 minutes

 1. Write *conspiracy theory* on the board. Direct students' attention to the photo. Ask: *What do you see?* [astronauts on the moon] Call on students to read aloud the examples of conspiracy theories. Ask: *Have you heard these theories? Why do you think people believe them?*

2. Group students and assign roles: manager, fact checker, recorder, and reporter. Explain that students will work with their team to define *conspiracy theory* and discuss examples.

3. Check comprehension of the activity. Ask: *Who will check the definition and other facts?* [fact checker] *Who will take notes on the team's ideas?* [recorder] *Who will share team ideas with the class?* [reporter] *Who will keep the team on track?* [manager]

4. Set a time limit (three minutes) and have students work together to complete the task.

5. Call time and have the reporters from each team take turns calling out their definitions. Then elicit examples of conspiracy theories. Record students' ideas on the board. If groups disagree with the definition, ask fact checkers to check their sources.

Guided Practice I
15–20 minutes

 1. Read the directions aloud. Check comprehension. Ask: *What are you skimming for?* [the concept that the text is explaining]

What is the title of the text? [*Why People Believe Conspiracy Theories and False Information*] *Do you think the writer has a positive or negative opinion about conspiracy theories?* [negative] *Why?* [The term is linked with *false information.*]

2. Set a time limit (five minutes). Direct students to underline the concept when they find it.

3. Elicit the answer.

Answer
confirmation bias

TIP

Explain that words and phrases have both denotations and connotations. The denotation is the word's meaning, but the connotation has to do with the feeling or attitude associated with the word. Provide examples such as *fat, obese, heavy, big, chubby, plump* and *overweight.* Point out that all these words mean someone who weighs more than is healthy. Ask: *Which word(s) seem more neutral?* [*overweight, big, heavy*] *Which word(s) are used sometimes in a more positive way?* [*chubby, plump*] *Which word is usually negative?* [*fat*] Write words from the article on the board: *conspiracy, uncertain, contradict, relieve, penalized, biased, incompetent, objectively.* Have students discuss which words think have a negative connotation and which have a positive connotation.

 1. Read the directions aloud. Check comprehension. Ask: *What is confirmation bias?*

2. Set a time limit (five minutes). Direct students to answer the question.

3. Elicit ideas from the whole class.

Answer
Confirmation bias is the tendency for people to only accept as true information that fits with their existing worldview or beliefs. Confirmation bias makes it difficult for people to judge information objectively.

Communicative Practice
10–20 minutes

D 1. Read the questions aloud.

2. Ask students to think about and mark their answers in the text.

3. Set a time limit (five minutes) for students to discuss their answers with a partner.

4. Invite pairs to share their responses. Check answers as a class.

> **Answers**
>
> 1. People dislike being confronted with information that contradicts their worldview or that makes them feel uncertain.
> 2. They might ignore bad calls that a referee has made in the past and only remember the good calls.
> 3. having received a penalty—related to *penalty* in previous sentence

Presentation II
20–25 minutes

 1. Tell students to rejoin their teams from 1A.

2. Explain that students will work with their team to discuss the questions.

3. Set a time limit (three minutes) and have students work together to complete the task.

4. Call time and have the reporters from each group take turns calling out their examples. Record students' examples on the board. If teams disagree, direct the fact checkers to look for information online.

> **EXTENSION ACTIVITY**
>
> **Identifying Worldviews**
>
> 1. Write questions on the board: *What is most important to you? Do you think people are mostly good or mostly bad? Whom do you trust to help you form opinions? What kind of lifestyle do you want? What is the role of people in the world?*
>
> 2. Model the activity. Tell students your answer to one of the questions. Then say how you think it might create confirmation bias for you. For example, if you trust scientists to help you form opinions, then you might believe all supposedly scientific reports without looking at them closely.
>
> 3. Tell students to work individually to answer the questions.
>
> 4. Pair students to share one aspect of their worldviews.

2 Listen and take notes

Guided Practice II
20–25 minutes

 1. Say: *Now we're going to listen to a lecture about evaluating sources.*

2. Set a time limit (five minutes). Direct students to brainstorm predictions about what the speaker might say.

3. Elicit ideas from the whole class. Write their ideas on the board.

B  1. Direct students' attention to the Listening Note. Write on the board: *Why do people believe conspiracy theories?* Elicit answers from the class. Point out that the text on page 26 could begin with that question.

2. Play the beginning of the audio. Direct students to listen without writing.

3. Replay the audio. Ask students to write the key question.

4. Set a time limit (five minutes). Direct students to brainstorm what the rest of the lecture will be about.

5. Elicit ideas from the whole class. Write their ideas on the board.

> **Answer**
>
> How can you be sure the information you're looking at online is accurate?

C  1. Direct students to look at the chart. Ask: *What is the first part of the lecture?* [the introduction] *How many key words or ideas are addressed?* [3]

2. Play the whole audio. Direct students to write notes in the chart as they listen.

Answers	
Employability Skills Lecture Series: Evaluating Sources	
Key question: <u>How can you be sure the information you're looking at online is accurate?</u>	
Notes	Key words/Questions
Introduction:	Quantity of info = no prob Quality of info = prob Must learn eval info
P: <u>purpose</u>	Why did author write? selling something? political? evidence? trying to persuade? biased language?
A: authoritative	expert? or established source? URL: .edu = school, .gov = gov't, .com may = selling s/thing
C: <u>current</u>	recent? old may = out of date

- **Pre-level** Allow students to read the script as they listen.
- **Higher-level** Suggest that students create a system of abbreviations for key words in the lecture. Ask them to share their symbols with the class.

Communicative Practice
10–20 minutes

 1. Set a time limit (five minutes) for students to discuss their answers with a partner.

2. Replay the audio. Ask students to add any information they were missing to their chart.

Presentation II
20–25 minutes

 1. Read the questions aloud. Ask: *What does the first set of questions focus on?* [the problem] *What does the second set focus on?* [the solution] *How many parts are there to each item?* [three] *What are they?* [the speaker's ideas, the student's opinion, and reasons for the student's opinion]

2. Direct students' attention to the sentence frames. Explain or elicit that *suggests* is the weakest reporting verb and *maintains* is the strongest.

3. Elicit responses from the class. Encourage students to use the sentence frames for reporting speech.

Possible Answers
1. The speaker maintains that the problem is that there is a lot of unreliable information. Opinions will vary. 2. The speaker suggests that the solution is to apply the PAC test. Reasons will vary.

TIP

Write the sentence frames from 2E on the board. Label each part: *Subject + reporting verb + that...* Point out that the reporting verbs are in the present tense, so students can simply repeat the speaker's ideas instead of the ellipses.

Evaluation
10–15 minutes

SELF-ASSESSMENT

1. Read each item. Have students raise their hands if they have difficulty.

2. Pair students who have difficulty with those who do not to review ways to achieve each objective.

Lesson Overview

Lesson Notes

MULTILEVEL OBJECTIVES

On-level: Identify and analyze bias; combine others' ideas and express own ideas with adjective clauses to create complex sentences

Pre-level: Identify bias; practice combining ideas with adjective clauses to create complex sentences

Higher-level: Identify and analyze bias; combine others' ideas and express own ideas with adjective clauses to create complex sentences

LANGUAGE FOCUS

Grammar: Adjective clauses

Vocabulary: *coerce, scheme,* emotive language

For vocabulary support, see this **Oxford Picture Dictionary** topic: Feelings, pages 42–43

STRATEGY FOCUS

Identify bias by recognizing emotive language.

READINESS CONNECTION

In this lesson, students work with others to discuss examples of biased language.

PACING

To compress this lesson: Assign 2B and 2C for homework.

To extend this lesson: Have students find examples of bias online (see page 59); Have students find articles with examples of a grammar point (see page 60).

And/or have students complete **Multilevel Activities 5 Unit 3, Lesson 3**.

CORRELATIONS

CCRS: SL.8.1.a. Come to discussions prepared, having read or researched material under study; explicitly draw on that preparation by referring to evidence on the topic, text, or issue to probe and reflect on ideas under discussion.

SL.8.1.c. Pose questions that connect the ideas of several speakers and respond to others' questions and comments with relevant evidence, observations, and ideas.

SL.8.1.d. Acknowledge new information expressed by others, and, when warranted, qualify or justify their own views in light of the evidence presented.

L.6.1/8.1.j. Explain the function of phrases and clauses in general and their function in specific sentences.

L.6.1/8.1.l. Place phrases and clauses within a sentence, recognizing and correcting misplaced and dangling modifiers.

L.6.4.c. Consult reference materials (e.g., dictionaries, glossaries, thesauruses), both print and digital, to find the pronunciation of a word or determine or clarify its precise meaning or its part of speech.

L.8.6 Acquire and use accurately level-appropriate general academic and domain-specific words and phrases; gather vocabulary knowledge when considering a word or phrase important to comprehension or expression.

ELPS: ELP Standard 2

- participate in conversations, extended discussions, and written exchanges about a range of substantive topics, texts, and issues
- build on the ideas of others
- express his or her own ideas clearly and persuasively

ELP Standard 8

using context, questioning, and consistent knowledge of English morphology,

- determine the meaning of general academic and content-specific words and phrases, figurative and connotative language, and idiomatic expressions in spoken and written texts about a variety of topics, experiences, or events

ELP Standard 10

- use complex phrases and clauses
- produce and expand simple, compound, and complex sentences

Warm-up and Review
10–15 minutes (books closed)

1. Write verbs on the board that express likes and dislikes in random order: *like, am fond of, enjoy, love, adore, be crazy about, dislike, hate, can't stand, loathe, detest.*

2. Give examples of things you like or dislike using several different verbs (for example, *I like vanilla ice cream, but I'm crazy about chocolate. I can't stand loud music. I don't really like concerts.*) Ask: *Which verbs express greater emotion?*

3. Tell students to rank the verbs in order of the degree of emotion they express.

Introduction
5 minutes

1. Say: *Emotive language can reveal bias.*

2. State the objective: *Today we are going to identify bias and combine ideas with adjective clauses to create complex sentences.*

1 Vocabulary: Recognize emotive language

Presentation and Guided Practice I
20–25 minutes

 1. Write *emotive language* on the board. Ask: *What does* emotive language *refer to?* Elicit examples from the warm-up and other examples.

2. Read the directions aloud. Point out that students may need to change the form of the word in the box.

3. Direct students to complete the task independently.

4. Call on students to read the new sentences aloud.

Answers
1. confronted with
2. dislike
3. affects
4. plan
5. persuaded

TIP

Call on students to read the sentences aloud. Elicit the part of speech for each underlined word. [four verbs and one noun] Then elicit the form of each verb. [1. present passive, 2. simple present, 3. simple present, 5. past passive] Say each word in the box and elicit the part of speech. [all can be verbs, and *plan* can also be a noun]

Communicative Practice
15–20 minutes

 1. Read the prompts aloud.

2. Set a time limit (five minutes) for students to complete the activity with a partner.

3. Invite pairs to share their responses. Check answers as a class.

Presentation II
20–25 minutes

 1. Read the questions aloud. Write *more biased* and *less biased* on the board. Ask: *Why is* scheme *more biased than* plan? [It suggests a plot or conspiracy, something tricky.]

2. Pair students to discuss the questions.

3. Elicit responses from the class.

EXTENSION ACTIVITY
Text Analysis
1. Have students go online to find one of the places they thought might have more biased language in 1C.
2. Tell students to look for examples of bias and then compare ideas with a partner.
3. Elicit examples from the class.

2 Grammar: Adjective clauses

Presentation and Guided Practice II
20–25 minutes

A 1. Demonstrate how to read the first grammar chart. Read each sentence aloud and have students repeat them after you.

2. Write the sentences in the chart as two separate sentences—for example, *Some information contradicts people's worldview. People dislike being confronted with some information.* Underline the noun(s) in both sentences.

3. Demonstrate how the sentences have been combined and some words removed or replaced.

4. Repeat with the second grammar chart.

5. Have students complete the Language Connection paragraph about adjective clauses. Go over the answers with the class.

Answers
combine, noun, subject, an object, cannot, can

MULTILEVEL STRATEGIES

To adapt 2A:

- **On-level** Have students work independently.

- **Pre-level** Have higher-level classmates assist these students.

- **Higher-level** Have these students work with pre-level classmates to write each sentence in the chart as two separate sentences and demonstrate how to combine them.

Guided Practice III
20–25 minutes

B 1. Read the directions aloud. Ask: *Which pronouns should be omitted?* [object relative pronouns]

2. Ask students to work individually to complete the task and then compare answers with a partner.

3. Ask volunteers to write the sentences on the board and mark them as directed.

4. Ask: *In which adjective clauses is the noun the subject?* [1, 4, 5] *In which adjective clauses is the noun the object of the verb in the clause?* [2, 3, 6]

Answers
1. People ignore **information** that doesn't fit with their beliefs.
2. For example, fans might ignore all of **the good calls** that a referee has made in the past.
3. As you're reading, you need to consider any **biases** that the writer may have.
4. Look for an article by **someone** who has the right credentials.
5. **A medical article** that was published ten years ago is probably out of date by now.
6. **A confirmation bias** that you may not be aware of will affect your judgment.

C Ask students to work individually to rewrite the summary using adjective clauses.

Answers
The speaker discusses a problem that many people have because of the Internet. It's easy to find bad information online. A lot of articles online are written by non-professionals who don't have any experience or authority. The speaker has a system (that) people can use to make sure (that) they are getting good information. She calls her system PAC. The *P* stands for *purpose*. Every writer has a purpose that influences the way they present their information. The A stands for *authority*. It's important to look for people with experience or credentials who have the authority to talk about the subject. C stands for *current*. Information that isn't current won't be very useful.

D 1. Set a time limit (five minutes) for students to discuss their revised summary with a partner.

2. Elicit the pairs of sentences that can be combined and write them together on the board.

3. Ask volunteers to combine them using adjective clauses.

EXTENSION ACTIVITY

Examples from the News

1. Have students work in pairs to find news articles.

2. Ask them to locate three to five sentences in the articles with adjective clauses and break them into shorter sentences.

3. Elicit examples from the class.

Evaluation
10–15 minutes

SELF-ASSESSMENT

1. Have students complete the self-assessment.

2. Provide additional practice as needed.

Lesson Overview

MULTILEVEL OBJECTIVES

On-level: Interpret statistics in a text; identify and discuss bias in a text that cites statistics

Pre-level: Recognize statistics in a text; identify bias in a text that cites statistics

Higher-level: Interpret statistics in a text; identify and lead discussion of bias in a text that cites statistics

LANGUAGE FOCUS

Grammar: Complex sentences

Vocabulary: *convincing*, *manipulate*, emotive language

For vocabulary support, see this **Oxford Picture Dictionary** topic: Mathematics, pages 204–205

STRATEGY FOCUS

Use phrases to introduce ideas.

READINESS CONNECTION

In this lesson, students work in a team to analyze different forms of bias.

PACING

To compress this lesson: Assign 2B for homework.

To extend this lesson: Have students practice checking sources (see page 64); Have students analyze an infographic for bias (see page 66).

And/or have students complete **Multilevel Activities 5 Unit 3, Lesson 4**.

Lesson Notes

CORRELATIONS

CCRS: RI/RL.6.2 Determine a theme or central idea of a text and how it is conveyed through particular details; provide a summary of the text distinct from personal opinions or judgments.

RST.6-8.2 Application: determine the central ideas or conclusions of a text; provide an accurate summary of the text distinct from prior knowledge or opinions.

RI.8.3 Analyze how a text makes connections among and distinctions between individuals, ideas, or events (e.g., through comparisons, analogies, or categories).

RI/RL.6.4 Determine the meaning of words and phrases as they are used in a text, including figurative, connotative, and technical meanings; analyze the impact of a specific word choice on meaning and tone.

RI.6.7 Integrate information presented in different media or formats (e.g., in charts, graphs, photographs, videos, or maps) as well as in words to develop a coherent understanding of a topic or issue.

RST.6-8.7 Integrate quantitative or technical information expressed in words in a text with a version of that information expressed visually (e.g., in a flowchart, diagram, model, graph, or table).

RI.8.9 Analyze a case in which two or more texts provide conflicting information on the same topic and identify where the texts disagree on matters of fact or interpretation.

W.7.7 Conduct short research projects to answer a question, drawing on several sources and generating additional related, focused questions for further research and investigation.

SL.8.1.a. Come to discussions prepared, having read or researched material under study; explicitly draw on that preparation by referring to evidence on the topic, text, or issue to probe and reflect on ideas under discussion.

SL.8.1.c. Pose questions that connect the ideas of several speakers and respond to others' questions and comments with relevant evidence, observations, and ideas.

SL.8.1.d. Acknowledge new information expressed by others, and, when warranted, qualify or justify their own views in light of the evidence presented.

SL.8.2 Analyze the purpose of information presented in diverse media and formats (e.g., visually, quantitatively, orally) and evaluate the motives (e.g., social, commercial, political) behind its presentation.

SL.8.4 Present claims and findings, emphasizing salient points in a focused, coherent manner with relevant evidence, sound valid reasoning, and well-chosen details; use appropriate eye contact, adequate volume, and clear pronunciation.

L.6.4.c. Consult reference materials (e.g., dictionaries, glossaries, thesauruses), both print and digital, to find the pronunciation of a word or determine or clarify its precise meaning or its part of speech.

ELPS: ELP Standard 1

use a wide range of strategies to:

- determine central ideas or themes in oral presentations and spoken and written texts
- cite specific details and evidence from texts to support the analysis

ELP Standard 2

- participate in conversations, extended discussions, and written exchanges about a range of substantive topics, texts, and issues
- build on the ideas of others
- express his or her own ideas clearly and persuasively
- refer to specific and relevant evidence from texts or research to support his or her ideas
- ask and answer questions that probe reasoning and claims

ELP Standard 6

- analyze and evaluate the reasoning in persuasive spoken and written texts

ELP Standard 7

- adapt language choices and style according to purpose, task, and audience with ease in various social and academic contexts
- use a wide variety of complex general academic and content specific words and phrases
- employ both formal and more informal styles and tones effectively in spoken and written texts, as appropriate

ELP Standard 8

using context, questioning, and consistent knowledge of English morphology,

- determine the meaning of general academic and content-specific words and phrases, figurative and connotative language, and idiomatic expressions in spoken and written texts about a variety of topics, experiences, or events

Warm-up and Review
10–15 minutes (books closed)

Provide students with examples of articles with numbers. Ask them to scan for the numbers and then identify the kinds they see (for example, dates, ages, percentages, fractions, decimals, temperatures, statistics). Elicit examples and have students say why they think each number is used in the article.

Introduction
5 minutes

1. Say: *Writers use numbers to give examples, describe people or places, talk about past events, and present statistics to support a position.*

2. State the objective: *Today we will learn to interpret statistics in a text and identify and discuss bias in a text that cites statistics.*

1 Get ready to read

Presentation I
20–25 minutes

A 🔊 **1.10** 1. Say: *Now we're going to listen to workers discuss a company email.* Read the question aloud. Check comprehension.

2. Play the audio. Direct students to listen silently without writing.

3. Elicit answers from the class.

Answer
The man says they are too confusing and should be explained. The woman says they show where the information is coming from and help people understand the conclusions.

B 🔊 **1.10** 1. Replay the audio. Ask students to check the ways the speakers introduce their ideas.

2. Check answers as a class.

Answers
For one thing... Another reason... It's clear that...

C 1. Write *Reasons for statistics in texts* on the board.

2. Group students and assign roles: manager, fact checker, recorder, and reporter. Explain that students will work with their team to make a list of important reasons to include statistics in texts.

3. Check comprehension of the activity. Ask: *Who checks examples in texts and looks up unfamiliar words?* [fact checker] *Who takes notes?* [recorder] *Who reports to the class?* [reporter] *Who keeps the team on time and on task?* [manager]

4. Set a time limit (three minutes) and have students work together to complete the task.

5. Call time and have the reporters from each team take turns calling out where they see statistics. Then elicit reasons. Record students' answers on the board. If teams disagree, ask the fact checkers to find examples.

Answers
Answers will vary.

MULTILEVEL STRATEGIES

To adapt 1C:

- **On-level** Assign these students the roles of fact checker and recorder.
- **Pre-level** Assign these students the role of reporter.
- **Higher-level** Assign these students the role of manager.

TIP

Suggest that students pull up a source for news they know about to scan for examples of statistics. Each team member should find at least one example. Then the fact checker can double-check how the statistic is used.

EXTENSION ACTIVITY

Source Check

1. When students find examples of statistics in texts in 1C, direct them to evaluate each source.

2. Review PAC: purpose, authority, currency. Tell students to take notes on each for their examples.

3. Call on students to share examples with the class.

2 Preview and read

Guided Practice I
20–25 minutes

A 1. Read the directions aloud. Ask: *What should you look at when you skim an article?* [titles, headings, visuals (charts, graphs, photos), first and last paragraphs/sentences] *What is the title?* [*Statistics to Watch Out For*] *What are the two headings?* [*Correlation is not causation* and *Survey data is easy to manipulate and misrepresent*] *What three things are connected in the chart?* [warm weather, ice cream purchases, bathing suit sales] *How are they connected?* [Warm weather is linked to the other two by causation, and ice cream sales and bathing suit sales are linked by correlation.] *What do you see in the other visual?* [a toothpaste ad with a child brushing teeth and a dentist]

2. Have students answer the question individually, and then check answers with the class. If any students answer incorrectly, ask them to support their answer. Establish the correct answer. Ask: *Is the main idea directly stated anywhere?* [yes] *Where?* [the last sentence of the article]

Answer
Statistics may be misleading, and it is critical that we read the numbers as carefully as the text.

B 1. Direct students' attention to the Reader's Note. Write *dashes* on the board. Elicit what they are used for. Have students scan the text to find the dashes. Ask: *What information follows a dash?* [warm weather; that is, used only the most beneficial numbers] *Which introduces a definition?* [the second] *Which one is an explanatory phrase?* [warm weather]

2. Ask students to read the article silently, answer the question, and then compare answers with a partner. Check answers as a class.

Answer
Correlation is not causation, and survey data is easy to manipulate and misrepresent.

Presentation II
20–25 minutes

C 1. Have students rejoin their teams from 1C.

2. Set a time limit (five minutes) and have students work together to complete the task.

3. Call time and have the reporters from each team take turns calling out the answers. Then elicit where the answer is located in the text. Record students' answers on the board. If teams disagree, ask fact checkers to explain how the text supports their answer.

Answers

1. *Correlation* tells us how closely two sets of data are related. *Cherry picking* is using only the most beneficial numbers.
2. The fact that two things have a connection or occur together doesn't mean that one causes the other.
3.

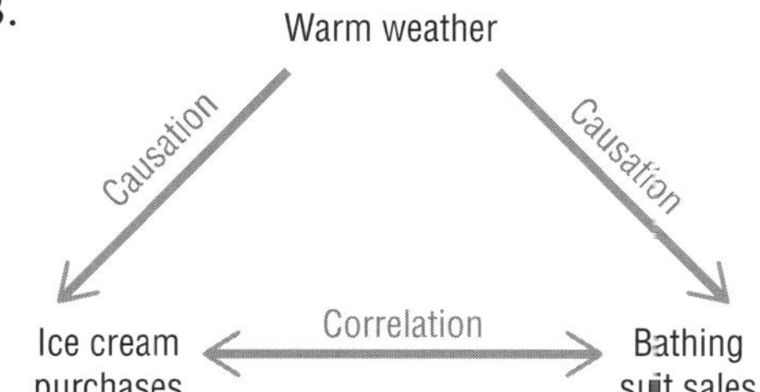

4. ask questions in a way to get the answers they want, cherry-pick the data, use a small sample size, only survey people who would recommend the product (for example, because they got a free sample)
5. only asking 10 dentists about a toothpaste
6. That the majority of dentists recommend the toothpaste. It relies on a small or biased sample size.

WORD STUDY

D

1. Ask students to stay in their teams from 2C. Write the four words on the board. Direct students to find *blare* in the text. Elicit the meaning.

2. Set a time limit (five minutes) and have students work together to complete the task.

3. Call time. Have the reporters from each team take turns calling out the definitions to the words in 2D item 1. Then elicit whether the words are neutral or emotive and why.

E

1. Read the directions aloud.

2. Direct students' attention to the Speaking Note.

3. Read each question and elicit discussion. Remind students to use the expressions to introduce ideas when they explain their ideas.

Possible Answers

1. Possibly—if researchers already believed that nightlights were bad for eyesight, they may have wanted to see them as the cause of the children's nearsightedness.
2. They can look for other factors that might cause both things. They can try to rule out other causes.

3 Build on it

Presentation I
20–25 minutes

A 

1. Have students look at the graphs. Ask: *What do the graphs show?* [absences due to illness and Ferndale crime rate] Draw a simple graph on the board with an *x*-axis and *y*-axis and explain what each is. Ask: *In the first graph, what is on the* x*-axis?* [the number of absences] *What is on the* y*-axis?* [the months of September through December] Repeat with the second graph.

2. Direct students' attention to the beginning of the two articles and elicit the titles.

3. Set a time limit (ten minutes). Have students work individually to complete the task and then compare answers with a partner. Ask volunteers to share their answers with the class.

Possible Answers

1. They accurately state the numbers in the graphs.
2. The first article says the absences are caused by stress, but there's no evidence for that in the chart; the second article doesn't mention that crime also went down last September.

MULTILEVEL STRATEGIES

• **On-level** Have students complete the task individually.

• **Pre-level** Work with these students to read the beginning of the articles together and answer the questions.

• **Higher-level** Ask students to answer this question: *What are other explanations for the patterns you see?*

TIP

Have students identify emotive language in each article in 3A. Elicit examples and write them on the board (for example, *excessive, obsessed, suffering, catastrophe, tough-but-fair, accomplishing, steadily, significantly*). Elicit whether the word is positive or negative and add a + or – next to each.

 **B** 1. Ask students to return to their teams. Explain that students will work with their team to discuss the questions. Remind students to use expressions to introduce their ideas.

2. Set a time limit (three minutes) and have students work together to complete the task.

3. Call time and have the reporters from each team take turns calling out the answers to the questions.

> **Possible Answers**
>
> 1. In the first article, something else could be causing the absences, like the winter cold season. In the second article, something else could be causing the crime drop, like cooler weather.
> 2. It only mentions the most recent part of the data.
> 3. Opinions will vary.

PROBLEM SOLVING

C 1. Read the directions aloud.

2. Direct students' attention to the photo. Ask: *What do you see?* [a man looking at an ad on a computer] Ask: *Is this a good way to get unbiased information? Why or why not?* Elicit responses from the class.

3. Read the email aloud or call on a higher-level student to read it. Call on other students to read the questions aloud.

4. Set a time limit (three minutes) and have students discuss the questions in their teams.

5. Call time and have the reporters from each team take turns calling out the problems. Then elicit their ideas for improvement. Record students' answers on the board.

> **Possible Answers**
>
> 1. He doesn't provide any statistics, he was biased in favor of the printer because he liked the way it looked, he checked a biased source of information (company website), and he just talked to one person who has had one for a short time (small sample size).
> 2. He could include some statistics in his email and research less-biased reviews. He could compare data about this printer with another printer.

APPLY YOUR KNOWLEDGE 

D 1. Ask students to complete the activity individually as an out-of-class assignment.

2. Write *bias, emotive language, cherry picking, sample size, correlation,* and *causation* on the board. Tell students to refer to these ideas if appropriate.

3. Pair students to discuss their articles. Reinforce expressions for introducing ideas.

4. Call on students to share their ideas with the class.

> **EXTENSION ACTIVITY**
>
> **Apply Your Knowledge**
>
> 1. Bring in or show an infographic.
> 2. Pair students to analyze it for bias.
> 3. Call on students to share their ideas.

Evaluation
10–15 minutes

SELF-ASSESSMENT

1. Have students check the boxes individually.

2. Ask students to identify the objective they had the most difficulty with. Then pair or group students accordingly.

3. Ask students to come up with two solutions to address the problem they are having. Provide additional practice as necessary.

Lesson Overview

MULTILEVEL OBJECTIVES

On-level: Use the writing process to summarize an article

Pre-level: Write sentences

Higher-level: Summarize an article and include sentences with adjective clauses

LANGUAGE FOCUS

Grammar: Simple present

Vocabulary: For vocabulary support, see this **Oxford Picture Dictionary** topic: English Composition, pages 202–203

STRATEGY FOCUS

Use verbs to paraphrase examples.

READINESS CONNECTION

In this lesson, students work with a partner to give and receive feedback.

PACING

To compress this lesson: Assign 2C for homework.

To extend this lesson: Have work in pairs to summarize text with numbers (see page 69).

And/or have students complete **Multilevel Activities 5 Unit 3, Lesson 5**.

Lesson Notes

CORRELATIONS

CCRS: W/WHST.6-8.2.a. Introduce a topic clearly, previewing what is to follow; organize ideas, concepts, and information, using strategies such as definition, classification, comparison /contrast, and cause/effect; include formatting (e.g., headings), graphics (e.g., charts, tables), and multimedia when useful to aiding comprehension.

W/WHST.6-8.2.b. Develop the topic with relevant facts, definitions, concrete details, quotations, or other information and examples.

W/WHST.6-8.2.c. Use appropriate transitions to create cohesion and clarify the relationships among ideas and concepts.

W/WHST.6-8.2.d. Use precise language and domain-specific vocabulary to inform about or explain the topic.

W/WHST.6-8.2.f. Provide a concluding statement or section that follows from and supports the information or explanation presented.

W/WHST.6-8.4 Produce clear and coherent writing in which the development and organization and style are appropriate to task, purpose, and audience.

W/WHST.6-8.5 With some guidance and support from peers and others, develop and strengthen writing as needed by planning, revising, editing, rewriting, or trying a new approach, focusing on how well purpose and audience have been addressed.

L.6.3/7.3.c. Choose language that expresses ideas precisely and concisely, recognizing and eliminating wordiness and redundancy.

L.8.6 Acquire and use accurately level-appropriate general academic and domain-specific words and phrases; gather vocabulary knowledge when considering a word or phrase important to comprehension or expression.

ELPS: ELP Standard 7

* adapt language choices and style according to purpose, task, and audience with ease in various social and academic contexts
* use a wide variety of complex general academic and content specific words and phrases
* employ both formal and more informal styles and tones effectively in spoken and written texts, as appropriate

<table>
<tr><td>

ELP Standard 9

- recount a complex and detailed sequence of events or steps in a process, with an effective sequential or chronological order
- introduce and effectively develop an informational topic with facts, details, and evidence
- use complex and varied transitions to link the major sections of speech and text and to clarify relationships among events and ideas
- provide a concluding section or statement

</td><td>

ELP Standard 10

- produce and expand simple, compound, and complex sentences

</td></tr>
</table>

Warm-up and Review
10–15 minutes (books closed)

Write details from the article on pages 30–31 on the board in random order (for example, *survey of 10 dentists, nightlights and nearsighted children, bathing suits and ice cream, 80 percent of dentists recommend*). Have students put the details in order from memory. Elicit the order, and then allow students to check the text.

Introduction
5 minutes

State the objective: *Today we will use the writing process to summarize an article.*

1 Write a summary

Presentation I
20–25 minutes

A 1. Have students revisit the article on pages 30–31. Check comprehension. Ask: *What is the article about? What are the most important ideas?*

2. Elicit responses. Record students' answers on the board.

Guided Practice I
15–20 minutes

B 1. Direct students to look at the chart. Focus students' attention on the left column. Elicit what students will note there. [first and second reasons] Then focus attention on the right column. Ask: *What will you take notes on in this column?* [examples]

2. Check comprehension of the activity. Ask: *Do you need to write complete sentences in the chart?* [no]

3. Have students work individually to complete their charts.

C 1. Read the directions aloud. Check comprehension. Ask: *What will your first sentence in the summary do?* [introduce the main idea of the article]

2. Write the sentence frame on the board.

3. Have students work individually to write their statements. Encourage students to use the frame provided.

D 1. Check comprehension. Ask: *Where is the conclusion of the article?* [in the last paragraph]

2. Write the following sentence frame on the board: *In the conclusion of the article, the author states that...*

3. Have students work individually to write their summary of the article's conclusion.

TIP

Direct students' attention to the last paragraph of the article on pages 30–31. Elicit synonyms and other word forms for key words in the conclusion. [*objectivity, bias, leading, critical, carefully*] Remind students that they can use synonyms and different word forms to rephrase ideas.

E 1. Read the directions aloud. Check comprehension. Ask: *What will you include in your summary?* [introduction, notes from the chart, conclusion]

2. Draw students' attention to the Writer's Note. Ask: *Why do writers give examples?* [to show something, to explain an idea more fully] Point out that the verbs refer to showing.

3. Write the sentence frame from the Writer's Note on the board. Point out that students can write the reason in place of the first ellipses and give examples in place of the second ellipses.

4. Have students work individually to write their summaries.

2 Get feedback and revise

Guided Practice II
10–15 minutes

A Direct students to check their writing using the editing checklist. Tell them to read each item in the list and check their papers before moving onto the next item. Explain that students should not edit their writing at this stage. They should just use the checklist to check their work and mark any areas they want to revise.

Communicative Practice
10–15 minutes

B 1. Read the directions aloud. Emphasize to students that they are responding to their partners' work, not correcting it.

2. Direct students to exchange papers with a partner and follow the instructions.

C Allow students time to edit and revise their writing using the editing checklist and their partner's feedback. If necessary, have students complete this task as homework.

Evaluation
10–15 minutes

SELF-ASSESSMENT

1. Call on students to read their completed sentences aloud.

2. Use the responses to the second statement to plan follow-up activities.

Lesson Overview

MULTILEVEL OBJECTIVES

On-level: Students conduct and present research

Pre-level: Students help conduct and present research

Higher-level: Students organize, conduct and present research

LANGUAGE FOCUS

Grammar: Adjective clauses

Vocabulary: Emotive language

For vocabulary support, see these **Oxford Picture Dictionary** topics: Feelings, pages 42–43; Internet Research, pages 212–213

STRATEGY FOCUS

Create an interesting opening to get an audience's attention.

READINESS CONNECTION

In this lesson, students work with a team to research and report on an example of bad information.

PACING

To compress this lesson: Assign 1C for homework. Alternatively, provide students with topics to expedite 1A.

To extend this lesson: Have students discuss the concept of hooks (see page 72); Have students practice interviewing a partner (see page 73).

And/or have students complete **Multilevel Activities 5 Unit 3, Lesson 6**.

Lesson Notes

CORRELATIONS

CCRS: W.7.7 Conduct short research projects to answer a question, drawing on several sources and generating additional related, focused questions for further research and investigation.

W.7.8 Gather relevant information from multiple print and digital sources, using search terms effectively; assess the credibility and accuracy of each source; and quote or paraphrase the data and conclusions of others while avoiding plagiarism and following a standard format for citation.

SL.8.4 Present claims and findings, emphasizing salient points in a focused, coherent manner with relevant evidence, sound valid reasoning, and well-chosen details; use appropriate eye contact, adequate volume, and clear pronunciation.

SL.8.6 Adapt speech to a variety of contexts and tasks, demonstrating command of formal English when indicated or appropriate.

L.6.3/7.3.b. Maintain consistency in style and tone.

L.6.3/7.3.c. Choose language that expresses ideas precisely and concisely, recognizing and eliminating wordiness and redundancy.

L.8.6 Acquire and use accurately level-appropriate general academic and domain-specific words and phrases; gather vocabulary knowledge when considering a word or phrase important to comprehension or expression.

ELPS: ELP Standard 2

- participate in conversations, extended discussions, and written exchanges about a range of substantive topics, texts, and issues
- build on the ideas of others
- express his or her own ideas clearly and persuasively

ELP Standard 3

- deliver oral presentations
- compose written informational texts
- fully develop the topic with relevant details, concepts, examples, and information
- integrate graphics or multimedia when useful about a variety of texts, topics, or events

<table>
<tr><td>

ELP Standard 5

- carry out both short and more sustained research projects to answer a question or solve a problem
- gather information from multiple print and digital sources
- use advanced search terms effectively
- synthesize information from multiple print and digital sources
- analyze and integrate information into clearly organized spoken and written texts
- include illustrations, diagrams, or other graphics as appropriate

</td><td>

ELP Standard 7

- adapt language choices and style according to purpose, task, and audience with ease in various social and academic contexts
- use a wide variety of complex general academic and content specific words and phrases
- employ both formal and more informal styles and tones effectively in spoken and written texts, as appropriate

</td></tr>
</table>

Warm-up and Review
10–15 minutes (books closed)

1. Write the following quotes on the board:

"Information is not knowledge." —Albert Einstein

"Opinion is usually something which people have when they lack comprehensive information." —Idries Shah

"Knowledge is of two kinds. We know a subject ourselves, or we know where we can find information on it." —Samuel Johnson

2. Discuss the quotes as a class.

Introduction
5 minutes

1. Point out that information can be bad for a number of different reasons.

2. State the objective: *Today we will conduct and present research related to information.*

1 Research an example of bad information

Communicative Practice
40–45 minutes

A 1. Group students but do not assign roles yet. Explain that students will work with their team to narrow their topics.

2. Go over the bulleted suggestions. Elicit examples of each.

3. Set a time limit (three minutes) and have students work together to complete the task.

B 1. Check comprehension of the task. Ask: *How many sources do you need?* [four or more] *How many sources will each team member take notes on?* [one]

2. Have students work in their teams to find at least four sources.

TIP

Suggest that students look for variations on two of the key words in 1A: *scam (fraud)* and *bad science (pseudoscience, flawed science, faulty science)*. They should find plenty of information on popular conspiracy theories.

C 1. Draw students' attention to the Research Tip. Ask: *What two things should you note?* [URL and main source of the information]

2. Check comprehension of the task. Ask: *In addition to the URL and source, what else should you take notes on?* [visual elements]

3. Have students work individually to take notes on their sources.

MULTILEVEL STRATEGIES

To adapt 1C for pre-level students, provide them with a chart in which they can take their notes.

Topic	
URL	
Main source	
What happened	
When	
# of people affected	
Visual elements	

D
1. Check comprehension of the task. Ask: *What three things will you do?* [collect everyone's information, organize it according to the bullets, choose visuals, and decide how to present]

2. Have students report on the information from their sources in their teams.

3. Assign roles: manager, fact checker, recorder, and IT specialist. Explain that students will work with their team to complete the task.

4. Check comprehension of the activity. Ask: *Who checks that the URL and source are correct?* [fact checker] *Who compiles the information from all sources?* [recorder] *Who creates the slide show with visual elements?* [IT specialist] *Who keeps the team on time and on task?* [manager]

5. Set a time limit (ten minutes) and have students work together to answer the questions.

EXTENSION ACTIVITY

Hooks

1. Write on the board:

How many of you have believed an article only to learn it was completely false?

"Information is not knowledge." —Albert Einstein

Why can you never trust atoms? They make up everything!

What if we suddenly lost the Internet? How would we get information?

According to a recent survey, 60 percent of Britons believe at least one conspiracy theory.

2. Say: *These are some ways to introduce a topic, also called hooks.*

3. Pair students to discuss the ideas and say which they find most interesting.

---

2 Present your research

Presentation
40–45 minutes

A
1. Have students stay in their teams from the 1D. Check comprehension of the task. Ask: What does the outline include? [introduction, body, and conclusion] *What should you do in the conclusion?* [answer one or more of these questions: *What can the audience learn? Why is it important or interesting? How does it connect to the ideas in the unit?*]

2. Draw students' attention to the Presentation Strategy. Read it aloud. Ask students to match each description with the correct example in the Extension Activity.

3. Set a time limit (five to ten minutes) and have students work as a team to outline their oral report and choose a hook idea.

B
1. Have students assign roles for the presentation: researcher, writer, IT specialist, and editor. Explain that students will work with their team to give a presentation on their topic.

2. Check comprehension of the activity. Ask: *Who will look up additional information?* [researcher] *Who will create text for the slides?* [writer] *Who will attach audio, video, or images?* [IT specialist] *Who makes sure spelling and grammar are correct?* [editor]

3. Set a time limit (five minutes) and have students work as a team to divide the roles and the sections of the presentation (for example, introduction, body 1, body 2, and conclusion).

MULTILEVEL STRATEGIES

To adapt 2B:
- **On-level** Assign these students the roles of IT specialist and writer.
- **Pre-level** Assign these students the role of researcher.
- **Higher-level** Assign these students the roles of editor or writer.

C
1. Read the bulleted items aloud.

2. Check comprehension of the activity. Ask: *Should you rehearse the presentation in exactly the way you will present to the class?* [yes]

3. Set a time limit (ten minutes) and have students rehearse their presentations in teams.

D
1. Draw a chart on the board, listing the teams in the first column. In the other columns, list the note-taking prompts or shortened forms of them: *Strategy, Transitions, Strengths, Advice.* Check comprehension of the activity. Ask: *What will you write under* Strategy? [the strategy the team used to get attention and whether it was effective] Remind students to just use words and phrases in the chart.

2. Set a time limit (five minutes) for each presentation, and ask each team to present in turn.

E 1. Have teams discuss their feedback for other teams. Ask each team to nominate a reporter to give feedback on the other teams' presentations.

2. Beginning with the first team to present, collect feedback from the reporters. Write feedback in the chart you drew on the board in 2D.

> **EXTENSION ACTIVITY**
>
> **Pair Interviews**
>
> 1. Pair students from different presentation groups/topics.
>
> 2. Tell students to take turns interviewing each other using the bulleted questions from step 2 of 1D.
>
> 3. Have pairs discuss the similarities and differences between their topics.

Evaluation
10–15 minutes

SELF-ASSESSMENT

1. Pair students to share their self-assessments.

2. Elicit suggestions from the class for developing more confidence in each of the three assessment areas.

4 Confidence

Unit Overview

This unit explores self-confidence and self-esteem and the roles that gender and social media play in self-confidence with a range of employability skills, and contextualizes collocations and noun clauses after verbs to add information. By the end of this unit, you will be able to conduct and present research related to self-confidence or self-esteem.

KEY OBJECTIVES

Lesson 1	Identify and discuss ways people demonstrate and gain confidence
Lesson 2	Consider the role of gender in perceptions of self-confidence and differentiate between self-confidence and self-esteem
Lesson 3	Recognize and use collocations so that your language sounds natural; use noun clauses after verbs to add information
Lesson 4	Read and discuss how social media affects self-confidence in teenagers
Lesson 5	Use the writing process to summarize an article
Lesson 6	Conduct and present research related to self-confidence or self-esteem

UNIT FEATURES

Academic Vocabulary	*assertively, disparity, empowering, confident, corollary, influence, inspiring, navigate, self-esteem, self-confidence*
Employability Skills	• Interpret and evaluate data in a bar graph • Evaluate an author's support • Analyze the complexities of social media on emotional health • Provide suggestions for resolving familial conflicts around social media use • Offer consequences of different approaches to solving a problem • Coordinate with a team to research an aspect of self-confidence or self-esteem • Collaborate to organize and present research with confidence
Resources	**Class Audio** CD1, Tracks 11-15 **Teacher Resource Center** Multilevel Activities 5 Unit 4 Multilevel Grammar Activities 5 Unit 4 Unit 4 Test **Oxford Picture Dictionary** Studying, Adults and Children, Feelings, Taking Care of Your Health, Soft Skills, English Composition, Internet Research

Lesson Overview

MULTILEVEL OBJECTIVES

On-level and pre-level: Identify and discuss ways people demonstrate and gain confidence

Higher-level: Identify, discuss and analyze ways people demonstrate and gain confidence

LANGUAGE FOCUS

Grammar: Conditional

Vocabulary: *disparity, confident, self-confidence*, words and phrases related to confidence

For vocabulary support, see these **Oxford Picture Dictionary** topics: Feelings, pages 42–43; Soft Skills, page 178

READINESS CONNECTION

In this lesson, students work together to research and discuss confidence.

PACING

To compress this lesson: Do 1D as a class.

To extend this lesson: Have students participate in a survey (see page 77).

And/or have students complete **Multilevel Activities 5 Unit 4, Lesson 1.**

Lesson Notes

CORRELATIONS

CCRS: RI.6.7 Integrate information presented in different media or formats (e.g., in charts, graphs, photographs, videos, or maps) as well as in words to develop a coherent understanding of a topic or issue.

SL.8.1.a. Come to discussions prepared, having read or researched material under study; explicitly draw on that preparation by referring to evidence on the topic, text, or issue to probe and reflect on ideas under discussion.

SL.8.1.c. Pose questions that connect the ideas of several speakers and respond to others' questions and comments with relevant evidence, observations, and ideas.

SL.8.1.d. Acknowledge new information expressed by others, and, when warranted, qualify or justify their own views in light of the evidence presented.

L.6.4.c. Consult reference materials (e.g., dictionaries, glossaries, thesauruses), both print and digital, to find the pronunciation of a word or determine or clarify its precise meaning or its part of speech.

L.6.4.c. Consult reference materials (e.g., dictionaries, glossaries, thesauruses), both print and digital, to find the pronunciation of a word or determine or clarify its precise meaning or its part of speech.

ELPS: ELP Standard 2

- participate in conversations, extended discussions, and written exchanges about a range of substantive topics, texts, and issues
- build on the ideas of others
- express his or her own ideas clearly and persuasively
- refer to specific and relevant evidence from texts or research to support his or her ideas
- ask and answer questions that probe reasoning and claim
- summarize the key points and evidence discussed

Warm-up and Review
10–15 minutes (books closed)

On the board, write the names of famous successful people who also show a lot of self-confidence (for example, Barack Obama, Mark Zuckerburg, Serena Williams, LeBron James, Lionel Messi, Oprah Winfrey, Elizabeth Warren). Brainstorm the qualities these people have in common.

Introduction
5 minutes

1. Say: *Many successful people have a lot of self-confidence.*

2. State the objective: *Today we're going to identify and discuss ways people demonstrate and gain confidence.*

1 Discuss confidence

Presentation I
20–25 minutes

A 1. Read the directions aloud. Put students in teams to share their examples. Assign roles: manager, fact checker, recorder, and reporter.

2. Call on reporters to share their teams' answers and write them on the board.

B 1. Direct students to look at the definition. Ask: *What are the key words in this definition?* [*belief, ability, successful*]

2. Write *confidence* on the board, and direct students to work with a partner to look up related words and phrases.

3. Elicit related words and phrases from the whole class. Write their ideas on the board. Point out the connection between their ideas and their responses in 1A.

Possible Answers
to have confidence, to lack confidence, to be confident, to lose/gain confidence, to have a high level of confidence, to be overly confident

MULTILEVEL STRATEGIES
To adapt 1C: • **Mixed-ability** Pair pre-level students with on- or higher-level students to generate lists of words and phrases. Then elicit ideas from the class.

C Direct students to look at the picture. Ask: *What do you see?* Elicit a description of the image including the speech bubble.

Guided Practice
10–20 minutes

D 1. Direct students to look at the first question. Check comprehension of the collocation. Ask: *What does it mean to have a* high level of confidence? [to feel very confident]

2. Set a time limit (five minutes). Direct students to work with in pairs to complete the activity. Have a volunteer from each pair give their responses. Check answers as a class.

Possible Answers
1. He seems very confident. 2. Not really. Their expressions make it look like they don't have confidence in him. 3. dropping the packages

Presentation II
20–25 minutes

E 1. Read the directions aloud.

2. Call on students to read the questions aloud.

3. Have students work individually to complete the task.

4. Elicit answers from the class. Then ask: *Can we sometimes look confident but actually not feel that way?* [yes] Explain that responses can show *apparent confidence.* Ask: *What are the possible problems with overconfidence?* [People may think you know what you are doing when you don't; your attitude might annoy others; you may make mistakes.]

Possible Answers
1. Start talking to people = probably confident; wait until someone talks to you = less confident 2. Upset = possible lack of confidence; doesn't bother you = possibly more confident 3. Yes = more confident; no = less confident. Note that students could point out that applying for a job without required qualifications may be considered inappropriate or even dishonest.

Draw out that all of these may show <u>apparent</u> confidence. Also, discuss possible problems with over-confidence.

MULTILEVEL STRATEGIES

To adapt 1E:

• **Pre-level** Group students to complete the task together.

F 1. Group students and assign roles: manager, fact checker, recorder, and reporter. Explain that students will work with their team to analyze the information. Verify students' understanding of the roles: the manager keeps the team on task and on time and asks the survey questions, the recorder takes notes, the fact checker checks numbers and definitions, and the reporter reports to the class.

2. Check comprehension of the task. Ask: *What do you do first?* [survey the team with questions from 1E] *When you analyze your results, how many questions will you answer?* [three]

3. Set a time limit (ten minutes) for teams to complete the task.

4. Call time and have the reporters take turns calling out their teams' findings.

Answers
Answers will vary.

MULTILEVEL STRATEGIES

To adapt 1E:

• **On-level** Assign these students the roles of fact checker and reporter.

• **Pre-level** Assign these students the role of recorder.

• **Higher-level** Assign these students the role of manager.

EXTENSION ACTIVITY

Class Results

1. On the board, create a chart with the headings *Social event, Social media,* and *Job application.* Under each heading, write the answers students mentioned in 1F (for example, *Social event: wait/talk to people; Social media: get upset/stay calm; Job application: apply/not apply*).

2. Say each response and ask for a show of hands. Tally the results on the board.

3. Direct students to make a graph or chart of the results. For example, they could make three pie charts or one bar graph.

Evaluation
10–15 minutes

SELF-ASSESSMENT

1. Ask students to spend some time reflecting on what they have learned.

2. Set a time limit (three minutes) for students to individually answer the questions. Ask for volunteers to share their thoughts.

3. Make a list of their questions to refer to at the end of the unit.

<table>
<tr><td>

Lesson Overview

</td><td>

Lesson Notes

</td></tr>
</table>

MULTILEVEL OBJECTIVES

On-level and Higher-level: Consider the role of gender in perceptions of self-confidence and differentiate between self-confidence and self-esteem

Pre-level: Learn about the role of gender in perceptions of self-confidence and about the difference between self-confidence and self-esteem

LANGUAGE FOCUS

Grammar: Noun clauses

Vocabulary: *assertive, influence, self-esteem,* words related to traits and giving examples

For vocabulary support, see this **Oxford Picture Dictionary** topic: Adults and Children, pages 30–31

STRATEGY FOCUS

Listen for how a speaker uses examples to support important points.

READINESS CONNECTION

In this lesson, students collaborate to analyze the differences between self-confidence and self-esteem.

PACING

To compress this lesson: Assign 1C and 1D for homework.

To extend this lesson: Have students summarize an article (see page 80); Have students role-play workplace scenarios (see page 81).

And/or have students complete **Multilevel Activities 5 Unit 4, Lesson 2**.

CORRELATIONS

CCRS: RI/RL.7.1 Cite several pieces of textual evidence to support analysis of what the text says explicitly as well as inferences drawn from the text.

RI/RL.6.2 Determine a theme or central idea of a text and how it is conveyed through particular details; provide a summary of the text distinct from personal opinions or judgments.

RST.6-8.2 Application: determine the central ideas or conclusions of a text; provide an accurate summary of the text distinct from prior knowledge or opinions.

RI.8.3 Analyze how a text makes connections among and distinctions between individuals, ideas, or events (e.g., through comparisons, analogies, or categories).

RI/RL.6.4 Determine the meaning of words and phrases as they are used in a text, including figurative, connotative, and technical meanings; analyze the impact of a specific word choice on meaning and tone.

SL.8.1.a. Come to discussions prepared, having read or researched material under study; explicitly draw on that preparation by referring to evidence on the topic, text, or issue to probe and reflect on ideas under discussion.

SL.8.1.c. Pose questions that connect the ideas of several speakers and respond to others' questions and comments with relevant evidence, observations, and ideas.

SL.8.1.d. Acknowledge new information expressed by others, and, when warranted, qualify or justify their own views in light of the evidence presented.

SL.8.2 Analyze the purpose of information presented in diverse media and formats (e.g., visually, quantitatively, orally) and evaluate the motives (e.g., social, commercial, political) behind its presentation.

L.6.3/7.3.c. Choose language that expresses ideas precisely and concisely, recognizing and eliminating wordiness and redundancy.

L.8.6 Acquire and use accurately level-appropriate general academic and domain-specific words and phrases; gather vocabulary knowledge when considering a word or phrase important to comprehension or expression.

ELPS: ELP Standard 1

use a wide range of strategies to:

- determine central ideas or themes in oral presentations and spoken and written texts
- cite specific details and evidence from texts to support the analysis
- summarize a text

<table>
<tr><td valign="top">

ELP Standard 2

- participate in conversations, extended discussions, and written exchanges about a range of substantive topics, texts, and issues
- build on the ideas of others
- express his or her own ideas clearly and persuasively

</td><td valign="top">

- refer to specific and relevant evidence from texts or research to support his or her ideas
- ask and answer questions that probe reasoning and claim
- summarize the key points and evidence discussed

</td></tr>
</table>

Warm-up and Review
10–15 minutes (books closed)

Write a list of traits on the board (for example, *confident, successful, assertive, kind, important, rude, sympathetic, intuitive, decisive, brave, shy, bossy*). Ask: *Do we use these words to describe mostly men, mostly women, or both equally?* Tell students to categorize the words as *more male, more female,* or *both*. Have students compare their ideas with a partner. Elicit ideas from the class and write *M, F,* or *B* next to the words on the board.

Introduction
5 minutes

1. Say: *Gender, or whether someone identifies as male or female, can affect many things.*

2. State the objective: *Today we will consider the role of gender in perceptions of self-confidence and differentiate between self-confidence and self-esteem.*

1 Read about confidence and gender

Presentation I
10–15 minutes

1. Put students in teams. Assign roles: manager, fact checker, recorder, and reporter.

2. Read the directions aloud.

3. Assign a time limit (three minutes) for teams to complete the task. Call on reporters to share their teams' ideas with the class.

Guided Practice I
15–20 minutes

B 1. Read the directions aloud. Check comprehension. Ask: *What are you going to do?* [skim the text] *What do you do when you skim?* [read quickly to find the general gist or main idea]

2. Set a time limit (five minutes). Direct students to underline the information that answers the question when they find it.

3. Elicit the answer.

Answer
no

TIP

Direct students' attention to the article and photo. Ask: *What is the title?* [*Is the Confidence Gap Real?*] *What do you think the confidence gap is?* [a difference in confidence between men and women] *What do you see in the photo?* [a woman talking to two men] *Do you think the photo presents a typical situation? Why or why not?*

C 1. Read the directions aloud. Check comprehension. Ask: *What key concept do you need to understand?* [the appearance of self-confidence]

2. Set a time limit (five minutes). Direct students to read the article and answer the question.

3. Elicit ideas from the whole class.

Answer
It isn't equal. For women, it was also linked to how warm and friendly they appear.

MULTILEVEL STRATEGIES

To adapt 1C:

- **Pre-level** Direct students to read the glossed words before they read and explain any unfamiliar words in the definitions.

Communicative Practice
10–20 minutes

D 1. Read the questions aloud.

2. Ask students to think about and mark their answers in the text.

3. Set a time limit (five minutes) for students to discuss their answers with a partner.

4. Invite pairs to share their responses. Check answers with the class.

<table>
<tr><td>

Answers

1. the idea that women would be more successful if they presented their ideas more assertively
2. They didn't differ consistently.
3. Researchers wanted to determine how much the appearance of confidence resulted in more influence in the company.
4. Among similarly high-performing employees, the appearance of confidence gave men more influence. For women, they had a double burden because they had to appear confident and they had to be warm and friendly.

</td></tr>
</table>

Presentation II
20–25 minutes

E 1. Read the directions and questions aloud.

2. Ask: *In question 1, what are the two most important, or key, words?* [*male* and *technology*] Suggest that students consider the impact of each factor separately. Ask: *Think about other industries. Which ones might be different, and why?*

3. Have students discuss their ideas in pairs, and then elicit ideas from the class.

<table>
<tr><td>

EXTENSION ACTIVITY

Summarizing Practice

1. Tell students to write a summary of the article using their own words. Pre-level students can write a group summary.

2. Ask two or three volunteers to write their summaries on the board. Correct or revise with the class as needed.

</td></tr>
</table>

2 Listen and take notes

Guided Practice II
20–25 minutes

 1. Say: *Now we're going to listen to a lecture about self-confidence versus self-esteem.*

2. Read the directions aloud.

3. Pair or group students. Set a time limit (three minutes). Direct students to complete the task.

4. Elicit ideas from the whole class. Write their ideas on the board.

B ◀)) **1.11** 1. Play the beginning of the audio. Direct students to listen without writing.

2. Replay the audio. Ask students to write what the speaker says about the two terms.

3. Point out any connection to students' ideas in 2A.

<table>
<tr><td>

Answer

They are related but not exactly the same.

</td></tr>
</table>

C ◀)) **1.12** 1. Copy the chart on the board.

2. Direct students to look at the chart. Tell students to complete the notes in the top section.

3. Direct students' attention to the Listening Note. Elicit the phrases that introduce examples.

4. Play the whole audio. Direct students to write notes in the chart as they listen.

Answers

Employability Skills Lecture Series: Self-confidence vs. Self-esteem	
Introduction: Self-confidence & self-esteem are <u>related terms, but they are different</u>	
Speaker's points	**Examples**
Self esteem = <u>general</u>	I am… <u>a decent person.</u> <u>a good friend.</u> <u>capable.</u>
Self confidence = <u>specific</u>	I can… <u>accomplish goals.</u> <u>get good job.</u> <u>do well on test.</u> <u>sing well.</u>
High confidence/ Low <u>self-esteem</u>	e.g., successful performer—<u>problems underneath, e.g., not good/attractive/rich enough</u>
High <u>self-esteem</u>/ Low <u>confidence</u>	e.g., not good cook—<u>friends will still like me</u>

Communicative Practice
10–20 minutes

 1. Set a time limit (five minutes) for students to discuss their notes with a partner.

2. Replay the audio. Ask students to confirm or add to their notes.

Presentation II
20–25 minutes

 1. Read the directions aloud.

2. Set a time limit (three minutes) and have pairs complete the task.

3. Elicit answers from the class.

4. Ask volunteers to write their summary statements on the board.

Answers
Answers will vary.

 1. Read the directions aloud. Direct students' attention to the expressions in the Listening Note again.

2. Pair students to discuss their answers using the expressions from the Listening Note.

3. Call on students to share their ideas with the class.

Answers
Answers will vary.

Evaluation
10–15 minutes

SELF-ASSESSMENT

1. Read each item. Have students raise their hands if they have difficulty.

2. Pair students who have difficulty with those who do not to review ways to achieve each objective.

<table>
<tr><td>

Lesson Overview

MULTILEVEL OBJECTIVES

On-level: Recognize and use collocations so that your language sounds natural; use noun clauses after verbs to add information

Pre-level: Recognize and use collocations so that your language sounds natural; recognize the use of noun clauses after verbs to add information

Higher-level: Recognize and use collocations so that your language sounds natural; explain and use noun clauses after verbs to add information

LANGUAGE FOCUS

Grammar: Noun clauses

Vocabulary: Collocations

For vocabulary support, see these **Oxford Picture Dictionary** topics: Studying, pages 8–9; Soft Skills, page 178

STRATEGY FOCUS

Use verbs connected with thinking and saying with *that*-clauses.

READINESS CONNECTION

In this lesson, students write and review sentences about self-confidence and self-esteem.

PACING

To compress this lesson: Assign 1B and/or 2C for homework.

To extend this lesson: Have students find examples of noun clauses in news sources (see page 84).

And/or have students complete **Multilevel Activities 5 Unit 4, Lesson 3**.

</td><td>

Lesson Notes

</td></tr>
</table>

CORRELATIONS

CCRS: SL.8.1.a. Come to discussions prepared, having read or researched material under study; explicitly draw on that preparation by referring to evidence on the topic, text, or issue to probe and reflect on ideas under discussion.

SL.8.1.c. Pose questions that connect the ideas of several speakers and respond to others' questions and comments with relevant evidence, observations, and ideas.

SL.8.1.d. Acknowledge new information expressed by others, and, when warranted, qualify or justify their own views in light of the evidence presented.

L.6.1/8.1.j. Explain the function of phrases and clauses in general and their function in specific sentences.

L.6.1/8.1.l. Place phrases and clauses within a sentence, recognizing and correcting misplaced and dangling modifiers.

L.8.6 Acquire and use accurately level-appropriate general academic and domain-specific words and phrases; gather vocabulary knowledge when considering a word or phrase important to comprehension or expression.

ELPS: ELP Standard 2

- participate in conversations, extended discussions, and written exchanges about a range of substantive topics, texts, and issues
- build on the ideas of others
- express his or her own ideas clearly and persuasively
- summarize the key points and evidence discussed

<table>
<tr><td>

ELP Standard 8

using context, questioning, and consistent knowledge of English morphology,

• determine the meaning of general academic and content-specific words and phrases, figurative and connotative language, and idiomatic expressions in spoken and written texts about a variety of topics, experiences, or events

</td><td>

ELP Standard 10

• use complex phrases and clauses

• produce and expand simple, compound, and complex sentences

</td></tr>
</table>

Warm-up and Review
10–15 minutes (books closed)

Draw a word web on the board with *take* in the center. Elicit words that often follow *take* and write them in the web (for example, *a class, a bus, control, a seat, a call, a test*). Explain or elicit that these are collocations, words that are often used together as a chunk. Point out that learning and using collocations makes our speech more natural and fluent. Pair or group students to list as many collocations as they can with the verb *make*. Set a time limit (three minutes). Call on each group to give a new collocation in turn. A group is out when it cannot list a new collocation. The group with the most turns wins.

Introduction
5 minutes

1. Say: *Collocations are groups of words, or chunks, that we often use together.*

2. State the objective: *Today we are going to recognize and use collocations so that your language sounds natural and use noun clauses after verbs to add information.*

1 Vocabulary: Collocations

Presentation and Guided Practice I
20–25 minutes

 **A** **1.13** **1.14** 1. Copy the chart onto the board.

2. Read the directions aloud.

3. Call on students to read the sentences from the article aloud.

4. Play the audio.

5. Tell students to listen and complete the chart.

6. Call on students to add words to the chart on the board.

Answers			
gather	reach	gain/lose	clarify
data information evidence	a conclusion a goal a decision	confidence influence value	distinctions differences information

Communicative Practice
15–20 minutes

B 1. Read the directions aloud.

2. Set a time limit (three minutes). Have students work individually to complete the sentences.

3. Call on students to read the completed sentences aloud.

Answers	
1. gather	4. gain
2. gain / lose	5. reach
3. clarify	

MULTILEVEL STRATEGIES

• **Pre-level** Pair students to complete the sentences.

• **Higher-level** Have students write an additional question for each verb using a different collocation (for example, *Do you like to gather a lot of information before you make a decision?*).

C 1. Read the directions aloud.

2. Set a time limit (five minutes) for students to complete the activity in pairs.

3. Call on students to share their ideas with the class.

2 Grammar: Noun clauses after verbs

Presentation and Guided Practice II
20–25 minutes

 1. Draw a stick figure on the board with a speech bubble. Label the stick figure *the speaker*. In the speech bubble, write: *Self-esteem and self-confidence are related but not the same.* Say: *The speaker* (point to the figure) *says that* (point to the bubble) *self-esteem and self-confidence are related but not the same.*

2. Demonstrate how to read the charts. Read each sentence aloud and have students repeat it after you.

3. Have students complete the sentences in the Language Connection about noun clauses after verbs. Go over the answers with the class.

Answers	
1. that	3. followed
2. not followed	4. indirect object

Guided Practice III
20–25 minutes

 1. Ask students to work individually to complete the task and then compare answers with a partner.

2. Ask volunteers to read sentences in the paragraph aloud.

Answers	
1. believe that	5. did not demonstrate that
2. suggests that	
3. persuaded them that	6. inform us that / inform them that / informed them that
4. show that / showed that	

C 1. Read the directions aloud.

2. Brainstorm a list of verbs students could use (for example, *say, learn, mention, find out*) to talk about what the speaker said and what they learned.

3. Set a time limit (three minutes). Tell students to work individually to write four sentences.

Answers
Answers will vary.

D 1. Set a time limit (five minutes) for students to share their sentences with a partner.

2. Ask volunteers to write sentences on the board.

3. If students disagree, ask them to look at the chart and explain their answers.

EXTENSION ACTIVITY

Examples from the News

1. Have students work in pairs to find articles or other texts online.

2. Ask them to locate five sentences using noun clauses.

3. Call on students to write their sentences on the board.

Evaluation
10–15 minutes

SELF-ASSESSMENT

1. Have students complete the self-assessment.

2. Provide additional practice as needed.

<table>
<tr><td>

Lesson Overview

</td><td>

Lesson Notes

</td></tr>
</table>

MULTILEVEL OBJECTIVES

On-level and Pre-level: Read and discuss how social media affects self-confidence in teenagers

Higher-level: Read, discuss and analyze how social media affects self-confidence in teenagers

LANGUAGE FOCUS

Grammar: Noun clauses

Vocabulary: *surge, empower, corollary, inspiring, navigate*

For vocabulary support, see these **Oxford Picture Dictionary** topics: Taking Care of Your Health, pages 116–117; Internet Research, pages 212–213

STRATEGY FOCUS

Use examples to support points and make ideas clearer.

READINESS CONNECTION

In this lesson, students interpret and evaluate data in a bar graph.

PACING

To compress this lesson: Assign 2B and/or 2C for homework.

To extend this lesson: Have students analyze speakers' relationships based on how they speak (see page 87); Have students role-play parent–teen conversations about social media (see page 89).

And/or have students complete **Multilevel Activities 5 Unit 4, Lesson 4**.

CORRELATIONS

CCRS: RI/RL.6.2 Determine a theme or central idea of a text and how it is conveyed through particular details; provide a summary of the text distinct from personal opinions or judgments.

RST.6-8.2 Application: determine the central ideas or conclusions of a text; provide an accurate summary of the text distinct from prior knowledge or opinions.

RI.8.3 Analyze how a text makes connections among and distinctions between individuals, ideas, or events (e.g., through comparisons, analogies, or categories).

RI/RL.6.4 Determine the meaning of words and phrases as they are used in a text, including figurative, connotative, and technical meanings; analyze the impact of a specific word choice on meaning and tone.

RI.6.7 Integrate information presented in different media or formats (e.g., in charts, graphs, photographs, videos, or maps) as well as in words to develop a coherent understanding of a topic or issue.

RST.6-8.7 Integrate quantitative or technical information expressed in words in a text with a version of that information expressed visually (e.g., in a flowchart, diagram, model, graph, or table).

W.7.7 Conduct short research projects to answer a question, drawing on several sources and generating additional related, focused questions for further research and investigation.

SL.8.1.a. Come to discussions prepared, having read or researched material under study; explicitly draw on that preparation by referring to evidence on the topic, text, or issue to probe and reflect on ideas under discussion.

SL.8.1.c. Pose questions that connect the ideas of several speakers and respond to others' questions and comments with relevant evidence, observations, and ideas.

SL.8.1.d. Acknowledge new information expressed by others, and, when warranted, qualify or justify their own views in light of the evidence presented.

SL.8.2 Analyze the purpose of information presented in diverse media and formats (e.g., visually, quantitatively, orally) and evaluate the motives (e.g., social, commercial, political) behind its presentation.

SL.8.4 Present claims and findings, emphasizing salient points in a focused, coherent manner with relevant evidence, sound valid reasoning, and well-chosen details; use appropriate eye contact, adequate volume, and clear pronunciation.

L.8.6 Acquire and use accurately level-appropriate general academic and domain-specific words and phrases; gather vocabulary knowledge when considering a word or phrase important to comprehension or expression.

ELPS: ELP Standard 1

use a wide range of strategies to:

- determine central ideas or themes in oral presentations and spoken and written texts
- cite specific details and evidence from texts to support the analysis
- summarize a text

ELP Standard 2

- participate in conversations, extended discussions, and written exchanges about a range of substantive topics, texts, and issues
- build on the ideas of others
- express his or her own ideas clearly and persuasively
- refer to specific and relevant evidence from texts or research to support his or her ideas
- ask and answer questions that probe reasoning and claims

ELP Standard 6

- analyze and evaluate the reasoning in persuasive spoken and written texts
- determine whether the evidence is sufficient to support the claim
- cite specific textual evidence to thoroughly support the analysis

ELP Standard 7

- adapt language choices and style according to purpose, task, and audience with ease in various social and academic contexts
- use a wide variety of complex general academic and content specific words and phrases
- employ both formal and more informal styles and tones effectively in spoken and written texts, as appropriate

ELP Standard 8

using context, questioning, and consistent knowledge of English morphology,

- determine the meaning of general academic and content-specific words and phrases, figurative and connotative language, and idiomatic expressions in spoken and written texts about a variety of topics, experiences, or events

Warm-up and Review
10–15 minutes (books closed)

Write *Social media* on the board, and under it write *Advantages* and *Disadvantages*. Brainstorm ideas with the class and write them on the board.

Introduction
5 minutes

State the objective: *Today we will read and discuss how social media affects self-confidence in teenagers.*

1 Get ready to read

Presentation I
20–25 minutes

 **A** ◀)) **1.15** 1. Say: *Now we're going to listen to a conversation between two friends.*

2. Play the audio. Direct students to answer the questions.

Answers
The parent is concerned that the son, Leo, is on his phone and social media too much.

 **B** ◀)) **1.15** 1. Replay the audio. Ask students to check the expressions.

2. Check answers as a class.

Answers
Here's why...   The main reason for that is...   Here's the thing...   Our priority is...

TIP

Pause the audio after each explanation or reason so students can pay attention to the content, not just the expression used.

 **C** 1. Read the directions aloud. Call on students to read the statements aloud.

2. Group students and assign roles: manager, fact checker, recorder, and reporter. Check comprehension of tasks. Ask: *Who keeps the team on task and on time?* [manager] *Who takes notes and writes any new statements?* [recorder] *Who takes notes on finding and citing textual evidence for answers?* [fact checker] *Who reports to the class?* [reporter]

3. Play the audio again if necessary.

4. Set a time limit (three minutes) and have students work together to complete the task.

5. Call time and have the reporters from each team take turns calling out their ideas.

Answers
Answers will vary.

To adapt 1C:

• **On-level** Assign these students the roles of recorder and manager.

• **Pre-level** Assign these students the role of reporter.

• **Higher-level** Assign these students the role of fact checker.

EXTENSION ACTIVITY

Analyzing a Relationship

1. Say: *You can tell a lot about a relationship by the way the speakers talk to each other. Listen again. Then describe the speakers' relationship in as much detail as you can.*

2. Play the audio again. Pair students to complete the task. Encourage them to use the expressions in 1B to explain their ideas.

3. Call on volunteers to share their ideas with the class.

2 Preview and read

Guided Practice I
20–25 minutes

1. Read the directions aloud. Ask: *What should you do when you preview an article?* [read the title and headings, look at visuals, skim the first and last paragraphs, skim first lines of other paragraphs]

2. Have students answer the question individually, and then check answers as a class.

Answer
The author argues that social media has a complex effect on teenagers.

Guide students in the preview process. Ask: *What is the title?* [*Teens and Social Media*] *What do you see in the picture?* [a teenager looking at a phone, a frustrated parent watching] Direct students to read the first and last paragraphs.

1. Ask students to read the article silently and answer the question and then compare answers with a partner.

2. Check the answer with the class. Say: *The first time you read an article, you should focus on the main idea or ideas.*

Answer
an individualized approach

To adapt 2B:

• **Pre-level** Work with pre-level students to read the article aloud. Stop after each paragraph and check comprehension.

• **On-level** Have students complete the activity as directed.

• **Higher-level** Direct students to write the main idea of the article in a statement using their own words.

Presentation II
20–25 minutes

C 1. Read the directions aloud. Call on students to read the questions aloud.

2. Set a time limit (ten minutes) and have students work individually to complete the task.

3. Call time. Have students compare answers in pairs.

4. Go over the answers as a class.

Possible Answers
1. increase in worry, loneliness, sleeplessness, increased suicide risk, pressures to post and get likes, FOMO, online bullying
2. It's possible that existing mental problems could lead to more social media use; there may be other problems that contribute to this.
3. People choose and post messages and images to give a certain impression (for example, that someone has a great social life, is very happy).
4. Teenagers had similar challenges before the digital age.
5. They suggest an individualized approach: don't just take device away, address underlying issues, involve teens in trying to manage.
6. Teenagers' habits may reflect the parents' habits.

WORD STUDY

D 1. Read the directions and the prompts aloud.

2. Write the chart on the board.

3. Set a time limit (five minutes). Have students work in pairs to complete the task.

4. Ask volunteers to write words in the chart on the board.

5. Elicit definitions.

Answers
surge: rise, uptick empowering: inspiring

E 1. Have students work with their teams from 1C. Assign roles: manager (keep team on time and on task), fact checker (check facts and look up words), recorder (take notes), and reporter (report to the class).

2. Set a time limit (five minutes) and have teams discuss the questions.

3. Call time. Ask reporters from each team to share their ideas.

Answers
Answers will vary.

3 Build on it

Presentation I
20–25 minutes

A 1. Have students stay in their teams from 2E and look at the graph. Ask: *What is the relationship between the ideas in each bar?* [opposites] *On which side are the more negative options?* [the top of each pair of lines] *Where are the more positive feelings or traits?* [on the bottom of each pair]

2. Set a time limit (five minutes). Have students work in teams to discuss the questions.

3. Call on reporters to share their ideas with the class.

Possible Answer
The data is biased because it only reflects the beliefs of the teens.

B 1. Have students stay in their teams with the same roles.

2. Direct students' attention to the Speaking Note. Read the directions and questions aloud.

3. Set a time limit (ten minutes). Have students work in teams to discuss the questions.

4. Elicit answers. Encourage students to use expressions to support their points and make ideas clearer.

Answers
1. Answers will vary. 2. Answers will vary. 3. Possible answer: The chart supports the idea that social media may have some positive effects on teenagers. However, it doesn't show any of the negative effects that the article suggests might be occurring. 4. Answers will vary.

PROBLEM SOLVING

C 1. Ask students to stay in their teams and suggest they change roles. Explain that students will work with their group to complete the task. Remind students to use examples to support points and make ideas clearer.

2. Set a time limit (five minutes) and have students work together to complete the task.

3. Call time and have the reporters from each group take turns calling out their answers.

Answers
Answers will vary.

APPLY YOUR KNOWLEDGE

D 1. Ask students to complete the research individually.

2. Students work in their teams from 3C with the same roles to share their research.

3. Call on reporters to share their teams' ideas with the class.

EXTENSION ACTIVITY

Role Play

1. Pair students. Tell pairs to create a role play in which a parent tries to convince a teen not to use social media so much.

2. Call on volunteers to role-play for the class.

Evaluation

10–15 minutes

SELF-ASSESSMENT

1. Direct students to complete the self-assessment individually.

2. Have students choose the one objective they had the most difficulty with.

3. Group students according to their weakest skill. Provide each group with suggestions or feedback.

Lesson Overview

| | Lesson Notes |

MULTILEVEL OBJECTIVES

On-level: Use the writing process to summarize an article

Pre-level: Work with others to summarize an article

Higher-level: Summarize an article using noun clauses

LANGUAGE FOCUS

Grammar: Noun clauses

Vocabulary: Positive and negative effects, introducing examples

For vocabulary support, see this **Oxford Picture Dictionary** topic: English Composition, pages 202–203

STRATEGY FOCUS

Use examples to give supporting ideas.

PACING

To compress this lesson: Assign 1A–E for homework.

To extend this lesson: Have students post and discuss each other's summaries (see page 92).

And/or have students complete **Multilevel Activities 5 Unit 4, Lesson 5**.

CORRELATIONS

CCRS: W/WHST.6-8.2.a. Introduce a topic clearly, previewing what is to follow; organize ideas, concepts, and information, using strategies such as definition, classification, comparison / contrast, and cause/effect; include formatting (e.g., headings), graphics (e.g., charts, tables), and multimedia when useful to aiding comprehension.

W/WHST.6-8.2.b. Develop the topic with relevant facts, definitions, concrete details, quotations, or other information and examples.

W/WHST.6-8.2.c. Use appropriate transitions to create cohesion and clarify the relationships among ideas and concepts.

W/WHST.6-8.2.d. Use precise language and domain-specific vocabulary to inform about or explain the topic.

W/WHST.6-8.2.f. Provide a concluding statement or section that follows from and supports the information or explanation presented.

W/WHST.6-8.4 Produce clear and coherent writing in which the development and organization and style are appropriate to task, purpose, and audience.

W/WHST.6-8.5 With some guidance and support from peers and others, develop and strengthen writing as needed by planning, revising, editing, rewriting, or trying a new approach, focusing on how well purpose and audience have been addressed.

L.6.3/7.3.c. Choose language that expresses ideas precisely and concisely, recognizing and eliminating wordiness and redundancy.

L.8.6 Acquire and use accurately level-appropriate general academic and domain-specific words and phrases; gather vocabulary knowledge when considering a word or phrase important to comprehension or expression.

ELPS: ELP Standard 7

- adapt language choices and style according to purpose, task, and audience with ease in various social and academic contexts
- use a wide variety of complex general academic and content specific words and phrases
- employ both formal and more informal styles and tones effectively in spoken and written texts, as appropriate

ELP Standard 9

- recount a complex and detailed sequence of events or steps in a process, with an effective sequential or chronological order
- introduce and effectively develop an informational topic with facts, details, and evidence
- use complex and varied transitions to link the major sections of speech and text and to clarify relationships among events and ideas
- provide a concluding section or statement

ELP Standard 10

- use complex phrases and clauses
- produce and expand simple, compound, and complex sentences

Warm-up and Review
10–15 minutes (books closed)

Go around the room and call on each student to say one thing he or she remembers from the article on social media in Lesson 4. Jot notes on the board.

Introduction
5 minutes

State the objective: *Today we will use the writing process to summarize an article.*

1 Write a summary

Presentation I
20–25 minutes

 1. Have students revisit the article on pages 42–43. Check comprehension. Ask: *What is the article about? What are the most important ideas?*

2. Elicit responses. Record any new information not mentioned in the warm-up on the board.

Guided Practice I
15–20 minutes

 1. Direct students to look at the chart. Ask about organization: *What paragraph is the introduction?* [the first] *The conclusion?* [the last]

2. Check comprehension of the activity. Ask: *Do you need to write complete sentences in the chart?* [no]

3. Have students work individually to complete their charts.

Answers	
Possible negative effects: • increase in worry, loneliness, sleeplessness • increased suicide risk • pressures to post and get likes, FOMO, online bullying	Possible positive effects: • empowering to connect with others around world • can raise awareness of issues important to them • share inspiring messages and images
Advice for parents: • take an individualized approach • don't just take device away • understand underlying issues • work together with teens	

C 1. Read the directions aloud. Check comprehension. Ask: *What do you need to include in a statement of the main idea?* [the topic, or what the article is about, and the controlling idea, or the writer's main focus/point]

2. Have students work individually to write their statements. Encourage students to use the sentence frame. Then ask students to compare statements in pairs.

> **TIP**
>
> Write the sentence frame from 1C on the board: *The article [title of article] examines...* Point out that the sentence frame uses a noun clause. Remind students that they identified the main idea in Lesson 4, 2A, but encourage them to use their own words.

D 1. Check comprehension. Ask: *What section do you need to reread?* [the last]

2. Have students work individually to write their conclusions.

> **TIP**
>
> Direct students' attention to the last paragraphs of the article. Elicit synonyms and other word forms for key words in the conclusion (for example, *individualized approach*). Remind students that they can use synonyms and different word forms to rephrase ideas.

E 1. Read the directions aloud. Check comprehension. Ask: *What will you include in your summary?* [introduction, notes from the chart, conclusion]

2. Draw students' attention to the Writer's Note. Ask: *What do these expressions introduce?* [examples]

3. Have students work individually to write their summaries.

> **MULTILEVEL STRATEGIES**
>
> To adapt 1E:
>
> • **On-level** Have students write summaries as directed.
>
> • **Pre-level** Work with students in a group to write the summary together.
>
> • **Higher-level** Direct students to add examples and details to their summaries.

2 Get feedback and revise

Guided Practice II
10–15 minutes

 Direct students to check their writing using the editing checklist. Tell them to read each item in the list and check their papers before moving onto the next item. Explain that students should not edit their writing at this stage. They should just use the checklist to check their work and mark any areas they want to revise.

Communicative Practice
10–15 minutes

 1. Read the directions aloud. Emphasize to students that they are responding to their partners' work, not correcting it.

2. Direct students to exchange papers with a partner and follow the instructions.

C Allow students time to edit and revise their writing using the editing checklist and their partner's feedback. If necessary, students could complete this task as homework.

MULTILEVEL STRATEGIES

To adapt 2C:

• **Mixed-ability** Pair pre-level students with on- and higher-level students. Have all students point out ideas that are not clear. Instruct on- and higher-level partners give feedback on spelling and grammar if helpful.

EXTENSION ACTIVITY

Discussion Board

1. Tell students to post their summaries to a discussion board.

2. Direct students to give feedback on two summaries.

Evaluation
10–15 minutes

SELF-ASSESSMENT

1. Call on students to read their completed sentences aloud.

2. Use the responses to the second statement to plan follow-up activities.

Lesson Overview

Lesson Notes

MULTILEVEL OBJECTIVES

On-level: Students conduct and present research related to self-confidence or self-esteem

Pre-level: Students help conduct and present research related to self-confidence or self-esteem

Higher-level: Students conduct and analyze research related to self-confidence or self-esteem and present it to the class

LANGUAGE FOCUS

Grammar: Noun clauses

Vocabulary: *self-confidence, self-esteem*

For vocabulary support, see these **Oxford Picture Dictionary** topics: Feelings, pages 42–43; Internet Research, pages 212–213

STRATEGY FOCUS

Project confidence when you speak.

READINESS CONNECTION

In this lesson, students collaborate to organize and present research with confidence.

PACING

To compress this lesson: Assign 1B and 1C for homework. Alternatively, assign students topics in 1A.

To extend this lesson: Have students work in pairs to debrief regarding the presentations (see page 95).

And/or have students complete **Multilevel Activities 5 Unit 4, Lesson 6**.

CORRELATIONS

CCRS: W.7.7 Conduct short research projects to answer a question, drawing on several sources and generating additional related, focused questions for further research and investigation.

W.7.8 Gather relevant information from multiple print and digital sources, using search terms effectively; assess the credibility and accuracy of each source; and quote or paraphrase the data and conclusions of others while avoiding plagiarism and following a standard format for citation.

SL.8.4 Present claims and findings, emphasizing salient points in a focused, coherent manner with relevant evidence, sound valid reasoning, and well-chosen details; use appropriate eye contact, adequate volume, and clear pronunciation.

SL.8.6 Adapt speech to a variety of contexts and tasks, demonstrating command of formal English when indicated or appropriate.

L.6.3/7.3.b. Maintain consistency in style and tone.

L.6.3/7.3.c. Choose language that expresses ideas precisely and concisely, recognizing and eliminating wordiness and redundancy.

L.8.6 Acquire and use accurately level-appropriate general academic and domain-specific words and phrases; gather vocabulary knowledge when considering a word or phrase important to comprehension or expression.

ELPS: ELP Standard 2

- participate in conversations, extended discussions, and written exchanges about a range of substantive topics, texts, and issues
- build on the ideas of others
- express his or her own ideas clearly and persuasively
- summarize the key points and evidence discussed

ELP Standard 3

- deliver oral presentations
- compose written informational texts
- fully develop the topic with relevant details, concepts, examples, and information
- integrate graphics or multimedia when useful about a variety of texts, topics, or events

<table>
<tr><td>

ELP Standard 5

- carry out both short and more sustained research projects to answer a question or solve a problem
- gather information from multiple print and digital sources
- use advanced search terms effectively
- synthesize information from multiple print and digital sources
- analyze and integrate information into clearly organized spoken and written texts
- include illustrations, diagrams, or other graphics as appropriate
- cite sources appropriately

</td><td>

ELP Standard 7

- adapt language choices and style according to purpose, task, and audience with ease in various social and academic contexts
- use a wide variety of complex general academic and content specific words and phrases
- employ both formal and more informal styles and tones effectively in spoken and written texts, as appropriate

</td></tr>
</table>

Warm-up and Review
10–15 minutes (books closed)

Say a series of statements that express either self-confidence or self-esteem. Tell students to raise their right hands for self-confidence and their left hands to indicate self-esteem. Use these statements or create your own: *I am a good friend, I can sing well, I'm good at fixing things, People generally like me, I'm responsible, I think I have a good sense of humor, My English speaking ability is good.*

Introduction
5 minutes

State the objective: *Today we will conduct and present research related to self-confidence or self-esteem.*

1 Research another aspect of self-confidence or self-esteem

Communicative Practice
40–45 minutes

A 1. Group students but do not assign roles yet. Explain that students will work with their team to narrow the topic.

2. Read the directions aloud.

3. Direct students' attention to the first Research Tip. Ask: *What are some other words you could search for to find different results for the other two topics?* [Possible answers: how self-esteem develops in children, developing children's self-esteem; technology's effect on self-confidence and self-esteem, impact of technology on self-confidence and self-esteem]

4. Set a time limit (ten minutes) and have students work together to complete the task.

B 1. Read the directions aloud.

2. Check comprehension of the task. Ask: *How many sources will the group find?* [at least four] *How many sources will each team member take notes on?* [at least one]

3. Draw students' attention to the second Research Tip. Check comprehension. Ask: *Why should you check the source's date of publication?* [to make sure it is up-to-date] *How recent do you think the information should be?* [preferably within a year or two]

4. Set a time limit (five minutes). Direct students to identify four or more recent sources as a group.

C 1. Read the directions aloud.

2. Set a time limit or assign research as an out-of-class task. Remind students to look for visual elements that they can include in their presentation.

D 1. Have students share their results in their teams.

2. Read the directions and questions aloud.

3. Assign roles: manager, IT specialist, recorder, and editor. Explain that students will work with their group to complete the task.

4. Check comprehension of the activity. Ask: *Who compiles the information from all sources?* [recorder] *Who checks that the sources and dates are accurate?* [IT specialist] *Who keeps the team on time and on task?* [manager] *Who checks that grammar and spelling are correct?* [editor]

5. Set a time limit (ten minutes) and have students work together to follow the steps and answer the questions.

2 Present your research

Presentation
40–45 minutes

A 1. Have students stay in their teams from 1D. Check comprehension of the task. Ask: *What does the outline include?* [introduction, body, and conclusion] *What should you do in the introduction?* [tell the audience the topic and why you chose it] *What do you need to include in the body?* [examples] *What should you explain in the conclusion?* [why the research is important or useful]

2. Draw students' attention to the Presentation Strategy. Call on students to read sentences aloud.

3. Check comprehension. Ask: *What makes you look more confident?* [standing tall with shoulders back] *What shouldn't you do?* [fidget] *Where should you look?* [at audience members in all parts of the room]

4. Set a time limit (five to ten minutes) and have students work as a team to outline their presentation.

B 1. Explain that students will work with their team to present their research.

2. Check comprehension of the activity. Ask: *Who will speak?* [everyone]

3. Set a time limit (five minutes) and have students work as a team to divide the roles and the sections of the presentation (for example, introduction and source 1, source 2, source 3, source 4 and conclusion).

C 1. Read the bulleted items aloud.

2. Check comprehension of the activity. Ask: *Should you rehearse the presentation in exactly the way you will present to the class?* [yes]

3. Set a time limit (ten minutes) and have students rehearse their presentations in teams.

D 1. Draw a chart on the board, listing the teams in the first column. In the other columns, list the note-taking prompts, or shortened forms of them: *Opening, Speaking, Transitions, Projecting confidence, Advice.* Check comprehension of the activity. Ask: *What will you write under* Opening? [whether the team included an interesting anecdote, quote, or statistic] Remind students to just use words and phrases in the chart.

2. Set a time limit (five minutes) for each presentation, and ask each team to present in turn.

E 1. Have each team discuss their feedback for other teams.

2. Ask each team to nominate a reporter to give feedback on the other teams' presentations.

3. Beginning with the first team to present, collect feedback from the reporters. Write feedback in the table you drew on the board in 2D.

Evaluation
10–15 minutes

SELF-ASSESSMENT

1. Pair students to share their self-assessments.

2. Elicit suggestions from the class for developing more confidence in each of the three assessment areas.

5 Communication

Unit Overview

This unit explores communication methods and styles as well as body language and communication breakdowns with a range of employability skills and contextualizes language with different levels of formality and gerunds. By the end of this unit, you will be able to conduct a survey and present results on communication.

KEY OBJECTIVES

Lesson 1	Rank communication methods
Lesson 2	Read about communication styles and discuss ways to communicate clearly
Lesson 3	Identify levels of formality; use gerunds in different sentence positions
Lesson 4	Read about body language and discuss how it can cause communication breakdowns
Lesson 5	Use the writing process to summarize an article
Lesson 6	Conduct a survey on communication problems and present survey results

UNIT FEATURES

Academic Vocabulary	*analytical, conclude, conduct, contradict, convey, encounter, excel, expertise, interpret, project*
Employability Skills	• Predict a lecture's content • Synthesize ideas across different sources • Draw conclusions based on survey results • Suggest ways to repair communication breakdown in the workplace • Divide work among peers and develop survey questions • Use technology to produce a shared presentation of survey results

Resources	**Class Audio** CD1, Tracks 16-18
	Teacher Resource Center
	    Multilevel Activities 5 Unit 5
	    Multilevel Grammar Activities 5 Unit 5
	    Unit 5 Test
	Oxford Picture Dictionary Everyday Conversation, The Telephone, Soft Skills, Interview Skills, English Composition, Digital Literacy, Internet Research

Lesson Overview	**Lesson Notes**

MULTILEVEL OBJECTIVES

On-level: Identify, rank, and discuss communication methods

Pre-level: Identify and rank communication methods

Higher-level: Identify, rank, and analyze communication methods

LANGUAGE FOCUS

Grammar: Simple present

Vocabulary: Modes of communication

For vocabulary support, see these **Oxford Picture Dictionary** topics: Everyday Conversation, page 12; The Telephone, pages 14–15; Soft Skills, page 178

READINESS CONNECTION

In this lesson, students draw conclusions based on survey results.

PACING

To compress this lesson: Do 1D as a whole-class activity and/or assign 2C for homework.

To extend this lesson: Have students role-play a breakdown in communication (see page 99).

And/or have students complete **Multilevel Activities 5 Unit 5, Lesson 1.**

CORRELATIONS

CCRS: RI.6.7 Integrate information presented in different media or formats (e.g., in charts, graphs, photographs, videos, or maps) as well as in words to develop a coherent understanding of a topic or issue.

SL.8.1.a. Come to discussions prepared, having read or researched material under study; explicitly draw on that preparation by referring to evidence on the topic, text, or issue to probe and reflect on ideas under discussion.

SL.8.1.c. Pose questions that connect the ideas of several speakers and respond to others' questions and comments with relevant evidence, observations, and ideas.

SL.8.1.d. Acknowledge new information expressed by others, and, when warranted, qualify or justify their own views in light of the evidence presented.

L.6.4.c. Consult reference materials (e.g., dictionaries, glossaries, thesauruses), both print and digital, to find the pronunciation of a word or determine or clarify its precise meaning or its part of speech.

L.6.4.c. Consult reference materials (e.g., dictionaries, glossaries, thesauruses), both print and digital, to find the pronunciation of a word or determine or clarify its precise meaning or its part of speech.

L.8.6 Acquire and use accurately level-appropriate general academic and domain-specific words and phrases; gather vocabulary knowledge when considering a word or phrase important to comprehension or expression.

ELPS: ELP Standard 2

- participate in conversations, extended discussions, and written exchanges about a range of substantive topics, texts, and issues
- build on the ideas of others
- express his or her own ideas clearly and persuasively
- refer to specific and relevant evidence from texts or research to support his or her ideas
- ask and answer questions that probe reasoning and claim

ELP Standard 8

using context, questioning, and consistent knowledge of English morphology,

- determine the meaning of general academic and content-specific words and phrases, figurative and connotative language, and idiomatic expressions in spoken and written texts about a variety of topics, experiences, or events

Warm-up and Review
10–15 minutes (books closed)

Draw a mind map on the board. Label the circle in the middle *Who I talk to*. Tell the class who you talk to on a regular basis, and add connecting lines and labels for each person. For example, draw a line to a circle and write *Work*. Then add the names of people you talk to at work. Continue with other categories, for example, *Family, Friends, Neighbors*). Tell students to draw their own talking maps and then describe them to a partner.

Introduction
5 minutes

1. Tell students the ways you usually communicate with the people in your talking map.

2. State the objective: *Today we're going to think about and rank different communication methods.*

1 Discuss communication

Presentation I
20–25 minutes

 1. Group students and assign roles: manager, fact checker, recorder, and reporter. Explain that students will work with their team to brainstorm ways that people communicate and categorize their list.

2. Check comprehension of the activity. Ask: *Who looks up the words in a dictionary?* [fact checker] *Who sorts words into categories?* [recorder] *Who tells the class your answers?* [reporter] *Who keeps everyone on track and manages time?* [manager]

3. Set a time limit (three minutes) and have students work together to complete the task.

4. Call time and have the reporters from each team take turns calling out their categories. Then elicit words for each category. Record students' answers on the board. If teams disagree, write each team's choice next to the word.

For 1A, use mixed-level groups.

- **On-level** Assign these students as fact checkers and reporters.
- **Pre-level** Assign these students as recorders.
- **Higher-level** Assign these students as leaders.

When setting up task-based activities, verify that students understand their roles using physical commands. For example: *If you report on your team's work, stand up.* [reporter] *If you keep the team on task, point to the clock.* [manager] *If you sort the words into categories, raise your hand.* [recorder] *If you look up words in the dictionary, hold up your dictionary/smartphone/tablet.*

B 1. Direct students to look at the definition. Ask: *According to the definition, what two kinds of activities does communication involve?* [expressing ideas and feelings, giving information]

2. Write *communication* on the board. Elicit examples of synonyms and word forms from the whole class and write their ideas on the board. Point out the connection between their ideas and their responses in 1A.

Answers
synonyms: *conversation, expression, connection, contact* forms: *communicate, communicative, communicator*

C 1. Direct students to look at the chart. Ask: *How many methods of workplace communication does it list?* [four] *What does each column show?* [frequency] *In what form are the results?* [percentages] *What method of communication do people use the most every day?* [email] *What do they use the next most?* [phone]

2. Elicit examples from the whole class. Write their ideas on the board. Point out the connection between their ideas and the definition in 1B.

Answers
email followed by phone

Guided Practice
10–20 minutes

 1. Direct students to look at the first question. Check comprehension of the collocation. Ask: *Is* effective communication *a good or bad thing?* [good] *What makes communication effective?* [It transmits the idea well.]

2. Set a time limit (five minutes). Direct students to work with their partners to complete the activity. Have a volunteer from each pair give their responses. Check answers as a class.

Answers
Answers will vary.

Presentation II
20–25 minutes

E 1. Group students and assign roles: manager, recorder, reporter, and editor. Explain that students will work with their team to analyze the information. Verify students' understanding of the roles: the reporter reports back to the class, the manager keeps track of time, the recorder writes the statements, and the editor checks grammar and spelling.

2. Survey the class. Say each method of communication and ask for a show of hands if students use the method most days. Tally the results on the board.

3. Set a time limit (ten minutes) for the discussions. Write the following sentence frame on the board: *A communication breakdown that can happen with ______ is ______.*

4. Call time and have the reporters from each team take turns calling out their examples. If examples aren't clear, have students ask questions to clarify.

EXTENSION ACTIVITY

Role-play a Communication Breakdown

1. Ask students to work with a partner and role-play a breakdown in one communication method.

2. Set a time limit (three minutes). Have pairs prepare their role plays.

3. Have students act out their role plays for the class.

4. Ask the class to find similarities and differences in the breakdowns. Ask: *Which method of communicating leads to the most breakdowns? Why?*

Evaluation
10–15 minutes

SELF-ASSESSMENT

1. Ask students to spend some time reflecting on what they have learned. Set a time limit (three minutes).

2. Ask volunteers to share their thoughts.

Lesson Overview

MULTILEVEL OBJECTIVES

On-level: Read about communication styles and discuss ways to communicate clearly

Pre-level: Read about communication styles and learn ways to communicate clearly

Higher-level: Read about communication styles and analyze ways to communicate clearly

LANGUAGE FOCUS

Grammar: Gerunds

Vocabulary: *analytical, contradict, excel, expertise,* words related to communications styles

For vocabulary support, see these **Oxford Picture Dictionary** topics: Everyday Conversation, page 12; Soft Skills, page 178

STRATEGY FOCUS

Using imperatives to make suggestions.

READINESS CONNECTION

In this lesson, students work together to identify communication styles.

PACING

To compress this lesson: Assign 1C and 1D for homework.

To extend this lesson: Have students complete a jigsaw activity about communication styles (see page 104); Have students role-play how to solve problems related to communication styles (see page 105).

And/or have students complete **Multilevel Activities 5 Unit 5, Lesson 2.**

Lesson Notes

CORRELATIONS

CCRS: RI/RL.7.1 Cite several pieces of textual evidence to support analysis of what the text says explicitly as well as inferences drawn from the text.

RI.8.3 Analyze how a text makes connections among and distinctions between individuals, ideas, or events (e.g., through comparisons, analogies, or categories).

RI/RL.6.4 Determine the meaning of words and phrases as they are used in a text, including figurative, connotative, and technical meanings; analyze the impact of a specific word choice on meaning and tone.

SL.8.1.a. Come to discussions prepared, having read or researched material under study; explicitly draw on that preparation by referring to evidence on the topic, text, or issue to probe and reflect on ideas under discussion.

SL.8.1.c. Pose questions that connect the ideas of several speakers and respond to others' questions and comments with relevant evidence, observations, and ideas.

SL.8.1.d. Acknowledge new information expressed by others, and, when warranted, qualify or justify their own views in light of the evidence presented.

SL.8.2 Analyze the purpose of information presented in diverse media and formats (e.g., visually, quantitatively, orally) and evaluate the motives (e.g., social, commercial, political) behind its presentation.

SL.8.3 Delineate a speaker's argument and specific claims, evaluating the soundness of the reasoning and relevance and sufficiency of the evidence and identifying when irrelevant evidence is introduced.

L.6.3/7.3.c. Choose language that expresses ideas precisely and concisely, recognizing and eliminating wordiness and redundancy.

L.6.4.a. Use context (e.g., the overall meaning of a sentence or paragraph; a word's position or function in a sentence) as a clue to the meaning of a word or phrase.

L.6.4.d. Verify the preliminary determination of the meaning of a word or phrase (e.g., by checking the inferred meaning in context or in a dictionary).

L.8.6 Acquire and use accurately level-appropriate general academic and domain-specific words and phrases; gather vocabulary knowledge when considering a word or phrase important to comprehension or expression.

ELPS: ELP Standard 1

use a wide range of strategies to:

- determine central ideas or themes in oral presentations and spoken and written texts
- cite specific details and evidence from texts to support the analysis
- summarize a text

ELP Standard 2

- participate in conversations, extended discussions, and written exchanges about a range of substantive topics, texts, and issues
- build on the ideas of others
- express his or her own ideas clearly and persuasively
- refer to specific and relevant evidence from texts or research to support his or her ideas
- ask and answer questions that probe reasoning and claim

ELP Standard 4

- construct a substantive claim about a variety of topics

ELP Standard 8

using context, questioning, and consistent knowledge of English morphology,

- determine the meaning of general academic and content-specific words and phrases, figurative and connotative language, and idiomatic expressions in spoken and written texts about a variety of topics, experiences, or events

Warm-up and Review
10–15 minutes (books closed)

1. Write *Communication breakdowns* on the board. Review the breakdowns that result from each communication method. Ask: *What causes the communication breakdown? How does a speaker or writer help or hurt the communication process?*

2. Elicit ideas and write them.

Introduction
5 minutes

1. Summarize any examples of communication styles that students mentioned in the warm-up (for example, *You mentioned that a speaker who is too impatient or gives too few details can contribute to a communication breakdown.*).

2. State the objective: *Today we are going to read about communication styles and discuss ways to communicate clearly.*

1 Read about communication styles

Presentation I
20–25 minutes

A 1. Write *Communication styles* on the board. Elicit a definition or explanation of each adjective.

2. Model the activity. To give an example, describe the communication style of a person you know using one of the adjectives.

3. Pair students to complete the task.

4. Set a time limit (three minutes) and have students work together to complete the task.

5. Call time and call on students to share examples. Record students' ideas on the board.

MULTILEVEL STRATEGIES

To adapt 1A:

- **Cross-ability** Pair pre-level and higher-level students. The higher-level student gives a general description of a person with each style (for example, *If you have a warm communication style, you are friendly and caring. You show concern for the other person and express positive feelings.*). The pre-level student gives an example of someone they know or a famous person and adds specific details.

Guided Practice I
15–20 minutes

B 1. Read the directions aloud. Check comprehension. Ask: *What are you skimming for?* [the definition of each communication style] *What is the title of the text?* [*What Is Your Communication Style?*] *How many styles does the writer describe?* [four]

2. Set a time limit (five minutes). Direct students to underline the definition of each communication style when they find it.

3. Elicit the answer.

 1. Read the directions aloud. Check comprehension. Ask: *What are you looking for?* [advice] *What tells you that writers are giving advice?* [using imperatives, *should, ought to, it's a good idea*]

2. Set a time limit (five minutes). Direct students to answer the question.

3. Elicit ideas from the whole class.

TIP

Tell students to read each paragraph again. Ask: *Does the writer give both positive and negative information about each style?* [yes] *Where is the positive information?* [at the beginning of each paragraph] *Where is the negative information?* [at the end of each paragraph] *What words or phrases does the writer use to show a switch to the negative information?* [*however, but, on the negative side*]. Draw a chart on the board with the column headings *Positive* and *Negative*. Write the names of the communication styles in a column on the left. Tell students to make their own charts and complete them with notes from the text.

Communicative Practice
10–20 minutes

 1. Read the questions aloud.

2. Ask students to think about and mark their answers in the text if possible.

3. Set a time limit (five minutes) for students to discuss their answers with a partner.

4. Invite pairs to share their responses. Check answers with the class.

Presentation II
20–25 minutes

 1. Call on students to read the questions aloud.

2. Set a time limit (three minutes) and have students work individually to complete the task.

3. Call time and ask volunteers to share their answers.

EXTENSION ACTIVITY

Jigsaw Conversation

1. Group students according to their communication style. Have each group brainstorm advantages and disadvantages of their style.

2. Form new groups with members who represent different communication styles, preferably one from each style. Tell team members to share their lists of advantages and disadvantages. Other members can add to the lists.

2 Listen and take notes

Guided Practice II
20–25 minutes

 1. Say: *Now we're going to listen to a lecture about communication breakdowns at work.*

2. Set a time limit (five minutes). Pair students to list three problems and possible solutions.

3. Elicit ideas from the whole class. Write their ideas.

B 🔊 **1.16** 1. Direct students to read the prompts.

2. Play the beginning of the audio. Direct students to listen without writing.

3. Replay the audio. Ask students to respond to the prompts.

4. Set a time limit (five minutes). Direct students to brainstorm what the rest of the lecture will be about.

5. Elicit ideas from the whole class. Write their ideas.

Answers
1. make sure that you are not always communicating in the same way / adapt to other people's styles 2. Answers will vary.

C 🔊 **1.17** 1. Direct students to look at the chart. Ask: *How many problems will the speaker describe?* [four]

2. Play the whole audio. Direct students to write notes in the chart as they listen.

Answers
Employability Skills Lecture Series: Developing Communication Skills
Communication problem:	**Solution:**	**Specific suggestions:**
people have diff comm. prefs	be aware of & vary comm methods	
not checking for comprehension	In email, encourage response	Say, "Please let me know if you have questions" or "Feel free to contact me about this"
easy to offend	address	Check that you didn't hit Reply All. Double-check attachments
carelessly-written emails look bad	rev, edit, read aloud to self	

D 🔊 **1.17** 1. Direct students' attention to the Listening Note.

2. Play the audio. Direct students to add specific suggestions to the chart. (If higher-level students completed the right column in C, they can confirm their answers.)

Answers
See right column of chart in 1C.

Communicative Practice
10–20 minutes

E 🔊 **1.17** 1. Set a time limit (five minutes) for students to discuss their answers with a partner.

2. Replay the audio. Ask students to confirm their answers.

F 1. Read the questions aloud. Direct students' attention to the expressions.

2. Pair students to share their ideas.

3. Elicit answers to the questions. Call on students to make a claim and support it by citing examples from the article and lecture notes using the sentence beginnings provided.

Possible Answers
1. because you can't see facial expressions, "Please let me know if you have questions" or "Feel free to contact me about this." 2. A personal communicator might prefer in-person interactions because they are focused on building relationships, which is easier to do when you see a person's face or hear his or her voice.

Evaluation

10–15 minutes

SELF-ASSESSMENT

1. Pair students to share their self-assessments.

2. Direct students to give advice to their partners as needed.

Lesson Overview

Lesson Notes

MULTILEVEL OBJECTIVES

On-level: Identify and use different levels of formality; use gerunds in different sentence positions

Pre-level: Recognize levels of formality; use gerunds in different sentence positions

Higher-level: Identify and use different levels of formality; use gerunds in different sentence positions and explain their use to classmates

LANGUAGE FOCUS

Grammar: Gerunds

Vocabulary: *conclude, conduct, encounter,* levels of formality

For vocabulary support, see these **Oxford Picture Dictionary** topics: Everyday Conversation, page 12; Soft Skills, page 178; Digital Literacy, pages 211–212

STRATEGY FOCUS

Recognize levels of formality.

READINESS CONNECTION

In this lesson, students work with a partner to discuss similarities and differences.

PACING

To compress this lesson: Assign 2B and 2C for homework.

To extend this lesson: Have students review examples of emotive language (see page 106); Have students practice rewriting with gerunds (see page 107).

And/or have students complete **Multilevel Activities 5 Unit 5, Lesson 3.**

CORRELATIONS

CCRS: SL.8.1.a. Come to discussions prepared, having read or researched material under study; explicitly draw on that preparation by referring to evidence on the topic, text, or issue to probe and reflect on ideas under discussion.

SL.8.1.c. Pose questions that connect the ideas of several speakers and respond to others' questions and comments with relevant evidence, observations, and ideas.

SL.8.1.d. Acknowledge new information expressed by others, and, when warranted, qualify or justify their own views in light of the evidence presented.

L.6.1/8.1.f. Explain the function of verbals (gerunds, participles, infinitives) in general and their function in particular sentences.

L.8.6 Acquire and use accurately level-appropriate general academic and domain-specific words and phrases; gather vocabulary knowledge when considering a word or phrase important to comprehension or expression.

ELPS: ELP Standard 2

• participate in conversations, extended discussions, and written exchanges about a range of substantive topics, texts, and issues

• build on the ideas of others

• express his or her own ideas clearly and persuasively

• summarize the key points and evidence discussed

ELP Standard 7

• employ both formal and more informal styles and tones effectively in spoken and written texts, as appropriate

ELP Standard 8

using context, questioning, and consistent knowledge of English morphology,

• determine the meaning of general academic and content-specific words and phrases, figurative and connotative language, and idiomatic expressions in spoken and written texts about a variety of topics, experiences, or events

<table>
<tr><td>

ELP Standard 10
• produce and expand simple, compound, and complex sentences

</td><td></td></tr>
</table>

Warm-up and Review
10–15 minutes (books closed)

1. Tell students to write two texts to say they will be late: one to a good friend and one to a boss.

2. Pair students to share their texts.

3. Call on several students to write their texts on the board. Elicit differences between the two kinds of texts.

Introduction
5 minutes

1. Say: *We use different communication styles and different language depending on the situation and the person we are talking to.*

2. State the objective: *Today we are going to identify levels of formality and use gerunds in different sentence positions.*

1 Vocabulary: Recognize levels of formality

Presentation and Guided Practice I
20–25 minutes

 1. Write *Formal* and *Less formal* on the board. Elicit examples from the warm-up and other examples.

2. Read the directions aloud.

3. Direct students to complete the task independently.

4. Call on students to read the new sentences aloud.

Answers	
1. excel at	4. verify
2. encountered	5. conclude
3. is conducted	

• **On-level** Have students complete the activity as directed without looking up words first.

• **Pre-level** Have students look up the definitions of any words they don't know.

• **Higher-level** Have students replace the underlined words in two ways if possible, with words provided and with other formal vocabulary.

Write the underlined words and phrases in the sentences in 1A on the board. Point out that most are phrases and that phrases, including phrasal verbs, often have more formal counterparts. Write other common examples (*turn in* paperwork, *get on* a plane, *go back* to work) and elicit more formal substitutes (*submit, board, return*).

Communicative Practice
15–20 minutes

 1. Read the prompts aloud.

2. Set a time limit (ten minutes) for students to complete the activity with a partner.

3. Invite pairs to share their responses. Check answers as a class.

EXTENSION ACTIVITY

Emotive Language Review

1. Have students analyze the text examples they found in 1B for evidence of emotive language or bias. Tell them to list any words that reveal a positive or negative attitude.

2. Elicit examples from the class. Ask: *Is there any relationship between levels of formality and emotive language? How can people use levels of formality to support a particular bias?*

 ## 2 Grammar: Gerunds

Presentation and Guided Practice II
20–25 minutes

A 1. Demonstrate how to read the grammar chart. Read each sentence aloud and have students repeat after you.

2. Have students complete the Language Connection about adjective clauses. Go over the answers with the class.

Answers
A gerund is a <u>noun</u>. When you use a gerund as a subject, the verb is <u>singular</u>. You can use a gerund after the verb be and after verbs such as *continue* and *stop*. You can also use a gerund after expressions like *spend time* and *have difficulty*. In addition, a gerund can follow prepositions like *of* and *without*.

MULTILEVEL STRATEGIES

To adapt 2A:

- **On-level** Have students work independently.

- **Pre-level** Have higher-level classmates assist these students.

- **Higher-level** Have these students work with pre-level classmates.

TIP

Point out that *-ing* words can be different parts of speech. Write examples on the board: *I enjoy swimming. Tony was sleeping when I called. We had an exciting experience on the way to class today.* Underline the *-ing* words and elicit the part of speech. Point out that a gerund looks like a verb but functions as a noun.

Guided Practice III
20–25 minutes

 1. Ask students to work individually to complete the task and then compare answers with a partner.

2. Ask volunteers to write the sentences on the board.

3. Elicit the pattern (from the left column of the chart).

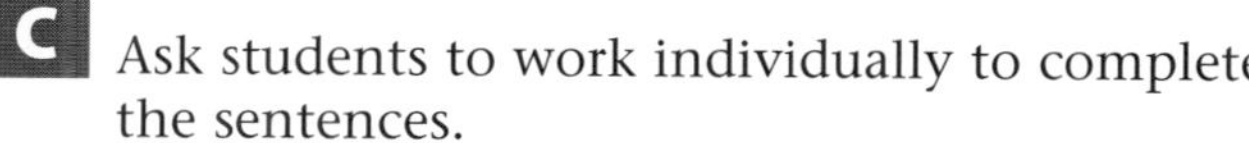

Answers
1. focusing on the big ideas rather than the details 2. adjusting your communication style to fit the situation 3. getting along well with more personal communicators 4. skipping any details 5. Focusing on facts

C Ask students to work individually to complete the sentences.

Possible Answers
1. sending your email to the wrong person 2. proofreading carefully 3. checking your email 4. reading it aloud to yourself 5. sending them the wrong attachment

 1. Set a time limit (five minutes) for students to discuss their answers with a partner.

2. Call on students to share their ideas.

EXTENSION ACTIVITY

Practice Rewriting with Gerunds

1. Have students work in pairs to find text online that they can rewrite with gerunds.

2. After students rewrite, elicit examples from the class.

Evaluation
10–15 minutes

SELF-ASSESSMENT

1. Pair students of different ability.

2. Have them discuss their self-assessments. Higher-level students can provide additional examples and explanation.

Lesson Overview

| | Lesson Notes |

MULTILEVEL OBJECTIVES

On-level: Read about body language and discuss how it can cause communication breakdowns

Pre-level: Read about body language and understand how it can cause communication breakdowns

Higher-level: Read about body language and lead discussion on how it can cause communication breakdowns

LANGUAGE FOCUS

Grammar: Simple present

Vocabulary: *convey, interpret, project, body language*

For vocabulary support, see these **Oxford Picture Dictionary** topics: Everyday Conversation, page 12; Soft Skills, page 178; Interview Skills, page 179

STRATEGY FOCUS

Read for a writer's conclusion.

READINESS CONNECTION

In this lesson, students discuss how body language can contribute to communication breakdown.

PACING

To compress this lesson: Students do 2B as homework.

To extend this lesson: Have students role-play interviews (see page 111); Have students create infographics about body language (see page 112).

And/or have students complete **Multilevel Activities 5 Unit 5, Lesson 4.**

CORRELATIONS

CCRS: RI/RL.7.1 Cite several pieces of textual evidence to support analysis of what the text says explicitly as well as inferences drawn from the text.

RI.8.3 Analyze how a text makes connections among and distinctions between individuals, ideas, or events (e.g., through comparisons, analogies, or categories).

RI/RL.6.4 Determine the meaning of words and phrases as they are used in a text, including figurative, connotative, and technical meanings; analyze the impact of a specific word choice on meaning and tone.

RI.6.7 Integrate information presented in different media or formats (e.g., in charts, graphs, photographs, videos, or maps) as well as in words to develop a coherent understanding of a topic or issue.

RST.6-8.7 Integrate quantitative or technical information expressed in words in a text with a version of that information expressed visually (e.g., in a flowchart, diagram, model, graph, or table).

W.7.7 Conduct short research projects to answer a question, drawing on several sources and generating additional related, focused questions for further research and investigation.

SL.8.1.a. Come to discussions prepared, having read or researched material under study; explicitly draw on that preparation by referring to evidence on the topic, text, or issue to probe and reflect on ideas under discussion.

SL.8.1.c. Pose questions that connect the ideas of several speakers and respond to others' questions and comments with relevant evidence, observations, and ideas.

SL.8.1.d. Acknowledge new information expressed by others, and, when warranted, qualify or justify their own views in light of the evidence presented.

SL.8.2 Analyze the purpose of information presented in diverse media and formats (e.g., visually, quantitatively, orally) and evaluate the motives (e.g., social, commercial, political) behind its presentation.

SL.8.4 Present claims and findings, emphasizing salient points in a focused, coherent manner with relevant evidence, sound valid reasoning, and well-chosen details; use appropriate eye contact, adequate volume, and clear pronunciation.

L.6.4.c. Consult reference materials (e.g., dictionaries, glossaries, thesauruses), both print and digital, to find the pronunciation of a word or determine or clarify its precise meaning or its part of speech.

L.8.6 Acquire and use accurately level-appropriate general academic and domain-specific words and phrases; gather vocabulary knowledge when considering a word or phrase important to comprehension or expression.

ELPS: ELP Standard 1

use a wide range of strategies to:

- determine central ideas or themes in oral presentations and spoken and written texts
- cite specific details and evidence from texts to support the analysis
- summarize a text

ELP Standard 2

- participate in conversations, extended discussions, and written exchanges about a range of substantive topics, texts, and issues
- build on the ideas of others
- express his or her own ideas clearly and persuasively
- refer to specific and relevant evidence from texts or research to support his or her ideas
- ask and answer questions that probe reasoning and claims

ELP Standard 6

- analyze and evaluate the reasoning in persuasive spoken and written texts
- determine whether the evidence is sufficient to support the claim
- cite specific textual evidence to thoroughly support the analysis

ELP Standard 7

- adapt language choices and style according to purpose, task, and audience with ease in various social and academic contexts
- use a wide variety of complex general academic and content specific words and phrases
- employ both formal and more informal styles and tones effectively in spoken and written texts, as appropriate

ELP Standard 8

using context, questioning, and consistent knowledge of English morphology,

- determine the meaning of general academic and content-specific words and phrases, figurative and connotative language, and idiomatic expressions in spoken and written texts about a variety of topics, experiences, or events

Warm-up and Review
10–15 minutes (books closed)

1. Tell the class about a time when body language caused a communication breakdown for you.

2. Pair or group students to share their own experiences with body language and communication breakdowns.

3. Elicit examples from the class.

Introduction
5 minutes

1. Summarize the discussion from the warm-up.

2. State the objective: *Today we will read about body language and discuss further how it can cause communication breakdowns.*

1 Get ready to read

Presentation I
20–25 minutes

A 🔊 **1.18** 1. Say: *Now we're going to listen to managers discussing an employee.* Read the question aloud. Check comprehension.

2. Play the audio. Direct students to read along silently without writing.

Answers

The employee doesn't seem friendly and doesn't smile or talk to customers. The manager is going to talk to him about it. Sample answers: He may be shy or nervous, he may be from a culture that doesn't place a major importance on smiling and eye contact while working.

B 🔊 **1.18** 1. Replay the audio. Ask students to check the ways the woman paraphrases to show she understands.

2. Check answers as a class.

Answers

Are you saying that...
In other words...

C 1. Write *Unfriendly* and *Too friendly* on the board.

2. Group students and assign roles: manager, fact checker, recorder, and reporter. Explain that students will work with their group to make their lists.

3. Check comprehension of the activity. *Who looks up words?* [fact checker] *Who takes notes?* [recorder] *Who reports to the class?* [reporter] *Who keeps the team on time and on task?* [manager]

4. Set a time limit (three minutes) and have students work together to complete the task.

5. Call time and have the reporters from each group take turns calling out things that give the impression of being unfriendly. Then elicit things that give the impression of being too friendly. Record students' answers on the board. If groups disagree, ask the fact checkers to find examples.

> **Answers**
>
> Answers will vary.

MULTILEVEL STRATEGIES

To adapt 1C:

- **On-level** Assign these students the roles of fact checker and recorder.

- **Pre-level** Assign these students the role of reporter.

- **Higher-level** Assign these students the role of manager.

TIP

Point out that students should list actions, not characteristics, in 1C. Elicit an example of each (unfriendly and too friendly) before students work in teams. For example, *refusing to shake hands* might give the impression of being unfriendly, and *hugging a stranger* might be an example of being too friendly.

2 Preview and read

Guided Practice I
20–25 minutes

A 1. Read the directions aloud. Ask: *What should you look at when you preview an article?* [titles, headings, visuals (charts, graphs, photos), first and last paragraphs/sentences] *What is the title?* [*Reading Body Language*]

2. Have students answer the question individually, and then check answers as a class. Call on students to demonstrate an example of each type of body language.

> **Answers**
>
> facial expressions, posture, gestures, personal space

B 1. Direct students' attention to the Reader's Note. Ask: *Where do you conclude a text?* [at the end]

2. Ask students to read the article silently and answer the question and then compare answers with a partner. Check answer with the class.

> **Answer**
>
> Most people aren't aware of the impression they make, and understanding nonverbal signals is an important part of communication.

Presentation II
20–25 minutes

C 1. Group students and assign roles: manager, fact checker, recorder, and reporter. Explain that students will work with their group to answer the questions.

2. Check comprehension of the activity. Ask: *Who looks up definitions of unfamiliar words?* [fact checker] *Who writes the answers?* [recorder] *Who reports the team's answers to the class?* [reporter] *Who keeps the team on time and on task?* [manager]

3. Set a time limit (five minutes) and have students work together to complete the task.

4. Call time and have the reporters from each group take turns calling out the answers. Then elicit where the answer is located in the text. Record students' answers on the board. If groups disagree, ask fact checkers to read the sentences in the text aloud and clarify as needed.

> **Answers**
>
> 1. Answers will vary.
> 2. not looking someone in the eyes, slouching, not using any gestures
> 3. Possible answer: They thought she wasn't interested in the job because she was slouching, which can convey disinterest.
> 4. Possible answer: sit up straight, look interviewer in the eyes

WORD STUDY

 1. Ask students to stay in their teams from 2C. Write the underlined words from the reading on the board. Ask students what meaning they share. [to communicate]

2. Set a time limit (two minutes) and have students work individually to underline other words with similar meanings.

3. Call time. Team members share their words and the recorders list them. Have managers assign each team member one of the words or phrases to look up. The recorders should write the definitions.

4. Have the reporters from each group take turns calling out the definitions to the words they underlined in 2D.

Possible Answers
signal
convey
show
seem
reflect
can be interpreted as
appear
can be perceived as
Definitions will vary.

 1. Discuss the questions with your classmates.

2. Read the questions aloud and elicit discussion.

EXTENSION ACTIVITY
Role Play
1. Pair students to take turns playing an interviewer and a job applicant. They can use either helpful or problematic body language when they play the role of applicant.
2. Partners give feedback on their body language.
3. Call on volunteers to role-play for the class. Elicit examples of good or problematic body language.

3 Build on it

Presentation I
20–25 minutes

 1. Have students look at the visuals in the infographic. Ask: *What body language do you see?* [nodding, eye contact, gestures, waving, crossed legs] *Is this polite body language?* Elicit responses before students read the text.

2. Set a time limit (ten minutes). Have students work individually to complete the task and then compare answers with a partner. Ask volunteers to share their answers with the class.

MULTILEVEL STRATEGIES
To adapt 3A:
• **Mixed-ability** Pair pre-level students with higher- or on-level students to discuss the infographic.

TIP
Copy the categories on the board in a column. Add another column with the heading *U.S.* and a third with the heading *Other countries.* Suggest students take notes in the chart to help them answer the questions.

Possible Answers
1. The U.S. interviewer might think candidates from Finland or Japan are disinterested or dishonest because they don't maintain eye contact. The interviewer might misread an Italian's hand gestures.
2. *Head:* A person from the U.S. might find it difficult to convey agreement when nodding his head in response to a question from a Greek person.
Eyes: A person from the U.S. might be interpreted as aggressive for failing to look away after the beginning of a conversation with someone from Japan.
Arms: People from Northern Europe might find the person from the U.S. to be insincere or overly emotional because of her broad arm gestures.
Hands: While communicating with Latin Americans, the person from the U.S. might appear to be saying "no" when he waves "goodbye."
Legs: A person from the U.S. may unintentionally insult someone from the Middle East by crossing her legs in a way that shows the bottom of her shoes.

 1. Ask students to return to their teams with the same roles. Explain that students will work with their group to discuss the questions. Remind students to use expressions to introduce their ideas.

2. Check comprehension of the activity. Ask: *Who looks up words or checks the text?* [fact checker] *Who takes notes?* [recorder] *Who reports to the class?* [reporter] *Who keeps the team on task and on time?* [manager]

3. Direct students' attention to the Speaking Note.

4. Set a time limit (three minutes) and have students work together to complete the task. Remind students to use the expressions to paraphrase as appropriate in their discussion.

5. Call time and have the reporters from each group take turns calling out their ideas. Then elicit support for each answer.

PROBLEM SOLVING

C 1. Read the directions aloud.

2. Direct students' attention to the emails. Call on students to read them aloud.

3. Set a time limit (three minutes) and have students discuss the questions in their teams.

4. Call time and have each group take turns calling out the problems. Then elicit their ideas for improvement. Record students' answers on the board.

Possible Answers

1. He might have misread her body language or her tone of voice. Maybe she was looking him in the eyes and smiling and he mistook that for interest in his project.
2. It's too informal (Hey Bev), and he didn't proofread "you're," "gonna," "he." The email is not clear.
3. Pay more attention to body language clues, proofread email, use appropriately formal language

---

APPLY YOUR KNOWLEDGE

D 1. Ask students to complete the activity individually as an out-of-class assignment.

2. Pair students to discuss their examples. Remind students to use expressions for paraphrasing if appropriate.

3. Call on students to share their ideas with the class.

EXTENSION ACTIVITY

Apply Your Knowledge

1. Group students who researched different examples of body language.

2. Have them create an infographic like the one on page 56.

3. Call on each group to present their infographics.

Evaluation
10–15 minutes

SELF-ASSESSMENT

1. Read each objective aloud. Have students raise their hands if they still have difficulty.

2. Review the objectives with the class.

Lesson Overview

MULTILEVEL OBJECTIVES

On-level: Use the writing process to summarize an article.
Pre-level: Write sentences to summarize an article
Higher-level: Summarize an article using gerunds

LANGUAGE FOCUS

Grammar: Gerunds, noun clauses for quotations
Vocabulary: For vocabulary support, see this **Oxford Picture Dictionary** topic: English Composition, pages 202–203

STRATEGY FOCUS

Use direct quotations to copy an author's exact words.

PACING

To compress this lesson: Assign 1B–E for homework.

To extend this lesson: Have students create group summaries (see page 115).

And/or have students complete **Multilevel Activities 5 Unit 5, Lesson 5.**

Lesson Notes

CORRELATIONS

CCRS: W/WHST.6-8.2.a. Introduce a topic clearly, previewing what is to follow; organize ideas, concepts, and information, using strategies such as definition, classification, comparison /contrast, and cause/effect; include formatting (e.g., headings), graphics (e.g., charts, tables), and multimedia when useful to aiding comprehension.

W/WHST.6-8.2.b. Develop the topic with relevant facts, definitions, concrete details, quotations, or other information and examples.

W/WHST.6-8.2.c. Use appropriate transitions to create cohesion and clarify the relationships among ideas and concepts.

W/WHST.6-8.2.d. Use precise language and domain-specific vocabulary to inform about or explain the topic.

W/WHST.6-8.2.f. Provide a concluding statement or section that follows from and supports the information or explanation presented.

W/WHST.6-8.4 Produce clear and coherent writing in which the development and organization and style are appropriate to task, purpose, and audience.

W/WHST.6-8.5 With some guidance and support from peers and others, develop and strengthen writing as needed by planning, revising, editing, rewriting, or trying a new approach, focusing on how well purpose and audience have been addressed.

L.6.3/7.3.c. Choose language that expresses ideas precisely and concisely, recognizing and eliminating wordiness and redundancy.

L.8.6 Acquire and use accurately level-appropriate general academic and domain-specific words and phrases; gather vocabulary knowledge when considering a word or phrase important to comprehension or expression.

ELPS: ELP Standard 7

- adapt language choices and style according to purpose, task, and audience with ease in various social and academic contexts
- use a wide variety of complex general academic and content specific words and phrases
- employ both formal and more informal styles and tones effectively in spoken and written texts, as appropriate

ELP Standard 9

- recount a complex and detailed sequence of events or steps in a process, with an effective sequential or chronological order
- introduce and effectively develop an informational topic with facts, details, and evidence
- use complex and varied transitions to link the major sections of speech and text and to clarify relationships among events and ideas
- provide a concluding section or statement

ELP Standard 10

- use complex phrases and clauses
- produce and expand simple, compound, and complex sentences

Warm-up and Review
10–15 minutes (books closed)

Ask: *What is a good way to write a summary of an article?* Elicit the steps students have followed in previous units: rereading, a sentence about the introduction, main ideas and details for body paragraphs, sentence for the conclusion. Copy the chart from page 58 on the board.

Introduction
5 minutes

State the objective: *Today we will use the writing process to summarize an article.*

1 Write a summary

Presentation I
20–25 minutes

 1. Have students revisit the article on pages 54–55. Check comprehension. Ask: *What does the writer do in the introduction?* [describes an interview that goes wrong because of body language] *What is the first kind of body language the writer describes?* [facial expressions] *What examples of facial expressions does the writer give?*

2. Elicit the other types of body language. Record students' answers on the board in the chart.

Guided Practice I
15–20 minutes

 1. Direct students to look at the outline in the book. Point out that the class has completed steps 1–4 in the left column.

2. Check comprehension of the activity. Ask: *What do you need to add to the outline?* [notes for the introduction, examples, and the conclusion]

3. Have students work individually to complete the outline.

Answers	
Introduction: Body language = 50 to 70 percent of communication; influenced by culture + other factors	

Type of body language	Examples
1. Facial expressions	raised eyebrows + smile = friendly, confident looking away = not interested; look too long = aggression bite lips = nervous tighten lips = don't like something face/smile & words don't match = dishonest
2. Posture – position of body	sit/stand straight = paying attention slouching = not interested hunching/crossing arms = not friendly / anxious body exposed = friendly
3. Gestures – hand movements	different in different cultures: thumbs up = OK in U.S. but not in other too many gestures = emotional
4. Personal Space – how close you get to someone	U.S. 4– 12 feet, longer for strangers closer only for good friends

Conclusion:
Most people aren't aware of the impression they make, and understanding nonverbal signals is an important part of communication

C 1. Read the directions aloud.

2. Write the sentence frame on the board.

3. Have students work individually to write their sentences. Encourage students to use the frame provided.

D 1. Check comprehension. Ask: *What does a conclusion often do?* Elicit ideas from Reader's Note on page 55.

2. Have students work individually to write their conclusions.

 1. Read the directions aloud. Check comprehension. Ask: *What should you use to write your summary?*

2. Draw students' attention to the Writer's Note. Tell students to revisit the article and underline phrases they might like to quote.

3. Write possible sentence frames on the board: *The writer says...* or *According to the writer, ...*

4. Have students work individually to write their summaries with one direct quotation.

MULTILEVEL STRATEGIES

• **Pre-level** Pair pre-level students with on-level or higher-level students to complete Activities 1B-1E.

TIP

Have students look at the Writer's Note. Point out that we often use direct quotes when the speaker or writer says something in a unique or powerful way. Suggest students look for these kinds of phrases in the article.

2 Get feedback and revise

Guided Practice II
10–15 minutes

 Direct students to check their writing using the editing checklist. Tell them to read each item in the list and check their papers before moving onto the next item. Explain that students should not edit their writing at this stage. They should just use the checklist to check their work and mark any areas they want to revise.

Communicative Practice
10–15 minutes

 1. Read the directions aloud. Emphasize to students that they are responding to their partners' work, not correcting it.

2. Direct students to exchange papers with a partner and follow the instructions.

 Allow students time to edit and revise their writing using the editing checklist and their partner's feedback. If necessary, students could complete this task as homework.

MULTILEVEL STRATEGIES

To adapt 2B, put students in groups of mixed ability.

• **On-level** Have these students mark any informal language.

• **Pre-level** Ask these students to check quotes for accuracy

• **Higher-level** Instruct these students to mark places where gerunds could be included.

EXTENSION ACTIVITY

Group Summary

1. Put students in groups.

2. Each group member starts the summary, writes one sentence, and passes it to the right.

3. Students add one sentence to the summaries they receive.

4. When summaries are completed, call on volunteers to read them aloud.

Evaluation
10–15 minutes

SELF-ASSESSMENT

1. Call on students to read their completed sentences aloud.

2. Use their responses to focus the next writing assignment.

<table>
<tr><td>

Lesson Overview

MULTILEVEL OBJECTIVES

On-level: Students conduct a survey and present survey results

Pre-level: Students help conduct a survey and present survey results

Higher-level: Students organize, conduct, and present a survey and results

LANGUAGE FOCUS

Grammar: Simple present

Vocabulary: Formal language

For vocabulary support, see this **Oxford Picture Dictionary** topic: Internet Research, pages 212–213

STRATEGY FOCUS

Search with formal language, and survey a wide range of people.

READINESS CONNECTION

In this lesson, students divide work among peers and develop survey questions.

PACING

To compress this lesson: Assign 1B for homework and/or provide students with topics to expedite 1A.

To extend this lesson: Have students create graphs of class survey results (see page 119).

And/or have students complete **Multilevel Activities 5 Unit 5, Lesson 6.**

</td><td>

Lesson Notes

</td></tr>
</table>

CORRELATIONS

CCRS: W.7.7 Conduct short research projects to answer a question, drawing on several sources and generating additional related, focused questions for further research and investigation.

W.7.8 Gather relevant information from multiple print and digital sources, using search terms effectively; assess the credibility and accuracy of each source; and quote or paraphrase the data and conclusions of others while avoiding plagiarism and following a standard format for citation.

SL.8.4 Present claims and findings, emphasizing salient points in a focused, coherent manner with relevant evidence, sound valid reasoning, and well-chosen details; use appropriate eye contact, adequate volume, and clear pronunciation.

SL.8.5 Integrate multimedia and visual displays into presentations to clarify information, strengthen claims and evidence, and add interest.

SL.8.6 Adapt speech to a variety of contexts and tasks, demonstrating command of formal English when indicated or appropriate.

L.6.3/7.3.b. Maintain consistency in style and tone.

L.6.3/7.3.c. Choose language that expresses ideas precisely and concisely, recognizing and eliminating wordiness and redundancy.

L.8.6 Acquire and use accurately level-appropriate general academic and domain-specific words and phrases; gather vocabulary knowledge when considering a word or phrase important to comprehension or expression.

ELPS: ELP Standard 2

- participate in conversations, extended discussions, and written exchanges about a range of substantive topics, texts, and issues
- build on the ideas of others
- express his or her own ideas clearly and persuasively
- summarize the key points and evidence discussed

ELP Standard 3

- deliver oral presentations
- compose written informational texts
- fully develop the topic with relevant details, concepts, examples, and information
- integrate graphics or multimedia when useful about a variety of texts, topics, or events

ELP Standard 5

- carry out both short and more sustained research projects to answer a question or solve a problem
- gather information from multiple print and digital sources
- use advanced search terms effectively
- synthesize information from multiple print and digital sources
- analyze and integrate information into clearly organized spoken and written texts
- include illustrations, diagrams, or other graphics as appropriate

ELP Standard 7

- adapt language choices and style according to purpose, task, and audience with ease in various social and academic contexts
- use a wide variety of complex general academic and content specific words and phrases
- employ both formal and more informal styles and tones effectively in spoken and written texts, as appropriate

Warm-up and Review
10–15 minutes (books closed)

Write *Communication problems* in a circle in the middle of the board. Elicit categories of problems (for example, body language, mode, language formality) and add them in circles around the center circle. Then elicit examples and add them outside the categories.

Introduction
5 minutes

1. Point out that communication problems can come from a variety of sources.

2. State the objective: *Today we will conduct a survey and present survey results.*

1 Create a survey about communication problems

Communicative Practice
40–45 minutes

A 1. Group students but do not assign roles yet. Explain that students will work with their team to identify survey topics.

2. Go over the bulleted suggestions. Elicit examples of each.

3. Direct students' attention to the Research Tip. Read it aloud.

4. Set a time limit (ten minutes) and have students work in teams to search for more topics.

B 1. Read the directions and example questions aloud. Ask: *What do you need to include?* [a *yes/ no* question and follow-up]

2. Point out that the questions are quite specific. Instead of *Have you ever accidentally offended someone?* the example question adds *in an email or a text.* Suggest students add one such limiting factor to each question.

> **MULTILEVEL STRATEGIES**
>
> To adapt 1B for pre-level students:
>
> - **Mixed-ability** Pair students of different abilities to generate questions together.

C

1. Draw students' attention to the Research Tip. Ask: *Why do you think it's important to talk to a wide range of people?*

2. Check comprehension of the task. Ask: *What should you think about when you evaluate your questions?* [level of interest, how common the experience might be, if it will provide clear and informative answers]

3. Have students work in teams to choose questions for the survey and give it a title.

D

1. Check comprehension of the task. Ask: *How many people do you need to survey?* [four or five] *Who can you ask?* [classmates, colleagues, community members, family members] *What do you need to make sure to do?* [talk to a wide range of people]

2. Tell students to conduct their surveys outside class.

E

1. Check comprehension of the task. Ask: *What are you going to do to analyze the results?* [share results with the team, discuss similar or different experiences, draw conclusions]

2. Have students report on their results in their teams.

3. Assign roles: manager, editor, recorder, and IT specialist. Explain that students will work with their team to discuss the results of their surveys and write a summary of the team's conclusions.

4. Check comprehension of the activity. Ask: *Who leads the discussion and restates important points in the conclusion?* [manager] *Who checks spelling and grammar?* [editor] *Who compiles the results in one document?* [recorder] *Who converts numbers to percentages?* [IT specialist]

5. Set a time limit (ten minutes) and have students work together to answer the questions.

2 Present your results

Presentation
40–45 minutes

1. Have students stay in their teams from 1E. Check comprehension of the task. Ask: *What does the outline include?* [introduction, body, and conclusion] *What should you do in the introduction?* [tell the audience what area the team focused on] *Where do you summarize the results?* [in the body] *What do you do in the conclusion?* [describe your conclusions]

2. Draw students' attention to the Presentation Strategy. Read it aloud.

3. Set a time limit (five to ten minutes) and have students work as a team to outline their oral report and choose a graph or chart.

 1. Have students assign roles for the presentation: manager, researcher, writer, and IT specialist. Explain that students will work with their team to give a presentation on their topic.

2. Check comprehension of the activity. Ask: *Who will look up additional information?* [researcher] *Who will create text for the note cards or slides?* [writer] *Who will generate the graphs?* [IT specialist] *Who will keep the team on task and on time and ensure overall quality?* [manager]

3. Set a time limit (five minutes) and have students work as a team to divide the roles and the sections of the presentation (for example, introduction, body description of survey, body summary of results, and conclusion).

MULTILEVEL STRATEGIES

To adapt 2B:

• **On-level** Assign these students the roles of IT specialist and writer.

• **Pre-level** Assign these students the role of researcher.

• **Higher-level** Assign these students the role of manager.

C 1. Read the bulleted items aloud. Tell students how long the reports should be (five minutes).

2. Check comprehension of the activity. Ask: *What might be a good way to begin your report?* [with a surprising result] *How can you make clear transitions between speakers? What will help you project confidence?*

3. Set a time limit (ten minutes) and have students rehearse their presentations.

D 1. Draw a chart on the board, listing the teams in the first column. In the other columns, list the note-taking prompts or shortened forms of them: *Strategy, Transitions, Strengths, Advice.* Check comprehension of the activity. Ask: *What should you evaluate the presentations on?*

2. Set a time limit (five minutes) for each presentation, and ask each team to present in turn.

E 1. Discuss other teams' presentations in each group. Ask each team to nominate a reporter to give feedback on the other teams' presentations.

2. Beginning with the first team to present, collect feedback from the reporters. Write feedback in the table you drew on the board in 2D.

EXTENSION ACTIVITY

Class Results

1. Make a list of questions and results on the board. Compile similar questions.

2. Tell students to create graphs of the results of four questions.

3. Pair students to share their graphs.

Evaluation
10–15 minutes

SELF-ASSESSMENT

1. Pair students to share their self-assessments.

2. Elicit suggestions from the class for developing more confidence in each of the three assessment areas.

6 Collaboration

Unit Overview

This unit explores styles of collaboration, teamwork in the workplace, and famous partnerships with a range of employability skills and contextualizes adjectives for collaborative and independent work and parallel structure to make writing clearer. By the end of this unit, you will be able to conduct and present research related to teamwork.

KEY OBJECTIVES

Lesson 1	Identify and discuss different styles of collaboration
Lesson 2	Identify aspects of teamwork and explain its value in the workplace
Lesson 3	Categorize adjectives for collaborative or independent work; recognize and use parallel structure to make writing clearer
Lesson 4	Read about famous partnerships and discuss difficulties partnerships sometimes face
Lesson 5	Use the writing process to summarize an article
Lesson 6	Conduct and present research related to teamwork

UNIT FEATURES

Academic Vocabulary	*assemble, autonomous, cohesive, communal, complement, cooperative, isolated, supportive, synergy, unified*
Employability Skills	• Evaluate collaboration styles • Analyze factors that lead to success or failure in partnerships • Predict potential problems and offer suggestions for starting a business partnership • Research a successful partnership • Collaborate to organize and deliver a presentation

Resources	**Class Audio** CD2, Tracks 02-05
	Teacher Resource Center
	    Multilevel Activities 5 Unit 6
	    Multilevel Grammar Activities 5 Unit 6
	    Unit 6 Test
	Oxford Picture Dictionary Studying, A Hospital, Jobs and Occupations, Soft Skills, English Composition, Internet Research

Lesson Overview

MULTILEVEL OBJECTIVES

On-level and pre-level: Identify and discuss different styles of collaboration

Higher-level: Identify, discuss and analyze different styles of collaboration

LANGUAGE FOCUS

Grammar: Parallel structure

Vocabulary: Words and phrases related to collaboration

For vocabulary support, see these **Oxford Picture Dictionary** topics: Studying, pages 8–9; Soft Skills, page 178

READINESS CONNECTION

In this lesson, students work together to discuss collaboration styles.

PACING

To compress this lesson: Do 1D as a class.

To extend this lesson: Have students create a chart to summarize class data (see page 123).

And/or have students complete **Multilevel Activities 5 Unit 6, Lesson 1**.

Lesson Notes

CORRELATIONS

CCRS: RI.6.7 Integrate information presented in different media or formats (e.g., in charts, graphs, photographs, videos, or maps) as well as in words to develop a coherent understanding of a topic or issue.

SL.8.1.a. Come to discussions prepared, having read or researched material under study; explicitly draw on that preparation by referring to evidence on the topic, text, or issue to probe and reflect on ideas under discussion.

SL.8.1.c. Pose questions that connect the ideas of several speakers and respond to others' questions and comments with relevant evidence, observations, and ideas.

SL.8.1.d. Acknowledge new information expressed by others, and, when warranted, qualify or justify their own views in light of the evidence presented.

L.6.4.c. Consult reference materials (e.g., dictionaries, glossaries, thesauruses), both print and digital, to find the pronunciation of a word or determine or clarify its precise meaning or its part of speech.

SL.8.4 Present claims and findings, emphasizing salient points in a focused, coherent manner with relevant evidence, sound valid reasoning, and well-chosen details; use appropriate eye contact, adequate volume, and clear pronunciation.

L.6.4.c. Consult reference materials (e.g., dictionaries, glossaries, thesauruses), both print and digital, to find the pronunciation of a word or determine or clarify its precise meaning or its part of speech.

L.8.6 Acquire and use accurately level-appropriate general academic and domain-specific words and phrases; gather vocabulary knowledge when considering a word or phrase important to comprehension or expression.

ELPS: ELP Standard 2

- participate in conversations, extended discussions, and written exchanges about a range of substantive topics, texts, and issues
- build on the ideas of others
- express his or her own ideas clearly and persuasively
- refer to specific and relevant evidence from texts or research to support his or her ideas
- ask and answer questions that probe reasoning and claim

ELP Standard 8

using context, questioning, and consistent knowledge of English morphology,

- determine the meaning of general academic and content-specific words and phrases, figurative and connotative language, and idiomatic expressions in spoken and written texts about a variety of topics, experiences, or events

Warm-up and Review
10–15 minutes (books closed)

Divide the class into two teams. Write words and phrases from the unit or related to collaboration on slips of paper (for example, *surgery, the Beatles, mechanic, the Wright Brothers*). Call a member of each team to the board to draw or act out the idea while the rest of their team guesses. Each correct guess earns the team a point.

Introduction
5 minutes

1. Say: *To succeed in many things, like winning a game, you need good teamwork.*

2. State the objective: *Today we're going to identify and discuss different styles of collaboration.*

1 Discuss collaboration styles

Presentation I
20–25 minutes

 1. Read the directions aloud. Put students in teams to brainstorm. Assign roles: manager, fact checker, recorder, and reporter.

2. Elicit categories from the class (for example, sports teams, group projects, family activities, work groups). Call on reporters to share their team's answers and write them on the board under the correct category.

B 1. Direct students to look at the definition. Ask: *How is collaboration different from teamwork?* [It includes creation or production.]

2. Write *collaboration* on the board, and elicit related words and phrases from the whole class. Write their ideas. Point out the connection between their ideas and their responses in 1A.

> **Possible Answers**
>
> synonyms: *partnership, alliance, cooperation*
> forms: *collaborate, collaborative*

> **MULTILEVEL STRATEGIES**
>
> To adapt 1B:
> • **Pre-level** Encourage students to use reference tools and/or work together.

C  1. Direct students to look at the pie chart. Ask: *What does the chart show?* [collaboration types] *How many are there?* [five] Call on students to read the description of each type aloud.

2. Point out any connections between the descriptions and students' ideas in 1A.

Guided Practice
10–20 minutes

D 1. Direct students to look at the first question. Check comprehension of the collocation. Ask: *What is a* collaboration style*?* [the way you work with other people]

2. Set a time limit (five minutes). Direct students to work with their partners to complete the activity. Have a volunteer from each pair give their responses. Check answers as a class.

> **Possible Answers**
>
> 1. Possibly two or three: Jorge seems to be taking care of the team and gathering resources to share. Tim and Ana may represent those who are always prepared, those who keep detailed notes, or those who understand every detail and help streamline the process.
> 2. She's sitting away from the others. He could be wrong. The team might have assigned her to research something independently and report back.
> 3. Tim and Ana appear like to collaborate closely. Pam may not. It is unclear what style Jorge prefers.
> 4. They could have problems if they didn't understand differences in working style. However, they might work well together if one understands every detail and helps streamline the process while the other keeps detailed notes and records.
> 5. The highest percentage is for the person who is always prepared. The other divisions are much closer. Answers will vary for conclusions.

Presentation II
20–25 minutes

 1. Group students and assign roles: manager, fact checker, recorder, and reporter. Explain that students will work with their team to analyze the information. Verify students' understanding of the roles: the manager keeps the team on task and on time and asks the survey questions, the recorder takes notes, the fact checker checks numbers and definitions, the reporter reports to the class.

2. Check comprehension of the task. Ask: *What do you need to write down for each of the five styles in the chart?* [strengths and weaknesses]

3. Set a time limit (five minutes) for groups to complete the task.

4. Call time and have the reporters from each team take turns calling out their answers.

Answers
Answers will vary.

MULTILEVEL STRATEGIES

To adapt 1E:

- **On-level** Assign these students the roles of fact checker and reporter.

- **Pre-level** Assign these students the role of recorder.

- **Higher-level** Assign these students the role of manager.

EXTENSION ACTIVITY

Class Results

1. Create a chart with headings for the color of each slice of the pie chart.

2. Ask: *Which is your style?* Read each description and ask for a show of hands. Tally the results on the board.

3. Direct students to make a bar graph or pie chart of the results.

Evaluation
10–15 minutes

SELF-ASSESSMENT

1. Ask students to spend some time reflecting on what they have learned. Set a time limit (three minutes).

2. Ask for volunteers to share their thoughts.

3. Make a list of their questions to refer to at the end of the unit.

Lesson Overview

MULTILEVEL OBJECTIVES

On-level and Higher-level: Identify aspects of teamwork and explain its value in the workplace

Pre-level: Identify aspects of teamwork and understand its value in the workplace

LANGUAGE FOCUS

Grammar: Complex sentences

Vocabulary: *assemble, synergy*

For vocabulary support, see these **Oxford Picture Dictionary** topics: A Hospital, pages 122–123; Soft Skills, page 178

STRATEGY FOCUS

Listen for expressions that signal a definition.

READINESS CONNECTION

In this lesson, students compare and discuss definitions of teamwork.

PACING

To compress this lesson: Assign 1C and 1D for homework.

To extend this lesson: Have students work in groups to summarize an article (see page 126); Have students create lists of pros and cons (see page 127).

And/or have students complete **Multilevel Activities 5 Unit 6, Lesson 2**.

Lesson Notes

CORRELATIONS

CCRS: RI/RL.7.1 Cite several pieces of textual evidence to support analysis of what the text says explicitly as well as inferences drawn from the text.

RI.8.3 Analyze how a text makes connections among and distinctions between individuals, ideas, or events (e.g., through comparisons, analogies, or categories).

RI/RL.6.4 Determine the meaning of words and phrases as they are used in a text, including figurative, connotative, and technical meanings; analyze the impact of a specific word choice on meaning and tone.

RI.6.5 Analyze how a particular sentence, paragraph, chapter, or section fits into the overall structure of a text and contributes to the development of the ideas.

SL.8.1.a. Come to discussions prepared, having read or researched material under study; explicitly draw on that preparation by referring to evidence on the topic, text, or issue to probe and reflect on ideas under discussion.

SL.8.1.c. Pose questions that connect the ideas of several speakers and respond to others' questions and comments with relevant evidence, observations, and ideas.

SL.8.1.d. Acknowledge new information expressed by others, and, when warranted, qualify or justify their own views in light of the evidence presented.

SL.8.2 Analyze the purpose of information presented in diverse media and formats (e.g., visually, quantitatively, orally) and evaluate the motives (e.g., social, commercial, political) behind its presentation.

SL.8.3 Delineate a speaker's argument and specific claims, evaluating the soundness of the reasoning and relevance and sufficiency of the evidence and identifying when irrelevant evidence is introduced.

L.6.3/7.3.c. Choose language that expresses ideas precisely and concisely, recognizing and eliminating wordiness and redundancy.

L.8.6 Acquire and use accurately level-appropriate general academic and domain-specific words and phrases; gather vocabulary knowledge when considering a word or phrase important to comprehension or expression.

ELPS: ELP Standard 1

use a wide range of strategies to:

- determine central ideas or themes in oral presentations and spoken and written texts
- cite specific details and evidence from texts to support the analysis

ELP Standard 2

- participate in conversations, extended discussions, and written exchanges about a range of substantive topics, texts, and issues
- build on the ideas of others
- express his or her own ideas clearly and persuasively
- refer to specific and relevant evidence from texts or research to support his or her ideas
- ask and answer questions that probe reasoning and claim
- summarize the key points and evidence discussed

ELP Standard 8

using context, questioning, and consistent knowledge of English morphology,

- determine the meaning of general academic and content-specific words and phrases, figurative and connotative language, and idiomatic expressions in spoken and written texts about a variety of topics, experiences, or events

ELP Standard 10

- produce and expand simple, compound, and complex sentences

Warm-up and Review
10–15 minutes (books closed)

Write *Emergency situation* on the board. Brainstorm different kinds of emergencies and list them on the board. Ask: *Who deals with these situations? How can teamwork help the situation?* Elicit responses from the class.

Introduction
5 minutes

1. Say: *In many situations, a team of people working together can achieve success.*

2. State the objective: *Today we will identify aspects of teamwork and explain its value in the workplace.*

1 Read about teamwork in an emergency room

Presentation I
10–15 minutes

A 1. Put students in teams. Assign roles: manager, fact checker, recorder, and reporter.

2. Read the directions aloud.

3. Assign a time limit (three minutes). Call on reporters to share their ideas. Write the people on the board.

Guided Practice I
15–20 minutes

B 1. Read the directions aloud. Check comprehension. Ask: *What are you going to do?* [skim the text] *What do you do when you skim?* [read quickly to find the general gist or main idea] *Where should you look for the outcome?* [probably the end]

2. Set a time limit (three minutes). Direct students to underline the information that answers the question when they find it.

3. Elicit the answer.

Answer
positive

TIP

Direct students' attention to the article and photo. Ask: *What is the title?* [*Teamwork Saves Lives in the ER*] *What do the letters* ER *stand for?* [emergency room] *What do you see in the photo?* [an emergency room, doctors and nurses] *Have you been to an emergency room?*

C 1. Read the directions aloud. Check comprehension. Ask: *What does* essential *mean?* [necessary, critical]

2. Set a time limit (five minutes). Direct students to answer the question.

3. Elicit ideas from the whole class.

Possible Answer
Several different specialists and areas of expertise were necessary because of the complexity of the situation. The specialists needed to collaborate and work together to achieve the best outcome for the patients.

MULTILEVEL STRATEGIES

To adapt 1C:

- **Pre-level** Direct students to read the glossed words before they read and explain any unfamiliar words in the definitions.

Communicative Practice
10–20 minutes

D 1. Read the questions aloud.

2. Ask students to think about and mark their answers in the text.

3. Set a time limit (five minutes) for students to discuss their answers with a partner.

4. Invite pairs to share their responses. Check answers as a class.

Answers
1. Linda offered to stay late because of the emergency. 2. Even after the car accident, it seemed like the pregnancy was OK, but then the ultrasound showed problems. This changed how the staff needed to handle the situation. 3. *Tragic* refers to a negative, sad, or bad outcome. Linda feels that teamwork was very important in helping this situation end positively rather than negatively.

Presentation II
20–25 minutes

 **E** 1. Read the directions and question aloud.

2. Call on students to share their ideas.

EXTENSION ACTIVITY
Summarizing Practice
1. Tell students to write a summary of the article using their own words. Pre-level students can write a group summary.
2. Ask two or three volunteers to write their summaries on the board. Correct or revise with the class as needed.

2 Listen and take notes

Guided Practice II
20–25 minutes

 **A** 1. Say: *Now we're going to listen to a lecture about why self-esteem matters in the workplace.*

2. Read the directions aloud.

3. Direct students' attention to the chart. Ask: *What does the lecturer give at the beginning?* [a definition of teamwork] *How many reasons teamwork matters will the speaker give?* [five] *How many things does teamwork improve?* [four]

Possible Answers
the definition of teamwork, reasons teamwork matters, specific examples of why teamwork matters

B 🔊 **2.02** 1. Play the beginning of the audio. Direct students to listen without writing.

2. Replay the audio. Ask students to complete the definition.

3. Elicit the answer.

Answer
achieve a common goal

C 🔊 **2.03** 1. Copy the chart on the board.

2. Play the whole audio. Direct students to write notes in the chart as they listen.

Answers	
Employability Skills Lecture Series: Teamwork	
Definition of teamwork: The ability and willingness of a group of people to work together, using their individual skills to <u>achieve a common goal</u>.	
Reasons teamwork matters	Specifics
1. Improves <u>efficiency</u> and <u>productivity</u>. Also improves <u>performance</u> and <u>job satisfaction</u>	tasks—on time ↓ pressure individuals ↓ pressure/stress for team
2. <u>More unified, cohesive</u>	work harder cooperate support each other
3. <u>Support network</u>	discuss concerns, share ideas If no = bad atmosphere
4. Opportunities for <u>brainstorming</u>, <u>collaborating</u>, and <u>sharing ideas</u>	Multiple <u>thoughts</u>, <u>perspectives</u>, and <u>ideas</u> = <u>better results</u>
5. <u>Synergy, group working together</u>	Shared goals + respect + support = <u>increased sense accomplishment for all</u>

MULTILEVEL STRATEGIES
• **On-level** Have students complete the activity as described.
• **Pre-level** Allow students to read the script as they listen.
• **Higher-level** Tell students to take notes on additional examples or explanations.

Communicative Practice
10–20 minutes

 **2.03** 1. Set a time limit (five minutes) for students to discuss their answers with a partner.

2. Replay the audio. Ask students to confirm or add to their notes.

3. Ask volunteers to complete the chart on the board.

Presentation II
20–25 minutes

 **2.04** 1. Read the directions aloud.

2. Direct students' attention to the Listening Note. Elicit the phrases that introduce definitions.

3. Set a time limit (three minutes). Pair students to complete the task.

4. Elicit definitions from the class.

Answers
1. Getting multiple thoughts, perspectives, and ideas—rather than just one person's—is likely to produce better results, no matter what kind of job you're doing. 2. the idea that the whole is more than its parts

 1. Read the directions aloud.

2. Remind students to use the noun clause structure.

3. Write the sentence frames on the board. Elicit completions from the class.

 1. Read the directions aloud.

2. Have students rejoin their teams from 1A with the same roles.

3. Set a time limit (ten minutes) for teams to complete the task.

4. Call on reporters to share their team's experiences with the class.

EXTENSION ACTIVITY
Pros and Cons
1. Point out that students work in teams in class all the time.
2. Have students stay in their teams from 1G to make a list of advantages and possible disadvantages of working in a team.
3. Call on teams to share their ideas. For each possible disadvantage (for example, some students are always in certain roles, or some people don't do the work on time), elicit suggestions to address the problem.
4. Write the ideas on the board so students can copy them. Encourage teams to use these suggestions when they run into difficulty on their teams.

Evaluation
10–15 minutes

SELF-ASSESSMENT

1. Read each item. Ask students to raise their hands if they have difficulty.

2. Pair students who have difficulty with those who do not to review ways to achieve each objective.

Lesson Overview

MULTILEVEL OBJECTIVES

On-level: Categorize adjectives for collaboration or independent work; recognize and use parallel structure to make writing clearer

Pre-level: Learn adjectives for collaboration or independent work; recognize the use of parallel structure to make writing clearer

Higher-level: Categorize adjectives for collaboration or independent work; recognize, use and correct parallel structure to make writing clearer

LANGUAGE FOCUS

Grammar: Parallel structure

Vocabulary: *analytical, autonomous, cohesive, collaborative, cooperative, creative, independent, isolated, productive, self-reliant, supportive, unified*

For vocabulary support, see these **Oxford Picture Dictionary** topics: Studying, pages 8–9; Soft Skills, page 178

STRATEGY FOCUS

Categorize adjectives related to collaboration and individualism.

READINESS CONNECTION

In this lesson, students work with a partner to prepare a quiz about parallel structure.

PACING

To compress this lesson: Assign 1B and/or 2C for homework.

To extend this lesson: Have students write a paragraph to answer comprehension questions (see page 130); Have students use a word web to create a description (see page 131).

And/or have students complete **Multilevel Activities 5 Unit 6, Lesson 3**.

Lesson Notes

CORRELATIONS

CCRS: SL.8.1.a. Come to discussions prepared, having read or researched material under study; explicitly draw on that preparation by referring to evidence on the topic, text, or issue to probe and reflect on ideas under discussion.

SL.8.1.c. Pose questions that connect the ideas of several speakers and respond to others' questions and comments with relevant evidence, observations, and ideas.

SL.8.1.d. Acknowledge new information expressed by others, and, when warranted, qualify or justify their own views in light of the evidence presented.

L.6.4.c. Consult reference materials (e.g., dictionaries, glossaries, thesauruses), both print and digital, to find the pronunciation of a word or determine or clarify its precise meaning or its part of speech.

L.8.6 Acquire and use accurately level-appropriate general academic and domain-specific words and phrases; gather vocabulary knowledge when considering a word or phrase important to comprehension or expression.

ELPS: ELP Standard 2

- participate in conversations, extended discussions, and written exchanges about a range of substantive topics, texts, and issues
- build on the ideas of others
- express his or her own ideas clearly and persuasively

<table>
<tr><td>

ELP Standard 8

using context, questioning, and consistent knowledge of English morphology,

- determine the meaning of general academic and content-specific words and phrases, figurative and connotative language, and idiomatic expressions in spoken and written texts about a variety of topics, experiences, or events

</td><td>

ELP Standard 10

- produce and expand simple, compound, and complex sentences

</td></tr>
</table>

Warm-up and Review
10–15 minutes (books closed)

Write a word web on the board with *Emergency room staff* in the middle and several outer circles: *Activities, Traits,* and *Jobs.* Put students in groups to brainstorm as many examples of each outer circle category as they can. Point out that the activities must be expressed as gerunds, the traits as adjectives, and the jobs as nouns. Set a time limit (three minutes). Call on students to share their total number of examples of each. Then elicit the examples and write them in the word web. Save the examples to use in the Extension Activity at the end of the lesson.

Introduction
5 minutes

1. Say: *In school, or at work, people work collaboratively, or independently. Both have positives and negatives.*

2. State the objective: *Today we are going to categorize adjectives for collaborative or independent work and recognize and use parallel structure to make writing clearer.*

1 Vocabulary: Adjectives for ways to work

Presentation and Guided Practice I
20–25 minutes

A 1. Copy the Venn diagram on the board. Ask: *What is collaboration?* [working together] *What is individualism?* [working alone]

2. Read the directions aloud. Say each word and have students repeat.

3. Set a time limit (three minutes). Direct students to work individually to complete the diagram and then compare answers with a partner.

4. Call on students to add words to the diagram on the board.

<table>
<tr><td>

Possible Answers

Working together: *cohesive, collaborative, cooperative, supportive, unified*
Working alone: *autonomous, independent, isolated, self-reliant*
Overlapping: *analytical, creative, productive*

</td></tr>
</table>

MULTILEVEL STRATEGIES

To adapt 1A:

- **Pre-level** Pair students to complete the task. Encourage them to each look up half the words in a dictionary.

TIP

Use this list of adjectives as an opportunity to review common suffixes for adjectives. Tell students to underline the suffixes and then elicit the adjectives in groups according to their endings (*-ical, -ive, -ent/-ant, -ous, -ed*).

Communicative Practice
15–20 minutes

B 1. Read the directions aloud.

2. Call on a student to read item 1. Elicit other possible completions. [*cooperative, supportive, cohesive, unified*]

3. Set a time limit (three minutes). Direct students to work individually to complete the sentences.

4. Call on students to read their completed sentences aloud.

MULTILEVEL STRATEGIES

To adapt 1B:

- **Pre-level** Pair students to complete the sentences.

- **Higher-level** Have students identify all the words that could correctly complete the sentence.

 **C** 1. Read the directions aloud.

2. Put students in teams. Assign roles: manager, fact checker, recorder, and reporter.

3. Set a time limit (five minutes) for students to complete the activity in teams.

4. Call on reporters to tell the class about their answers and ask them to explain their choices.

D 1. Read the directions aloud.

2. Ask each question and elicit responses from the class.

EXTENSION ACTIVITY

Writing Practice

1. Tell students to choose one of the questions to answer in paragraph form.

2. Have students post their paragraphs on a discussion board.

2 Grammar: Parallel structure

Presentation and Guided Practice II
20–25 minutes

A 1. Call on students to read the examples aloud. Check comprehension. Ask: *What phrases are underlined in item 1? What structure do they share?* Repeat with each example. Write the structures on the board: *1. Being + adjective + infinitive + adverb; 2. That + it needs to be + -ed/passive; 3. Gerund; 4. Be + adjective.*

2. Have students complete the paragraph about parallel structure in the Language Connection box. Go over the answers with the class.

Answers
use
and, but

MULTILEVEL STRATEGIES

To adapt 2A:

- **On-level** Have students work independently.
- **Pre-level** Have higher-level classmates assist these students
- **Higher-level** Have these students work with pre-level classmates.

TIP

To help students see parallel structure, elicit at least one more example of each structure in 2A (for example, *being able to work independently, being able to cooperate*).

Guided Practice III
20–25 minutes

 **B** 1. Read the directions aloud.

2. Ask students to work individually to complete the task and then compare answers with a partner.

3. Ask volunteers to read sentences aloud.

Answers
1. Good teamwork improves productivity and <u>efficiency</u>.
2. When you work together, you can brainstorm, collaborate and <u>share</u> information.
3. It's fine to be independent and to be self-reliant, but it's not good <u>to be isolated</u>.
4. Workers who are supportive and <u>cooperative</u> usually make good team members.
5. Already parallel.
6. When people work on shared goals and they <u>do</u> it with respect, the team will be more cohesive.

TIP

Write the first sentence on the board. Elicit the structure of the sentence and write it above the words: *subject A + verb + noun + and + subject B + be + adjective.* Tell students to focus on the structures on each side of *and*. Circle *productivity* and *efficient*. Ask: *Are these the same parts of speech?* [no] *How can we make them the same?* [change *efficient* to *efficiency*]. Make the change on the board and cross out *people are.*

To adapt 2A:

• **On-level** Have students work independently.

• **Pre-level** Group pre-level students to complete the task together.

• **Higher-level** Direct students to add another parallel element to each sentence.

C 1. Read the directions aloud.

2. Write a sentence using parallel structure on the board. Then cross out parallel elements and replace them with phrases that are not parallel but express the same idea.

3. Ask students to work in pairs to complete the task. Set a time limit (five minutes).

4. Direct each pair to join another pair to exchange and correct sentences. Set a time limit (five minutes).

5. Have each pair check the other pair's work.

6. Call on students to write their sentences on the board. Correct as necessary.

Answers

Answers will vary.

MULTILEVEL STRATEGIES

To adapt 2C:

• **Pre-level** Work with this group to create the sentences in the quiz.

TIP

If students have difficulty, suggest that they follow the models of incorrect sentences in 2B.

EXTENSION ACTIVITY

Describe an Emergency Room

1. Show students the word web they created in the warm-up activity. Point out that the examples in each category are the same part of speech.

2. Direct students to write a description of an emergency room using examples from the word web and parallel structure.

3. Ask volunteers to write sentences from their descriptions on the board. Correct with the class as necessary.

Evaluation

10–15 minutes

SELF-ASSESSMENT

1. Have students complete the self-assessment.

2. Provide additional practice as needed.

Lesson Overview

MULTILEVEL OBJECTIVES

On-level and Pre-level: Read about famous partnerships and discuss difficulties partnerships sometimes face

Higher-level: Read about famous partnerships and analyze difficulties partnerships sometimes face

LANGUAGE FOCUS

Grammar: Parallel structure

Vocabulary: *complement*, collocations with *diametrically*, *tremendously*, *meteoric*, and *devoted*

For vocabulary support, see this **Oxford Picture Dictionary** topic: Jobs and Occupations, pages 170–173

STRATEGY FOCUS

Use expressions to suggest and respond.

READINESS CONNECTION

In this lesson, students discuss difficulties in business partnerships.

PACING

To compress this lesson: Assign 2B and/or 2C for homework.

To extend this lesson: Have students role-play a conversation including expressions from the lesson (see page 134); Have students role-play a discussion (see page 136).

And/or have students complete **Multilevel Activities 5 Unit 6, Lesson 4**.

Lesson Notes

CORRELATIONS

CCRS: RI/RL.7.1 Cite several pieces of textual evidence to support analysis of what the text says explicitly as well as inferences drawn from the text.

RI.8.3 Analyze how a text makes connections among and distinctions between individuals, ideas, or events (e.g., through comparisons, analogies, or categories).

RI/RL.6.4 Determine the meaning of words and phrases as they are used in a text, including figurative, connotative, and technical meanings; analyze the impact of a specific word choice on meaning and tone.

RI.6.7 Integrate information presented in different media or formats (e.g., in charts, graphs, photographs, videos, or maps) as well as in words to develop a coherent understanding of a topic or issue.

SL.8.1.a. Come to discussions prepared, having read or researched material under study; explicitly draw on that preparation by referring to evidence on the topic, text, or issue to probe and reflect on ideas under discussion.

SL.8.1.c. Pose questions that connect the ideas of several speakers and respond to others' questions and comments with relevant evidence, observations, and ideas.

SL.8.1.d. Acknowledge new information expressed by others, and, when warranted, qualify or justify their own views in light of the evidence presented.

SL.8.2 Analyze the purpose of information presented in diverse media and formats (e.g., visually, quantitatively, orally) and evaluate the motives (e.g., social, commercial, political) behind its presentation.

SL.8.4 Present claims and findings, emphasizing salient points in a focused, coherent manner with relevant evidence, sound valid reasoning, and well-chosen details; use appropriate eye contact, adequate volume, and clear pronunciation.

L.6.4.a. Use context (e.g., the overall meaning of a sentence or paragraph; a word's position or function in a sentence) as a clue to the meaning of a word or phrase.

L.6.4.d. Verify the preliminary determination of the meaning of a word or phrase (e.g., by checking the inferred meaning in context or in a dictionary).

L.8.6 Acquire and use accurately level-appropriate general academic and domain-specific words and phrases; gather vocabulary knowledge when considering a word or phrase important to comprehension or expression.

ELPS: ELP Standard 1	**ELP Standard 7**

<table>
<tr><td>

ELPS: ELP Standard 1

use a wide range of strategies to:

- determine central ideas or themes in oral presentations and spoken and written texts
- cite specific details and evidence from texts to support the analysis
- summarize a text

ELP Standard 2

- participate in conversations, extended discussions, and written exchanges about a range of substantive topics, texts, and issues
- build on the ideas of others
- express his or her own ideas clearly and persuasively
- refer to specific and relevant evidence from texts or research to support his or her ideas
- ask and answer questions that probe reasoning and claims
- summarize the key points and evidence discussed

</td><td>

ELP Standard 7

- adapt language choices and style according to purpose, task, and audience with ease in various social and academic contexts
- use a wide variety of complex general academic and content specific words and phrases
- employ both formal and more informal styles and tones effectively in spoken and written texts, as appropriate

ELP Standard 8

using context, questioning, and consistent knowledge of English morphology,

- determine the meaning of general academic and content-specific words and phrases, figurative and connotative language, and idiomatic expressions in spoken and written texts about a variety of topics, experiences, or events

</td></tr>
</table>

Warm-up and Review
10–15 minutes (books closed)

Draw a word web on the board and write *partners* in the middle. Model the activity by telling the class about different partners you have (for example, a spouse or a running partner). Direct students to create mind maps of their partners. Encourage them to think broadly about different aspects of their lives: work, family, sports, entertainment, etc. When students finish, have them compare word webs in pairs. Call on students to tell the class about their partners' other partners.

Introduction
5 minutes

State the objective: *Today we will read about famous partnerships and discuss difficulties partnerships sometimes face.*

1 Get ready to read

Presentation I
20–25 minutes

A  **2.05** 1. Say: *Now we're going to listen to two students plan for a project.*

2. Play the audio. Direct students to answer the questions.

Answer
meet and work together, work by email, send text messages

B **2.05** 1. Replay the audio. Ask students to check the expressions.

2. Check answers with the class.

Answers	
Don't forget that . . .	Definitely.
Let's...	Good idea.
Maybe we should	Let's do that.
think about...	Sure.
Remember that...	That's right.
That reminds me...	
We should...	

TIP

Suggest that students rank the expressions for suggesting in order of directness or strength. For example, *We should...* is more direct than *That makes me think of...* Students can also rank the responses in order of strength or enthusiasm. Elicit their ideas and write them in order. Discuss their reasons for ranking as they did.

C 1. Read the directions aloud.

2. Group students and assign roles: manager, fact checker, recorder, and reporter. Check comprehension of tasks. Ask: *Who keeps the team on task and on time?* [manager] *Who takes notes?* [recorder] *Who looks up information or unfamiliar words?* [fact checker] *Who reports to the class?* [reporter]

3. Set a time limit (three minutes) and have students work together to complete the task.

4. Call time and have the reporters from each group take turns calling out their ideas.

Answers
Answers will vary.

MULTILEVEL STRATEGIES

To adapt 1C:

• **On-level** Assign these students the roles of recorder and manager.

• **Pre-level** Assign these students the role of reporter.

• **Higher-level** Assign these students the role of fact checker.

EXTENSION ACTIVITY
Role Play

1. Put students in pairs to create a role play. Direct them to choose one of the research topics from a previous unit to present.

2. Tell students to use the conversation in 1A as a model. They should include at least ten expressions listed in 1B.

3. Set a time limit (five minutes). Call on pairs to perform their role plays for the class. Direct their classmates to check the expressions they hear.

2 Preview and read

Guided Practice I
20–25 minutes

1. Read the directions aloud. Ask: *Which sentences should you skim?* [the first of each paragraph]

2. Have students answer the question individually, and then check answers as a class.

Answers
Paragraph 1: aviation Paragraph 2: music Paragraph 3: technology / the Internet / the Web Paragraph 4: fitness

Ask students to read the article silently and answer the question and then compare answers with a partner. Check the answer as a class.

Possible Answers
Wright Bros—played and worked together because they were brothers Lennon and McCartney—both wrote songs Yang and Filo—did something they enjoyed together, which led to partnership Rice and Cutler—had same idea for good fitness experience

MULTILEVEL STRATEGIES

To adapt 2B:

• **Pre-level** Work with pre-level students to read the article aloud. Stop after each paragraph and check comprehension.

• **On-level** Have students complete the activity as directed.

• **Higher-level** Direct students to write the main idea of the article in a statement using their own words.

Presentation II
20–25 minutes

1. Read the directions aloud. Call on students to read the questions aloud.

2. Set a time limit (five minutes) and have students work individually to complete the task.

3. Call time. Have students compare answers in pairs.

4. Go over the answers with the class.

WORD STUDY

1. Read the directions and the prompts aloud.

2. Write the chart on the board.

3. Set a time limit (five minutes). Have students work in pairs to answer the questions.

4. Ask volunteers to write words in the chart.

5. Elicit definitions.

Answers

	Meaning based on context	Common collocation(s)
diametrically	completely or directly	opposed, different
tremendously	to a very great extent	grow, effective
meteoric	sudden and great increase (related to meteor)	rise, career
devoted	having great love and being loyal to someone	community, following, friend

TIP

Explain that students can find collocation dictionaries online. They can search for "collocations with" + one of the words in the chart.

E 1. Read the directions and the questions aloud.

2. Have students work with their teams from 1C. Assign roles: manager (keep team on time and on task), fact checker (check facts and look up words), recorder (take notes), and reporter (report to the class).

3. Set a time limit (five minutes) for teams to complete the task.

4. Call time. Ask reporters from each team to share their ideas.

Answers

Answers will vary.

3 Build on it

Presentation I
20–25 minutes

A 1. Have students look at the photo. Ask: *What are the two women doing?* [working at a laptop] *What kinds of projects might they be working on?* [planning, writing, looking for information, creating documents] *What are the two men doing?* [working on/repairing a car] *In what ways do you think they need to collaborate?* [problem-solving/troubleshooting, communicating, helping with tools]

2. Direct students' attention to the mind map. Read the directions aloud.

3. Ask: *What is an example of an unequal balance of power?* Elicit an idea or two.

4. Set a time limit (five minutes). Have students work in pairs to complete the activity.

5. Call on students to share their ideas with the class.

Possible Answers

Different values and vision: one cares about the environment
Financial disagreement: how much to spend on expansion
Unequal balance of power: only one controls the money
Difference in commitment: one works 60 hours a week, the other only 40
Communication problems: one tells the other what to do
Personality or relationship problems: one partner is a bully

 1. Have students rejoin their teams from 1C and 1E with the same roles.

2. Set a time limit (ten minutes). Have students work in teams to discuss the questions.

3. Call on reporters to share their team's ideas.

Possible Answers
1. Answers will vary. 2. They have a difference in vision (hiring a new employee) and commitment (Luis works long hours) and relationship problems (Luis's wife is angry). 3. Answers will vary.

PROBLEM SOLVING

C 1. Ask students to stay in their teams and switch roles.

2. Set a time limit (five minutes) and have students work together to discuss their advice.

3. Call time and each team join another team to compare ideas.

Answers
Answers will vary.

EXTENSION ACTIVITY
Role Play
1. Pair students to take turns playing Lena and Mari.
2. Tell students to create a role play in which they discuss their plan for a partnership and the potential problem areas listed on the mind map.
3. Call on volunteers to role-play for the class.

Evaluation
10–15 minutes

SELF-ASSESSMENT

1. Direct students to complete the self-assessment individually.

2. Have students choose the one objective they have the most difficulty with.

3. Group students according to their weakest skill. Provide each group with suggestions or feedback.

Lesson Overview

MULTILEVEL OBJECTIVES

On-level: Use the writing process to summarize an article

Pre-level: Work with others to summarize an article

Higher-level: Summarize the article using parallel structure and adjectives for working together

LANGUAGE FOCUS

Grammar: Parallel structure

Vocabulary: Types of collaboration

For vocabulary support, see this **Oxford Picture Dictionary** topic: English Composition, pages 202–203

STRATEGY FOCUS

Use transitions to give reasons.

PACING

To compress this lesson: Assign 1A–E for homework.

To extend this lesson: Have students write a summary of an article (see page 139).

And/or have students complete **Multilevel Activities 5 Unit 6, Lesson 5.**

Lesson Notes

CORRELATIONS

CCRS: W/WHST.6-8.2.a. Introduce a topic clearly, previewing what is to follow; organize ideas, concepts, and information, using strategies such as definition, classification, comparison /contrast, and cause/effect; include formatting (e.g., headings), graphics (e.g., charts, tables), and multimedia when useful to aiding comprehension.

W/WHST.6-8.2.b. Develop the topic with relevant facts, definitions, concrete details, quotations, or other information and examples.

W/WHST.6-8.2.c. Use appropriate transitions to create cohesion and clarify the relationships among ideas and concepts.

W/WHST.6-8.2.d. Use precise language and domain-specific vocabulary to inform about or explain the topic.

W/WHST.6-8.2.f. Provide a concluding statement or section that follows from and supports the information or explanation presented.

W/WHST.6-8.4 Produce clear and coherent writing in which the development and organization and style are appropriate to task, purpose, and audience.

W/WHST.6-8.5 With some guidance and support from peers and others, develop and strengthen writing as needed by planning, revising, editing, rewriting, or trying a new approach, focusing on how well purpose and audience have been addressed.

L.6.3/7.3.c. Choose language that expresses ideas precisely and concisely, recognizing and eliminating wordiness and redundancy.

L.8.6 Acquire and use accurately level-appropriate general academic and domain-specific words and phrases; gather vocabulary knowledge when considering a word or phrase important to comprehension or expression.

ELPS: ELP Standard 7

- adapt language choices and style according to purpose, task, and audience with ease in various social and academic contexts
- use a wide variety of complex general academic and content specific words and phrases
- employ both formal and more informal styles and tones effectively in spoken and written texts, as appropriate

ELP Standard 9

- recount a complex and detailed sequence of events or steps in a process, with an effective sequential or chronological order
- introduce and effectively develop an informational topic with facts, details, and evidence
- use complex and varied transitions to link the major sections of speech and text and to clarify relationships among events and ideas
- provide a concluding section or statement

ELP Standard 10

- produce and expand simple, compound, and complex sentences

Warm-up and Review
10–15 minutes (books closed)

Write a list of fields on the board: *Technology, Health, Fashion, Entertainment, Design/architecture, Music, Business.* Put students in pairs or small groups to list as many famous partnerships as they can. Set a time limit (three minutes). Elicit the number students can list in each category. Then elicit examples.

Introduction
5 minutes

State the objective: *Today we will use the writing process to summarize an article.*

1 Write a summary

Presentation I
20–25 minutes

 1. Have students revisit the article on pages 66–67. Check comprehension. Ask: *What is the article about? What are the most important ideas?*

2. Elicit responses and jot them on the board.

Guided Practice I
15–20 minutes

 1. Direct students to look at the chart. Ask about organization: *What do you see in the columns?* [the partners] *What information will you put in each row?* [what the partners did together and why it was successful]

2. Check comprehension of the activity. Ask: *Do you need to write complete sentences in the chart?* [no]

3. Have students work individually to complete their charts.

Answers				
	Wright Brothers	**Lennon & McCartney**	**Yang & Filo**	**Cutler & Rice**
What they did together	flight in airplane	The Beatles, music, song writing	started Yahoo! Inc.	Started SoulCycle
Why it was successful	Because they were brothers, they were able to collaborate at a time when it was difficult to do so.	They had very different personalities but were able to collaborate on song writing. They brought different talents to the songs, and that's why the songs were more interesting.	The company developed from a shared interest in using the Web. They identified a problem and working together to solve it.	They had a very similar vision for something different in the fitness industry.

C 1. Read the directions aloud.

2. Have students work individually to write their statements. Encourage students to use the sentence frame. Then ask students to compare statements in pairs.

> **TIP**
>
> Point out that a statement of the main idea often makes a reference to how the article was organized. Ask: *How was the article organized?* [four paragraphs, each one about a different partnership]

D 1. Read the directions aloud.

2. Have students work individually to write their conclusions.

> **TIP**
>
> Point out that usually an article will end with a conclusion. In that situation, students should reread the last paragraph and write one sentence that expresses the general idea. In this article, there is no conclusion. Encourage students to write their own conclusion in which they sum up the four paragraphs.

To adapt 2C:

• **Mixed-ability** Pair pre-level students with on- and higher-level students. Have all students point out ideas that are not clear. Instruct on- and higher-level partners to give feedback on spelling and grammar if helpful.

EXTENSION ACTIVITY

Summary Practice

1. Tell students to find an article online about one of the partnerships the class listed in the warm-up.

2. Direct students to write one paragraph to summarize the main points of the article.

E 1. Read the directions aloud. Check comprehension. Ask: *What will you include in your summary?* [introduction, notes from the chart, conclusion]

2. Draw students' attention to the Writer's Note. Ask: *What do these expressions introduce?* [reasons]

3. Have students work individually to write their summaries.

MULTILEVEL STRATEGIES

To adapt 1E:

• **On-level** Have students write summaries as directed.

• **Pre-level** Work with students in a group to write the summary together.

• **Higher-level** Have these students add one or two concluding sentences to their summaries to say what is important about the information in the article.

2 Get feedback and revise

Guided Practice II
10–15 minutes

A Direct students to check their writing using the editing checklist. Tell them to read each item in the list and check their papers before moving on to the next item. Explain that students should not edit their writing at this stage. They should just use the checklist to check their work and mark any areas they want to revise.

Communicative Practice
10–15 minutes

B 1. Read the directions aloud. Emphasize to students that they are responding to their partners' work, not correcting it.

2. Direct students to exchange papers with a partner and follow the instructions.

C Allow students time to edit and revise their writing using the editing checklist and their partner's feedback. If necessary, students could complete this task as homework.

Evaluation
10–15 minutes

SELF-ASSESSMENT

1. Call on students to read their completed sentences aloud.

2. Use the responses to the second statement to plan follow-up activities.

LESSON **6** TEAM RESEARCH

Lesson Overview

MULTILEVEL OBJECTIVES

On-level: Students conduct and present research related to teamwork

Pre-level: Students help conduct and present research related to teamwork

Higher-level: Students conduct and analyze research related to teamwork and present it to the class

LANGUAGE FOCUS

Grammar: Parallel structure

Vocabulary: For vocabulary support, see this **Oxford Picture Dictionary** topic: Internet Research, pages 212–213

STRATEGY FOCUS

Pace your presentation.

READINESS CONNECTION

In this lesson, students research a successful partnership.

PACING

To compress this lesson: Assign 1B and 1C for homework. Alternatively, assign students topics in 1A.

To extend this lesson: Have students debrief with a partner (see page 142).

And/or have students complete **Multilevel Activities 5 Unit 6, Lesson 6**.

Lesson Notes

CORRELATIONS

CCRS: W.7.7 Conduct short research projects to answer a question, drawing on several sources and generating additional related, focused questions for further research and investigation.

W.7.8 Gather relevant information from multiple print and digital sources, using search terms effectively; assess the credibility and accuracy of each source; and quote or paraphrase the data and conclusions of others while avoiding plagiarism and following a standard format for citation.

SL.8.4 Present claims and findings, emphasizing salient points in a focused, coherent manner with relevant evidence, sound valid reasoning, and well-chosen details; use appropriate eye contact, adequate volume, and clear pronunciation.

SL.8.5 Integrate multimedia and visual displays into presentations to clarify information, strengthen claims and evidence, and add interest.

SL.8.6 Adapt speech to a variety of contexts and tasks, demonstrating command of formal English when indicated or appropriate.

L.6.3/7.3.b. Maintain consistency in style and tone.

L.6.3/7.3.c. Choose language that expresses ideas precisely and concisely, recognizing and eliminating wordiness and redundancy.

L.8.6 Acquire and use accurately level-appropriate general academic and domain-specific words and phrases; gather vocabulary knowledge when considering a word or phrase important to comprehension or expression.

ELPS: ELP Standard 2
- participate in conversations, extended discussions, and written exchanges about a range of substantive topics, texts, and issues
- build on the ideas of others
- express his or her own ideas clearly and persuasively
- summarize the key points and evidence discussed

ELP Standard 3
- deliver oral presentations
- compose written informational texts
- fully develop the topic with relevant details, concepts, examples, and information
- integrate graphics or multimedia when useful about a variety of texts, topics, or events

<table>
<tr><td>

ELP Standard 5
- carry out both short and more sustained research projects to answer a question or solve a problem
- gather information from multiple print and digital sources
- use advanced search terms effectively
- synthesize information from multiple print and digital sources
- analyze and integrate information into clearly organized spoken and written texts
- include illustrations, diagrams, or other graphics as appropriate
- cite sources appropriately

</td><td>

ELP Standard 7
- adapt language choices and style according to purpose, task, and audience with ease in various social and academic contexts
- use a wide variety of complex general academic and content specific words and phrases
- employ both formal and more informal styles and tones effectively in spoken and written texts, as appropriate

</td></tr>
</table>

Warm-up and Review
10–15 minutes (books closed)

1. Have students exchange and read their summaries from the Extension Activity in Lesson 5.

2. Call on students to share one thing they learned from their partner's summary.

Introduction
5 minutes

1. Say: *A successful partnership depends on teamwork.*

2. State the objective: *Today we will conduct and present research related to teamwork.*

1 Research a successful partnership

Communicative Practice
40–45 minutes

1. Group students but do not assign roles yet. Explain that students will work with their team to narrow the topic.

2. Read the directions aloud.

3. Direct students' attention to the first Research Tip. Ask: *What are some other general terms you could use for this assignment?* [successful partnerships, famous partnerships] *What are some specific terms you can add?* [in arts, in sports, in business, now, in history]

4. Set a time limit (ten minutes) and have students work together to complete the task.

B 1. Read the directions aloud.

2. Tell students to each find at least one source on their team's topic.

3. Set a time limit (five minutes). Direct students to identify four or more recent sources as a team.

1. Read the directions aloud.

2. Set a time limit or assign research as an out-of-class task. Remind students to look for visual elements that they can include in their presentation.

3. Draw students' attention to the second Research Tip. Check comprehension. Ask: *What is an anecdote?* [a small story] *What kind of stories do you think might be interesting?*

4. Have students work individually to complete the research.

TIP
Find an article or essay that begins with an interesting anecdote. Remind students that an anecdote or story is one possible hook for a presentation.

D 1. Have students share their results in their teams.

2. Read the directions and questions aloud.

3. Assign roles: manager, IT specialist, recorder, and editor. Explain that students will work with their group to complete the task.

4. Check comprehension of the activity. Ask: *Who compiles the information from all sources?* [recorder] *Who checks that the sources and dates are accurate and downloads or creates visual elements?* [IT specialist] *Who keeps the team on time and on task and helps the team organize?* [manager] *Who checks that grammar and spelling are correct?* [editor]

5. Set a time limit (ten minutes) and have students work together to follow the steps and answer the questions.

2 Present your research

Presentation
40–45 minutes

A 1. Have students stay in their teams. Check comprehension of the task. Ask: *What does the outline include?* [introduction, body, and conclusion] *What should you do in the introduction?* [tell the audience the topic] *What do you need to do in the body?* [describe the partnership] *What should you summarize in the conclusion?* [the value of collaboration in this situation and what the audience can learn from it]

2. Ask: *What are some specific details you should include?* [the field, background, roles, contributions, challenges] Write the categories of details on the board as a reminder.

3. Set a time limit (five to ten minutes) and have students work as a team to outline their presentation.

B 1. Explain that students will work with their team to present their research.

2. Check comprehension of the activity. *Who will speak?* [everyone] *Who will check the slide show if there is one?* [IT specialist]

3. Draw students' attention to the Presentation Strategy. Call on students to read sentences aloud.

4. Check comprehension. Ask: *What are places where you should pause briefly?* [between clauses, phrases, or transitions] *What are some examples of fillers that you should avoid?* [*uh, um, OK, like, you know*]

5. Set a time limit (five minutes) and have students work as a team to divide the roles and the sections of the presentation (for example, introduction, field, background; roles and contributions; challenges; conclusion).

C 1. Read the bulleted items aloud.

2. Check comprehension of the activity. Ask: *Should you rehearse the presentation in exactly the way you will present to the class?* [yes]

3. Set a time limit (ten minutes) and have students rehearse their presentations in teams.

D 1. Draw a chart on the board, listing the teams in the first column. In the other columns, list the note-taking prompts or shortened forms of them: *Pacing, Visuals, Strengths, Advice.* Check comprehension of the activity. Ask: *What will you write under* pacing? [if they added pauses and avoided fillers] Remind students to just use words and phrases in the chart.

2. Set a time limit (five minutes) for each presentation, and ask each team to present in turn.

E 1. Have each team discuss their feedback for other teams. Ask each team to nominate a reporter to give feedback on the other teams' presentations.

2. Beginning with the first team to present, collect feedback from the reporters. Write feedback in the table you drew on the board in 2D.

Evaluation
10–15 minutes

SELF-ASSESSMENT

1. Pair students to share their self-assessments.

2. Elicit suggestions from the class for developing more confidence in each of the three assessment areas.

Unit Overview

This unit explores initiative, ways to increase it, and cultural differences with a range of employability skills, and contextualizes word families and passive forms. By the end of this unit, you will be able to conduct and present research related to initiative.

KEY OBJECTIVES	
Lesson 1	Identify ways to show initiative
Lesson 2	Identify ways to increase initiative
Lesson 3	Identify word families; use passive forms to avoid mentioning an agent
Lesson 4	Read and discuss cultural differences
Lesson 5	Use the writing process to summarize an article
Lesson 6	Conduct and present research related to initiative

UNIT FEATURES	
Academic Vocabulary	*attribute, criticize, Individualism, ingenuity, motivation, perceptive, philosophy, self-reliance, tendency, unique*
Employability Skills	• Compare and contrast worldviews • Synthesize ideas across texts and a lecture • Suggest solutions for improving workplace performance • Participate actively in philosophical discussions • Conduct research on self-directed learning • Plan and deliver a team presentation

Resources	**Class Audio** CD2, Tracks 06-08
	Teacher Resource Center
	    Multilevel Activities 5 Unit 7
	    Multilevel Grammar Activities 5 Unit 7
	    Unit 7 Test
	Oxford Picture Dictionary Succeeding in School, The Library, Jobs and Occupations, Career Planning, Soft Skills, Interview Skills, English Composition, U.S. History, World History, Internet Research

<table>
<tr><td>

Lesson Overview

</td><td>

Lesson Notes

</td></tr>
<tr><td>

MULTILEVEL OBJECTIVES

On-level: Identify ways to show initiative

Pre-level: Understand initiative and ways to show it

Higher-level: Lead discussion on ways to show initiative

LANGUAGE FOCUS

Grammar: Simple past, complex sentences

Vocabulary: *initiative, initiate, initiation,* and synonyms

For vocabulary support, see this **Oxford Picture Dictionary** topic: Soft Skills, page 178

READINESS CONNECTION

In this lesson, students work in a team to discuss ways to show initiative.

PACING

To compress this lesson: Do 1D as a class.

To extend this lesson: Have students role-play a situation showing initiative or lack of initiative (see page 146).

And/or have students complete **Multilevel Activities 5 Unit 7, Lesson 1.**

</td><td></td></tr>
</table>

CORRELATIONS

CCRS: RI.6.7 Integrate information presented in different media or formats (e.g., in charts, graphs, photographs, videos, or maps) as well as in words to develop a coherent understanding of a topic or issue.

SL.8.1.a. Come to discussions prepared, having read or researched material under study; explicitly draw on that preparation by referring to evidence on the topic, text, or issue to probe and reflect on ideas under discussion.

SL.8.1.c. Pose questions that connect the ideas of several speakers and respond to others' questions and comments with relevant evidence, observations, and ideas.

SL.8.1.d. Acknowledge new information expressed by others, and, when warranted, qualify or justify their own views in light of the evidence presented.

L.6.4.c. Consult reference materials (e.g., dictionaries, glossaries, thesauruses), both print and digital, to find the pronunciation of a word or determine or clarify its precise meaning or its part of speech.

SL.8.4 Present claims and findings, emphasizing salient points in a focused, coherent manner with relevant evidence, sound valid reasoning, and well-chosen details; use appropriate eye contact, adequate volume, and clear pronunciation.

L.6.4.c. Consult reference materials (e.g., dictionaries, glossaries, thesauruses), both print and digital, to find the pronunciation of a word or determine or clarify its precise meaning or its part of speech.

L.8.6 Acquire and use accurately level-appropriate general academic and domain-specific words and phrases; gather vocabulary knowledge when considering a word or phrase important to comprehension or expression.

ELPS: ELP Standard 2

- participate in conversations, extended discussions, and written exchanges about a range of substantive topics, texts, and issues
- build on the ideas of others
- express his or her own ideas clearly and persuasively
- refer to specific and relevant evidence from texts or research to support his or her ideas
- ask and answer questions that probe reasoning and claim

ELP Standard 8

using context, questioning, and consistent knowledge of English morphology,

- determine the meaning of general academic and content-specific words and phrases, figurative and connotative language, and idiomatic expressions in spoken and written texts about a variety of topics, experiences, or events

Warm-up and Review
10–15 minutes (books closed)

Ask: *How would you like to improve your academic or work situation? What can you do to achieve that goal?* Set a time limit (three minutes) for students to answer the questions in pairs. Call on students to share their ideas.

Introduction
5 minutes

1. Say: *Often, to get where we want to be, we need to show initiative.*

2. State the objective: *Today we're going to identify ways to show initiative.*

1 Discuss initiative

Presentation I
20–25 minutes

 1. Read the directions aloud. Ask: *What does motivate mean?* [generate enthusiasm for doing something]

2. Elicit ideas and write them on the board.

> **TIP**
>
> If students have trouble generating a lot of ideas, suggest that they think about not only ways to get excited before tackling something but also how they can stay motivated and how they can reward themselves after.

B 1. Direct students to look at the definition. Ask: *What do you think are the key words in the definition?* [*decide, act, on your own*]

2. Write *initiative* on the board, and elicit examples from the whole class. Write their ideas. Point out the connection between their ideas and their responses in 1A.

Answers
synonyms: *enterprise, inventiveness, resourcefulness, capability*   other forms of the word: *initiate* (v)

C Direct students to look at the quiz. Ask: *How many items are there?* [five] *If the statement is strongly true for you, what number should you give?* [4] Point out any connections between the items and students' ideas in 1A.

Guided Practice
10–20 minutes

 1. Direct students to look at the first question. Check comprehension of the collocation. Ask: *What does* display *mean?* [show]

2. Set a time limit (five minutes). Direct students to work with their partners to complete the activity.

3. Have a volunteer from each pair give their responses.

4. Check answers as a class.

Possible Answers
1. He displays initiative by finding ways to motivate himself.   2. He sometimes lacks initiative at work or school. He doesn't do more than is asked of him.   3. One example of demonstrating initiative is offering to help a co-worker with something he or she is having a problem with.

Presentation II
20–25 minutes

 1. Group students and assign roles: manager, recorder, reporter, and editor. Explain that students will work with their team to analyze the information. Verify students' understanding of the roles: the reporter reports back to the class, the manager keeps the team on task and on time, the recorder writes the statement, and the editor checks grammar and spelling.

2. Check comprehension of the task: *Which step will you do individually?* [1]

3. Set a time limit (ten minutes) for the discussions. Write the following sentence frame on the board: *We think _____ shows initiative because _____.*

4. Call time and have the reporters from each group take turns calling out their statements. If groups disagree, ask groups to explain their objections.

Evaluation

10–15 minutes

SELF-ASSESSMENT

1. Ask students to spend some time reflecting on what they have learned. Set a time limit (three minutes).

2. Ask for volunteers to share their thoughts.

Lesson Overview

Lesson Notes

MULTILEVEL OBJECTIVES

On-level and Higher-level: Identify ways to increase initiative and give examples

Pre-level: Identify ways to increase initiative

LANGUAGE FOCUS

Grammar: Simple past, simple present, complex sentences

Vocabulary: *individualism, ingenuity, motivation, philosophy, self-reliance*

For vocabulary support, see these **Oxford Picture Dictionary** topics: Jobs and Occupations, pages 170–173; U.S. History, page 208

STRATEGY FOCUS

Listen for how a speaker introduces important ideas.

READINESS CONNECTION

In this lesson, students work collaboratively to discuss initiative.

PACING

To compress this lesson: Assign 1C and 1D for homework.

To extend this lesson: Have students conduct online research about quotes and their meanings (see page 149); Have students set goals (see page 150).

And/or have students complete **Multilevel Activities 5 Unit 7, Lesson 2.**

CORRELATIONS

CCRS: RI/RL.7.1 Cite several pieces of textual evidence to support analysis of what the text says explicitly as well as inferences drawn from the text.

RI.8.3 Analyze how a text makes connections among and distinctions between individuals, ideas, or events (e.g., through comparisons, analogies, or categories).

RI/RL.6.4 Determine the meaning of words and phrases as they are used in a text, including figurative, connotative, and technical meanings; analyze the impact of a specific word choice on meaning and tone.

SL.8.1.a. Come to discussions prepared, having read or researched material under study; explicitly draw on that preparation by referring to evidence on the topic, text, or issue to probe and reflect on ideas under discussion.

SL.8.1.c. Pose questions that connect the ideas of several speakers and respond to others' questions and comments with relevant evidence, observations, and ideas.

SL.8.1.d. Acknowledge new information expressed by others, and, when warranted, qualify or justify their own views in light of the evidence presented.

SL.8.2 Analyze the purpose of information presented in diverse media and formats (e.g., visually, quantitatively, orally) and evaluate the motives (e.g., social, commercial, political) behind its presentation.

SL.8.3 Delineate a speaker's argument and specific claims, evaluating the soundness of the reasoning and relevance and sufficiency of the evidence and identifying when irrelevant evidence is introduced.

L.6.3/7.3.c. Choose language that expresses ideas precisely and concisely, recognizing and eliminating wordiness and redundancy.

L.8.6 Acquire and use accurately level-appropriate general academic and domain-specific words and phrases; gather vocabulary knowledge when considering a word or phrase important to comprehension or expression.

ELPS: ELP Standard 1

use a wide range of strategies to:

- determine central ideas or themes in oral presentations and spoken and written texts

- cite specific details and evidence from texts to support the analysis

<table>
<tr><td>

ELP Standard 2

- participate in conversations, extended discussions, and written exchanges about a range of substantive topics, texts, and issues
- build on the ideas of others
- express his or her own ideas clearly and persuasively
- refer to specific and relevant evidence from texts or research to support his or her ideas
- ask and answer questions that probe reasoning and claim
- summarize the key points and evidence discussed

</td><td>

ELP Standard 8

using context, questioning, and consistent knowledge of English morphology,

- determine the meaning of general academic and content-specific words and phrases, figurative and connotative language, and idiomatic expressions in spoken and written texts about a variety of topics, experiences, or events

</td></tr>
</table>

Warm-up and Review
10–15 minutes (books closed)

Write *American Dream* on the board. Ask: *What do you think the American Dream is?* Have students discuss the question in pairs, and then elicit ideas from the class.

Introduction
5 minutes

State the objective: *Today we will identify ways to increase initiative.*

1 Read about Franklin and Emerson

Presentation I
10–15 minutes

A 1. Write the quote on the board.

2. Read the directions aloud. Have students work in teams to complete the task.

3. Elicit students' ideas.

Guided Practice I
15–20 minutes

B 1. Read the directions aloud. Check comprehension. Ask: *What are you scanning for?* [the two names and what they did] *What is the title of the text?* [*Two American Individualists*] *What do you think an* individualist *is?*

2. Set a time limit (five minutes). Direct students to underline the information that answers the question when they find it.

3. Elicit the answer.

Answer

Franklin was an inventor, author, diplomat, and one of the founding fathers of the United States. Emerson was an essayist and philosopher.

TIP

Write *founding fathers* on the board. Explain or elicit that this term refers to a small group of wealthy, educated men who wrote important papers that helped create the United States. They included Benjamin Franklin and the first four presidents.

C 1. Read the directions aloud. Check comprehension. Ask: *What does* have in common *mean?* [similarities, things shared]

2. Set a time limit (five minutes). Direct students to answer the question.

3. Elicit ideas from the whole class.

Answer

They were both Americans, both philosophers and writers, and both believers in individualism and initiative.

MULTILEVEL STRATEGIES

To adapt 1C:

- **Mixed-ability:** Pair pre-level students with on- or higher-level students. Have pre-level students follow along while partners read the text aloud and explain any unfamiliar vocabulary.

Communicative Practice
10–20 minutes

D 1. Read the questions aloud.

2. Ask students to answer the questions and mark their answers to questions 1 and 2 in the text.

3. Set a time limit (five minutes) for students to discuss their answers with a partner.

Answers

1. *philosopher, philosophy, philosophical*; Responses about meaning may vary. *Philosophy is the study of the nature of and meaning of the universe and of human life.*
2. In text: "the idea that through hard work and ingenuity, anyone can succeed"
3. Possible answers: Just because you are moving around doesn't mean you're doing something useful. To be motivated, you can't just dream, you have to work for what you want. Do the things that you really want to do and are good at—don't do things just because other people do them.
4. Answers will vary.

EXTENSION ACTIVITY

Presenting Quotes

1. Revisit the ideas students generated in Lesson 1.

2. Tell students to search online for quotes on one of those ideas (motivation, initiative, reaching goals, resourcefulness, capability, success).

3. Call on students to present their quotes and explain what they think they mean.

2 Listen and take notes

Guided Practice II
20–25 minutes

A 1. Say: *Now we're going to listen to a lecture about showing initiative at work.*

2. Direct students' attention to the quote. Check comprehension: *What are the three kinds of people? Which is the most active?* [the first] *Which is the least involved?* [the last]

3. Pair or group students. Set a time limit (five minutes). Direct students to complete the task.

4. Elicit ideas from the whole class. Write their ideas on the board.

To adapt 2A:

• **Mixed-ability:** Group students of mixed ability. Higher-level students provide examples of each type of person.

B **2.06** 1. Play the beginning of the audio. Direct students to listen without writing.

2. Replay the audio. Ask students to write what the speaker will focus on.

3. Brainstorm with the class predictions about else what the speaker will say.

Answer

The speaker will focus on ways to show initiative.

C **2.07** 1. Direct students' attention to the Listening Note. Point out that these phrases signal that the speaker is adding another important idea. Elicit other signal words: *a second way, also, in addition, the last one.*

2. Direct students to look at the chart. Ask: *What are the three parts in the chart?* [*Ways to demonstrate it, One more thing,* and *Conclusion*]

3. Play the whole audio. Direct students to write notes in the chart as they listen.

Answers

Ways to demonstrate it:
One way, look for things to improve / ways to save $
Another way, be eager to learn
Finally, help others
One more thing:
Make sure you have a career goal
Reasons/Examples: makes you more eager to help/learn, for example, if you want to be a chef, you will help more in kitchen; with clear goals initiative is easier
Conclusion: Note examples of showing initiative for future job interviews

• **On-level** Have students complete the activity as described.

• **Pre-level** Provide students with the answers in random order so they can choose the correct one.

• **Higher-level** Tell students to take notes on additional examples or explanations.

Communicative Practice
10–20 minutes

 **2.07** 1. Set a time limit (five minutes) for students to discuss their answers with a partner.

2. Replay the audio. Ask students to confirm or add to their notes.

Presentation II
20–25 minutes

 1. Read the questions aloud. Direct students' attention to the sentence frames. Ask: *Which frames will you use in the first question?* [the first two] *Which can you use to answer the second question?* [the last one]

2. Model the first item. Describe someone you know who shows initiative and how it is similar.

3. Elicit responses from the class. Encourage students to use the expressions/frames provided.

Answers
Answers will vary.

TIP

You can broaden the topic in item 2 of 2D by following up with questions about other goals, for example, *How could having a personal goal like buying a house or biking across country help a student show initiative at school? How can having an academic goal help students show initiative in other aspects of their lives?*

EXTENSION ACTIVITY

Goal Setting

1. Tell students to write down three goals they want to achieve in the next five years.

2. For each goal, have them think of one way to show initiative at school or work that can help them achieve the goal.

3. Pair students to share their ideas.

Evaluation
10–15 minutes

SELF-ASSESSMENT

1. Read each item. Have students raise their hands if they have difficulty.

2. Pair students who have difficulty with those who do not to review ways to achieve each objective.

Lesson Overview

MULTILEVEL OBJECTIVES

On-level: Identify word families; use passive forms to avoid mentioning an agent

Pre-level: Identify word families; practice passive forms to avoid mentioning an agent

Higher-level: Identify word families; use and explain passive forms to avoid mentioning an agent

LANGUAGE FOCUS

Grammar: Passive forms

Vocabulary: *criticize, perceptive, philosophy*, word families

For vocabulary support, see these **Oxford Picture Dictionary** topics: Jobs and Occupations, pages 170–173; U.S. History, page 208

STRATEGY FOCUS

Use passive forms.

READINESS CONNECTION

In this lesson, students work with a partner to teach forms of a new word to the class.

PACING

To compress this lesson: Assign 1A and 1B for homework.

To extend this lesson: Have students work in pairs to find additional examples of word families (see page 152); Have students work in pairs to find examples of passive voice in the news (see page 153).

And/or have students complete **Multilevel Activities 5 Unit 7, Lesson 3.**

Lesson Notes

CORRELATIONS

CCRS: SL.8.1.a. Come to discussions prepared, having read or researched material under study; explicitly draw on that preparation by referring to evidence on the topic, text, or issue to probe and reflect on ideas under discussion.

SL.8.1.c. Pose questions that connect the ideas of several speakers and respond to others' questions and comments with relevant evidence, observations, and ideas.

SL.8.1.d. Acknowledge new information expressed by others, and, when warranted, qualify or justify their own views in light of the evidence presented.

L.6.1/8.1.g. Form and use verbs in the active and passive voice.

L.6.4.c. Consult reference materials (e.g., dictionaries, glossaries, thesauruses), both print and digital, to find the pronunciation of a word or determine or clarify its precise meaning or its part of speech.

L.8.6 Acquire and use accurately level-appropriate general academic and domain-specific words and phrases; gather vocabulary knowledge when considering a word or phrase important to comprehension or expression.

ELPS: ELP Standard 2

- participate in conversations, extended discussions, and written exchanges about a range of substantive topics, texts, and issues
- build on the ideas of others
- express his or her own ideas clearly and persuasively

ELP Standard 8

using context, questioning, and consistent knowledge of English morphology,

- determine the meaning of general academic and content-specific words and phrases, figurative and connotative language, and idiomatic expressions in spoken and written texts about a variety of topics, experiences, or events.

ELP Standard 10

- produce and expand simple, compound, and complex sentences

Warm-up and Review
10–15 minutes (books closed)

1. Write sentences on the board: *1. Showing initiative can help you be successful at work, in school, and in other aspects of your life. 2. For many people, the American Dream represents the idea that through hard work, you can achieve anything you want in life.*

2. Say: *You have already practiced restating or rephrasing ideas. Rewrite the sentences using synonyms, different word forms, and/or different sentence structures.*

3. Call on students to write their sentences on the board. Elicit the rephrasing strategies students used.

Introduction
5 minutes

1. Say: *One way to restate or rephrase ideas is to use different word forms. Another way can be to change the sentence from the active to passive voice.*

2. State the objective: *Today we are going to identify word families and use passive forms to avoid mentioning an agent.*

1 Vocabulary: Word families

Presentation and Guided Practice I
20–25 minutes

 1. Write *word families* on the board. Ask: *What is a word family?* [different forms/parts of speech with the same base word] Point out that students have been generating word families in the first lesson of every unit.

2. Copy the chart on the board.

3. Read the directions aloud. Call on students to read aloud the words in each part of speech.

4. Direct students to complete the task independently.

5. Call on students to add words to the chart on the board.

Answers		
Nouns	**Verbs**	**Adjectives**
action	act	active
critic	criticize	critical
motivation	motivate	motivational
perception		perceptive
philosophy / philosopher	perceive	philosophical
reliance	rely	reliable

- **On-level** Have students complete the activity as directed and then check the dictionary.
- **Pre-level** Have students use dictionaries.
- **Higher-level** Have students add definitions.

Communicative Practice
15–20 minutes

 1. Read the sentences aloud.

2. Set a time limit (five minutes) for students to complete the activity individually.

3. Call on students to read the completed sentences aloud.

Answers
1. philosopher, rely, critical
2. philosophical, reliance, active

Presentation II
20–25 minutes

 1. Read the directions aloud. Explain that students will find a word new to them in the previous lesson.

2. Pair students to complete the task. Set a time limit (ten minutes).

3. Call on students to present their words and sentences to the class.

MULTILEVEL STRATEGIES

To adapt 1C:

- **Pre-level** Assign each student or pair a word from the inputs in Lesson 2 (*individualism, advice, imitator, ingenuity, inefficiently, successful, diplomatic*).

EXTENSION ACTIVITY

Rephrasing Practice

1. Call on students to write one of their sentences from 1C on the board. Underline the target word.

2. Direct students to rewrite the sentences using a different word form but keeping the same idea.

3. Call on different students to write the rephrased statement next to the original.

 **2 Grammar: Passive forms**

Presentation and Guided Practice II
20–25 minutes

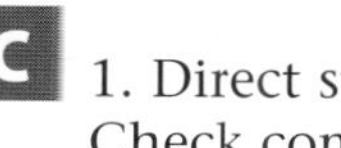

A 1. Demonstrate how to read the chart. Read each sentence aloud and have students repeat after you.

2. Write the sentences in the chart on the board. Elicit the forms of *be* in each sentence. Elicit the tense of each (simple present, simple past, modal, present perfect, future with *be going to*).

3. Have students complete the Language Connection about passive forms. Go over the answers as a class.

Answers
the action *be*, past participle present, past, present perfect, future *by*

MULTILEVEL STRATEGIES
To adapt 2A: • **On-level** Have students work independently. • **Pre-level** Have higher-level classmates assist these students • **Higher-level** Have these students work with pre-level classmates.

TIP
Explain or elicit the ways we use passive voice: to focus on the action or result rather than the actor, when we don't know who performed the action or it is not important, and when we want to be less direct and avoid blaming someone.

Guided Practice III
20–25 minutes

B 1. Have students work individually to complete the task and then compare answers with a partner.

2. Ask volunteers to write the sentences on the board.

Answers	
1. has been viewed	4. can be perceived
2. is, seen	5. were surveyed
3. are expected	6. will be evaluated

C 1. Direct students' attention to the memo. Check comprehension. Ask: *What voice/form does the memo use?* [active] *Is the tone positive and friendly?* [no]

2. Direct students' attention to the note.

3. Ask students to work individually to rewrite the sentences in the passive voice.

Answers
1. Too much food has been left in the break room lately. 2. Food that has been left in the refrigerator for more than 48 hours will be thrown away. 3. In addition, the counters must be cleaned. When they are not cleaned, we have a problem with ants. 4. All cleaning supplies can be found in the cabinet under the sink. Use them! 5. When foods with strong odors are microwaved, the smell bothers your coworkers. Please be considerate. 6. Tom can be reached anytime at (756) 555-0987 if you have any questions about these policies. 7. Answers will vary.

D 1. Set a time limit (five minutes) for students to share their sentences with a partner.

2. Ask volunteers to write sentences on the board.

3. If students disagree, ask them to look at the chart and explain their answers.

EXTENSION ACTIVITY
Examples from the News 1. Have students work in pairs to find articles or other texts online. 2. Ask them to locate three to five sentences in the passive voice. Have them rewrite in the active voice. 3. Ask volunteers to write both the original sentence and the rewrite on the board. Elicit the reason they think the passive voice was used.

Evaluation
10–15 minutes

SELF-ASSESSMENT

1. Have students complete the self-assessment.

2. Provide additional practice as needed.

Lesson Overview

MULTILEVEL OBJECTIVES

On-level: Read and discuss cultural differences; identify limiting factors

Pre-level: Read and discuss cultural differences

Higher-level: Read and discuss cultural differences; explain limiting factors

LANGUAGE FOCUS

Grammar: Active and passive forms

Vocabulary: *attribute, individualism, self-reliance, tendency, unique, individualistic, focused, selfish, trait*

For vocabulary support, see these **Oxford Picture Dictionary** topics: Soft Skills, page 178; U.S History, page 208; World History, page 209

STRATEGY FOCUS

Recognize limiting factors.

READINESS CONNECTION

In this lesson, students compare and contrast worldviews.

PACING

To compress this lesson: Assign 3B for homework.

To extend this lesson: Have students practice with comparative forms (see page 156); Have students role-play a breakdown in communication due to different traits (see page 158).

And/or have students complete **Multilevel Activities 5 Unit 7, Lesson 4.**

Lesson Notes

CORRELATIONS

CCRS: RI/RL.7.1 Cite several pieces of textual evidence to support analysis of what the text says explicitly as well as inferences drawn from the text.

RI/RL.6.2 Determine a theme or central idea of a text and how it is conveyed through particular details; provide a summary of the text distinct from personal opinions or judgments.

RST.6-8.2 Application: determine the central ideas or conclusions of a text; provide an accurate summary of the text distinct from prior knowledge or opinions.

RI/RL.6.4 Determine the meaning of words and phrases as they are used in a text, including figurative, connotative, and technical meanings; analyze the impact of a specific word choice on meaning and tone.

RI.6.7 Integrate information presented in different media or formats (e.g., in charts, graphs, photographs, videos, or maps) as well as in words to develop a coherent understanding of a topic or issue.

SL.8.1.a. Come to discussions prepared, having read or researched material under study; explicitly draw on that preparation by referring to evidence on the topic, text, or issue to probe and reflect on ideas under discussion.

SL.8.1.c. Pose questions that connect the ideas of several speakers and respond to others' questions and comments with relevant evidence, observations, and ideas.

SL.8.1.d. Acknowledge new information expressed by others, and, when warranted, qualify or justify their own views in light of the evidence presented.

SL.8.4 Present claims and findings, emphasizing salient points in a focused, coherent manner with relevant evidence, sound valid reasoning, and well-chosen details; use appropriate eye contact, adequate volume, and clear pronunciation.

L.6.4.c. Consult reference materials (e.g., dictionaries, glossaries, thesauruses), both print and digital, to find the pronunciation of a word or determine or clarify its precise meaning or its part of speech.

L.8.6 Acquire and use accurately level-appropriate general academic and domain-specific words and phrases; gather vocabulary knowledge when considering a word or phrase important to comprehension or expression.

<table>
<tr><td>

ELPS: ELP Standard 1

use a wide range of strategies to:

- determine central ideas or themes in oral presentations and spoken and written texts
- cite specific details and evidence from texts to support the analysis

ELP Standard 2

- participate in conversations, extended discussions, and written exchanges about a range of substantive topics, texts, and issues
- build on the ideas of others
- express his or her own ideas clearly and persuasively
- refer to specific and relevant evidence from texts or research to support his or her ideas
- ask and answer questions that probe reasoning and claims

</td><td>

ELP Standard 7

- adapt language choices and style according to purpose, task, and audience with ease in various social and academic contexts
- use a wide variety of complex general academic and content specific words and phrases
- employ both formal and more informal styles and tones effectively in spoken and written texts, as appropriate

ELP Standard 8

using context, questioning, and consistent knowledge of English morphology,

- determine the meaning of general academic and content-specific words and phrases, figurative and connotative language, and idiomatic expressions in spoken and written texts about a variety of topics, experiences, or events

</td></tr>
</table>

Warm-up and Review
10–15 minutes (books closed)

1. Revisit the quotes by Franklin and Emerson on page 74. Ask: *Are these ideas common in your culture? What ideas or quotes are similar in your native country? What ideas are more common?*

2. Group students to discuss. Then elicit their ideas.

Introduction
5 minutes

State the objective: *Today we will learn to read and discuss cultural differences.*

1 Get ready to read

Presentation I
20–25 minutes

A 🔊 **2.08** 1. Say: *Now we're going to listen to students discuss individualism.* Read the directions aloud. Check comprehension. Ask: *What is a trait?* [a quality or characteristic] *What question will you answer?* [*What do they conclude about individualistic people?*]

2. Play the audio. Direct students to listen without writing.

Answer
They conclude that individualistic people might be more selfish.

B 🔊 **2.08** 1. Replay the audio. Ask students to match the beginning and ending of each sentence.

2. Check answers with the class.

Answers	
1. e	4. d
2. a	5. b
3. c	

C 1. Write *Is individualism a positive or negative trait?* on the board.

2. Group students and assign roles: manager, editor, recorder, and reporter. Explain that students will work with their team to make a list of important reasons to include statistics in texts.

3. Check comprehension of the activity. *Who checks grammar in the comparisons?* [editor] *Who takes notes?* [recorder] *Who reports to the class?* [reporter] *Who keeps the team on time and on task?* [manager]

4. Set a time limit (three minutes) and have students work together to complete the task.

5. Call time and have the reporters from each group take turns calling out their ideas. Ask a few recorders to write sentences with comparisons on the board.

Answers
Answers will vary.

To adapt 1C:

• **On-level** Assign these students the roles of recorder and manager.

• **Pre-level** Assign these students the role of reporter.

• **Higher-level** Assign these students the role of editor.

EXTENSION ACTIVITY

Comparison Practice

1. Review ways to make comparisons.

2. Point out that adjectives in 1A are more than one syllable. Elicit the ways to make comparative forms with longer words.

3. Have students rewrite the sentences in 1B in a different way (for example, *Maybe if someone is less individualistic, they're less focused on being different.*).

2 Preview and read

Guided Practice I
20–25 minutes

 1. Read the directions aloud. Ask: *Where can you often find a statement of the main idea in an article?* [at the end of the first paragraph]

2. Have students answer the question individually, and then check answers with the class. Ask: *Is the main idea directly stated anywhere?* [yes] *Where?* [the last sentence]

Answers
Underlined in text: *Research suggests that differences in worldviews don't just affect behaviors and values—they actually influence basic reasoning and even perception.*

B 1. Ask students to read the article silently and answer the question and then compare answers with a partner.

2. Check answer with the class.

Possible Answers
Paragraph 2: People with a collectivist worldview focus more on context. People with an individualist worldview focus more on individuals. Paragraph 3: Worldview affects visual perception.

Presentation II
20–25 minutes

 1. Direct students' attention to the Reader's Note.

2. Check comprehension of the activity. Ask: *What will you underline?* [limiting expressions] *Why does a writer use these expressions?* [to indicate they are not describing all members of a group]

3. Set a time limit (five minutes) and have students work individually to complete the task.

4. Call time and elicit examples. Then ask students to explain why the writer used them.

Answers
Underlined in text: *the majority, tend to, more likely, seem to, usually, can, a tendency toward*

TIP

Explain or elicit that limiting expressions can include verbs (*seem to*), quantifiers (*the majority of*), adjectives (*likely*), adverbs (*often*), nouns (*a tendency*), and modals (*may, can, might*).

D 1. Read the directions aloud.

2. Have students work individually to answer the questions.

3. Pair students to compare answers.

4. Go over the answers as a class.

Answers
1. From text: *when given a story about a baseball player taking performance-enhancing drugs, they are more likely to talk about whether the player was under severe pressure to succeed.* Explanations will vary. 2. From text: *an eye-tracking study which found that the East Asian participants usually spent more time looking at the background of an image—exploring the context—than Americans, who were more likely to focus on the main elements.* Explanations will vary. 3. From text: *The children of immigrants generally adopt the worldview of the culture they move to. And a tendency toward individualism has been rising rapidly around the world as technology increases communication between cultures.* 4. Possible answer: A collectivist would group *train* and *track* because they are more likely to look at the relationships between things, like *cow* and *grass*.

WORD STUDY

E 1. Ask students to stay with their partners. Write the chart on the board. Ask: *What part of speech is* succeed? [verb] Tell students to write it under *Verbs* in the chart.

2. Set a time limit (five minutes) and have students work together to complete the task.

3. Call time. Have volunteers add words to the chart.

Answers		
Nouns	**Verbs**	**Adjectives**
success	succeed	successful
culture	acculturate	
reason	reason	reasonable
participant	participate	participatory

F 1. Direct students' attention to the Speaking Note. Read the directions and questions aloud.

2. Group students and assign roles: manager (keep team on time and on task), editor (check grammar of notes), recorder (take notes), and reporter (report to the class). Explain that students will work with their group to discuss the questions.

3. Set a time limit (five minutes) for teams to complete the task.

4. Call time and have the reporters from each group take turns calling out their examples. Record students' examples on the board. If groups disagree, direct the fact checkers to look for information online.

Answers
Answers will vary.

3 Build on it

Presentation I
20–25 minutes

A 1. Have students look at the chart. Ask: *How many worldviews are shown in the chart?* [two] *What are they?* [individualist and collectivist]

2. Call on students to explain each trait in the chart.

3. Set a time limit (ten minutes). Have students work individually to complete the task.

To adapt 3A:

• **Mixed-ability** Pair students of mixed ability to complete the task. Higher-level students can explain the traits and check comprehension.

TIP

Have students look up any words they don't understand before completing the task.

Answers	
1. C	6. I
2. I	7. I
3. I	8. I
4. C	9. C
5. C	

B 1. Have students compare their choices in pairs.

2. Elicit answers and ask students to explain why using the chart and article.

C 1. Ask students to return to their teams with the same roles. Explain that students will work with their group to discuss the questions. Remind students to use comparisons if appropriate.

2. Set a time limit (five minutes) and have students work together to complete the task.

3. Call time and have the reporters from each group take turns calling out their answers.

Possible Answers
1. Emerson focuses on the importance of the individual, of relying on yourself. The lecturer talks about setting personal goals and working to achieve them. Both reflect self-reliance and uniqueness.
2. teamwork, cooperation, good social skills
3. How well do you work with others? Can you give some examples of when you worked on a team? How would you rate your ability to get along with different kinds of people?

PROBLEM SOLVING

 1. Read the directions aloud.

2. Direct students' attention to the text.

3. Read the email aloud or call on a higher-level student to read it. Call on students to read the questions aloud.

4. Set a time limit (three minutes) and have students discuss the questions in their teams.

5. Call time and have each group take turns calling out the problems. Then elicit their ideas for improvement. Record students' answers on the board.

Possible Answers
1. Jasmine might have a more collectivist worldview. 2. The manager might have a more individualist worldview. 3. The manager should tell Jasmine what she is doing well and where she could improve. The manager could ask Jasmine for her ideas and input.

APPLY YOUR KNOWLEDGE

 1. Ask students to complete the research individually.

2. Students work in their teams from 1D with the same roles to discuss their research.

3. Call on reporters to share their teams' ideas with the class.

EXTENSION ACTIVITY
Role Play
1. Pair students to take turns playing someone with more individualistic traits and someone with more collectivist traits.
2. Tell students to choose a communication breakdown at work or at school to role-play.
3. Call on volunteers to role-play for the class.
4. For each role play, ask students what the cause of the breakdown was and what solutions they have.

Evaluation
10–15 minutes

SELF-ASSESSMENT

1. Direct students to complete the self-assessment individually.

2. Have students choose the one objective they have the most difficulty with.

3. Group students according to their weakest skill. Provide each group with suggestions or feedback.

Lesson Overview

MULTILEVEL OBJECTIVES

On-level: Use the writing process to summarize an article

Pre-level: Write sentences to summarize an article

Higher-level: Summarize an article and suggest ways they can apply their new knowledge

LANGUAGE FOCUS

Grammar: Connecting words and phrases for contrast?

Vocabulary: Connecting words that show contrast

For vocabulary support, see this **Oxford Picture Dictionary** topic: English Composition, pages 202–203

STRATEGY FOCUS

Use connecting words that show contrast.

PACING

To compress this lesson: Assign 2C for homework.

To extend this lesson: Have students write a summary of an article (see page 161).

And/or have students complete **Multilevel Activities 5 Unit 7, Lesson 5.**

Lesson Notes

CORRELATIONS

CCRS: W/WHST.6-8.2.a. Introduce a topic clearly, previewing what is to follow; organize ideas, concepts, and information, using strategies such as definition, classification, comparison /contrast, and cause/effect; include formatting (e.g., headings), graphics (e.g., charts, tables), and multimedia when useful to aiding comprehension.

W/WHST.6-8.2.b. Develop the topic with relevant facts, definitions, concrete details, quotations, or other information and examples.

W/WHST.6-8.2.c. Use appropriate transitions to create cohesion and clarify the relationships among ideas and concepts.

W/WHST.6-8.2.d. Use precise language and domain-specific vocabulary to inform about or explain the topic.

W/WHST.6-8.2.f. Provide a concluding statement or section that follows from and supports the information or explanation presented.

W/WHST.6-8.4 Produce clear and coherent writing in which the development and organization and style are appropriate to task, purpose, and audience.

W/WHST.6-8.5 With some guidance and support from peers and others, develop and strengthen writing as needed by planning, revising, editing, rewriting, or trying a new approach, focusing on how well purpose and audience have been addressed.

L.6.3/7.3.c. Choose language that expresses ideas precisely and concisely, recognizing and eliminating wordiness and redundancy.

L.8.6 Acquire and use accurately level-appropriate general academic and domain-specific words and phrases; gather vocabulary knowledge when considering a word or phrase important to comprehension or expression.

ELPS: ELP Standard 7

- adapt language choices and style according to purpose, task, and audience with ease in various social and academic contexts
- use a wide variety of complex general academic and content specific words and phrases
- employ both formal and more informal styles and tones effectively in spoken and written texts, as appropriate

ELP Standard 9

- recount a complex and detailed sequence of events or steps in a process, with an effective sequential or chronological order
- introduce and effectively develop an informational topic with facts, details, and evidence
- use complex and varied transitions to link the major sections of speech and text and to clarify relationships among events and ideas
- provide a concluding section or statement

ELP Standard 10

- produce and expand simple, compound, and complex sentences.

Warm-up and Review
10–15 minutes (books closed)

Write *Agree* on one side of the board and *Disagree* on the other. Call volunteers to the front of the class. Read a statement from 3A in Lesson 4 on page 80. Tell students to place themselves along a continuum from *Agree* to *Disagree* to show how much they agree with the statement. Call on students to explain their position. Repeat with other statements and other students.

Introduction
5 minutes

State the objective: *Today we will use the writing process to summarize an article.*

1 Write a summary

Presentation I
20–25 minutes

 **A** 1. Have students revisit the article on pages 78–79. Check comprehension. Ask: *What is the article about? What are the most important ideas?*

2. Elicit responses. Record students' answers on the board.

Guided Practice I
15–20 minutes

B 1. Direct students to look at the chart. Ask: *What will you write in the middle column?* [aspects of the collectivist worldview] *What goes in the right column?* [aspects of the individualist worldview]

2. Check comprehension of the activity. Ask: *Do you need to write complete sentences in the chart?* [no]

3. Have students work individually to complete their charts.

C 1. Read the directions aloud. Check comprehension. Ask: *What is your statement about?* [the main idea of the article]

2. Write the sentence frame on the board.

3. Have students work individually to write their statements. Encourage students to use the frame provided.

D 1. Check comprehension. Ask: *Where is the conclusion of the article?* [in the last paragraph]

2. Write the following sentence frame on the board: *In conclusion, the author states...*

3. Have students work individually to write their conclusions.

> **TIP**
>
> Direct students' attention to the last paragraph. Elicit synonyms and other word forms for key words in the conclusion (conflicting theories, learned, genetic, tendency, individualism, communication). Remind students that they can use synonyms and different word forms to rephrase ideas.

E 1. Read the directions aloud. Check comprehension. Ask: *What will you include in your summary?* [introduction, notes from the chart, conclusion]

2. Draw students' attention to the *Writer's Note*. Ask: *What do all these connecting words show?* [contrast] *When we contrast two things, are we talking about similarities or differences?* [differences]

3. Have students work individually to write their summaries.

> **MULTILEVEL STRATEGIES**
>
> To adapt 1E:
> - **On-level** Have students write summaries as directed.
> - **Pre-level** Work with students in a group to write the summary together.
> - **Higher-level** Have students add examples to their summaries.

2 Get feedback and revise

Guided Practice II
10–15 minutes

 **A** Direct students to check their writing using the editing checklist. Tell them to read each item in the list and check their papers before moving onto the next item. Explain that students should not edit their writing at this stage. They should just use the checklist to check their work and mark any areas they want to revise.

Communicative Practice
10–15 minutes

B
1. Read the directions aloud. Emphasize to students that they are responding to their partners' work, not correcting it.

2. Direct students to exchange papers with a partner and follow the instructions.

C
Allow students time to edit and revise their writing using the editing checklist and their partner's feedback. If necessary, have students complete this task as homework.

MULTILEVEL STRATEGIES

To adapt 2C:

• **Mixed-ability** Pair pre-level students with on- and higher-level students. Have all students point out ideas that are not clear. Instruct on- and higher-level partners to give feedback on spelling and grammar if helpful.

TIP

Remind students that they should note the positive feedback they receive so they can continue to do those things on future assignments.

EXTENSION ACTIVITY

Discussion Board

1. Tell students to post their summaries to a discussion board.

2. Direct students to give feedback on two summaries.

Evaluation
10–15 minutes

SELF-ASSESSMENT

1. Call on students to read their completed sentences aloud.

2. Use the responses to the second statement to plan follow-up activities.

Lesson Overview

MULTILEVEL OBJECTIVES

On-level: Students conduct and present research

Pre-level: Students help conduct and present research

Higher-level: Students organize, conduct, and present research

LANGUAGE FOCUS

Grammar: Simple present, passive

Vocabulary: Learning resource vocabulary

For vocabulary support, see these **Oxford Picture Dictionary** topics: Succeeding in School, page 10; The Library, page 135; Jobs and Occupations, pages 170–173; Career Planning, pages 174–175; Internet Research, pages 212–213

STRATEGY FOCUS

Create an interesting conclusion.

READINESS CONNECTION

In this lesson, student conduct research on self-directed learning.

PACING

To compress this lesson: Assign 1C for homework. Alternatively, provide students with topics to expedite 1A.

To extend this lesson: Have students practice interviewing each other (see page 165).

And/or have students complete **Multilevel Activities 5 Unit 7, Lesson 6.**

Lesson Notes

CORRELATIONS

CCRS: W.7.7 Conduct short research projects to answer a question, drawing on several sources and generating additional related, focused questions for further research and investigation.

W.7.8 Gather relevant information from multiple print and digital sources, using search terms effectively; assess the credibility and accuracy of each source; and quote or paraphrase the data and conclusions of others while avoiding plagiarism and following a standard format for citation.

SL.8.4 Present claims and findings, emphasizing salient points in a focused, coherent manner with relevant evidence, sound valid reasoning, and well-chosen details; use appropriate eye contact, adequate volume, and clear pronunciation.

SL.8.6 Adapt speech to a variety of contexts and tasks, demonstrating command of formal English when indicated or appropriate.

L.6.3/7.3.b. Maintain consistency in style and tone.

L.6.3/7.3.c. Choose language that expresses ideas precisely and concisely, recognizing and eliminating wordiness and redundancy.

L.8.6 Acquire and use accurately level-appropriate general academic and domain-specific words and phrases; gather vocabulary knowledge when considering a word or phrase important to comprehension or expression.

ELPS: ELP Standard 2

- participate in conversations, extended discussions, and written exchanges about a range of substantive topics, texts, and issues
- build on the ideas of others
- express his or her own ideas clearly and persuasively
- summarize the key points and evidence discussed

ELP Standard 3

- deliver oral presentations
- compose written informational texts
- fully develop the topic with relevant details, concepts, examples, and information
- integrate graphics or multimedia when useful about a variety of texts, topics, or events

<table>
<tr><td>

ELP Standard 5

- carry out both short and more sustained research projects to answer a question or solve a problem
- gather information from multiple print and digital sources
- use advanced search terms effectively
- synthesize information from multiple print and digital sources
- analyze and integrate information into clearly organized spoken and written texts
- include illustrations, diagrams, or other graphics as appropriate

</td><td>

ELP Standard 7

- adapt language choices and style according to purpose, task, and audience with ease in various social and academic contexts
- use a wide variety of complex general academic and content specific words and phrases
- employ both formal and more informal styles and tones effectively in spoken and written texts, as appropriate

</td></tr>
</table>

Warm-up and Review
10–15 minutes (books closed)

Write *Academic goals, Career goals,* and *Personal goals* on the board. Pair students to share one of each type of goal they have for themselves. Elicit examples and write them under the heading. Explain that students can repeat goals they mentioned earlier in the unit. Then elicit a skill or subject they can learn about to reach that goal.

Introduction
5 minutes

1. Remind students that taking initiative can help us meet our goals.

2. State the objective: *Today we will conduct and present research related to initiative.*

1 Research a resource for self-directed learning

Communicative Practice
40–45 minutes

 1. Group students but do not assign roles yet. Explain that students will work with their team to narrow their topics.

2. Read the directions aloud.

3. Set a time limit (three minutes) and have students work together to complete the task. Suggest that they use the ideas on the board if helpful.

 1. Draw students' attention to the Research Tip. Ask: *Why should you develop a set of questions before you research?* [to guide and focus the research]

2. Check comprehension of the task. Ask: *How many more questions do you need to write?* [four]

3. Have students work in their teams to write four more questions.

4. Elicit questions and write them on the board.

> **TIP**
>
> Point out that students can revise their questions as they do research.

 1. Ask: *How many questions should each team member research?* [two] *If you work in pairs, how many will each pair research?* [four]

2. Check comprehension of the task. Ask: *In addition to taking notes, what else will you do?* [identify images or video clips]

3. Have students work individually or in pairs to research their questions.

> **MULTILEVEL STRATEGIES**
>
> To adapt 1C:
>
> - **Pre-level** Provide students with a chart in which they can take their notes. Pair students to research their questions.
>
> | Who for | |
> | --- | --- |
> | How to access | |
> | Costs | |
> | Contact | |
> | When | |
> | | |
> | | |

D 1. Check comprehension of the task.
Ask: *What will you do?* [collect everyone's information, organize it, and then choose visuals and decide how to present]

2. Have students report on their research in their teams.

3. Assign roles: manager, fact checker, recorder, and IT specialist. Explain that students will work with their team to complete the task.

4. Check comprehension of the activity. *Who checks that the information is accurate?* [fact checker] *Who compiles the information from all sources?* [recorder] *Who creates the slide show with visual elements?* [IT specialist] *Who keeps the team on time and on task?* [manager]

5. Set a time limit (ten minutes) and have students work together.

> **MULTILEVEL STRATEGIES**
>
> To adapt 2B:
>
> • **On-level** Assign these students the roles of IT specialist and fact checker.
>
> • **Pre-level** Assign these students the role of recorder.
>
> • **Higher-level** Assign these students the role of manager.

2 Present your research

Presentation
40–45 minutes

A 1. Have students stay in their teams from 1D. Check comprehension of the task. Ask: *What does the outline include?* [introduction, body, and conclusion] *What should you do in the introduction?* [tell the audience the resource you chose to focus on and why] Remind students to use a hook (from Unit 5).

2. Draw students' attention to the Presentation Strategy. Read it aloud.

3. Set a time limit (five to ten minutes) and have students work as a team to outline their oral report and choose a way to connect with the audience.

> **TIP**
>
> Write three sentences on the board: *If you would like to know more about this resource, visit the website. Using this resource can help you achieve your dream of starting a small business. If you would like to use this resource, fill out an application either online or in person.* Have students work individually to identify which of the three bullet points in 2A each sentence exemplifies. Elicit answers from the class.

B 1. Have students assign roles for the presentation. Explain that students will work with their team to give a presentation on their topic.

2. Check comprehension of the activity. Ask: *Who will speak?* [everyone]

3. Set a time limit (five minutes) and have students work as a team to divide the roles and the sections of the presentation (for example, introduction, questions 1–4, questions 5–8, conclusion).

C 1. Read the bulleted items aloud.

2. Check comprehension of the activity. Ask: *Should you rehearse the presentation in exactly the way you will present to the class?* [yes]

3. Set a time limit (ten minutes) and have students rehearse their presentations in teams.

D 1. Draw a chart on the board, listing the teams in the first column. In the other columns, list the note-taking prompts or shortened forms of them: *Hook, Speaking, Transitions, Conclusion.* Check comprehension of the activity. Ask: *What will you write under* hook? [the hook the team used to get attention and whether it was effective] Remind students to just use words and phrases in the chart.

2. Set a time limit (five minutes) for each presentation, and ask each team to present in turn.

E   1. Have each team discuss their feedback for other teams.

2. Ask each team to nominate a Reporter to give feedback on the other teams' presentations.

3. Beginning with the first team to present, collect feedback from the Reporters. Write feedback in the table you drew on the board in 2D.

EXTENSION ACTIVITY

Pair Interviews

1. Pair students from different presentation groups/resources.

2. Tell students to take turns interviewing each other using their questions from 1B.

3. Have pairs discuss the similarities and differences between their resources.

Evaluation
10–15 minutes

SELF-ASSESSMENT

1. Pair students to share their self-assessments.

2. Elicit suggestions from the class for developing more confidence in each of the three assessment areas.

Unit Overview

This unit explores conflict, ways to resolve it, and its possible benefits with a range of employability skills and contextualizes synonyms and the use of modals to soften statements. By the end of this unit, you will be able to research and perform a role play to demonstrate how to resolve a conflict.

KEY OBJECTIVES

Lesson 1	Identify causes of workplace conflict
Lesson 2	Read about anger and identify ways to resolve conflict
Lesson 3	Identify and use synonyms to avoid repetition; use modals to soften statements
Lesson 4	Read about potential benefits of conflict
Lesson 5	Use the writing process to summarize an article
Lesson 6	Research and conduct a role play about conflict

UNIT FEATURES

Academic Vocabulary	*annoyance, assumption, confront, constructive, defuse, escalate, grudge, intimidating, irritating, resolve*
Employability Skills	• Analyze and draw conclusions from survey results • Translate survey results into a visual form • Offer advice on resolving conflict • Assess consequences of different approaches to conflict • Collaborate to research case studies • Write and perform a role play to exemplify how people might resolve a conflict • Use natural intonation and gestures when performing a role play
Resources	**Class Audio** CD2, Tracks 09-14 **Teacher Resource Center** Multilevel Activities 5 Unit 8 Multilevel Grammar Activities 5 Unit 8 Unit 8 Test **Oxford Picture Dictionary** Feelings, Personal Hygiene, Illnesses and Medical Conditions, Taking Care of Your Health, Soft Skills, English Composition, Internet Research

Lesson Overview

MULTILEVEL OBJECTIVES

On-level and pre-level: Identify causes of workplace conflict

Higher-level: Identify and analyze causes of workplace conflict

LANGUAGE FOCUS

Grammar: Simple present, gerunds

Vocabulary: *annoyance, resolve*

For vocabulary support, see these **Oxford Picture Dictionary** topics: Feelings, pages 42–43; Personal Hygiene, pages 108–109; Soft Skills, page 178

READINESS CONNECTION

In this lesson, students analyze and draw

conclusions from survey results.

PACING

To compress this lesson: Do 1C as a class.

To extend this lesson: Have students generate and graph data (see page 169).

And/or have students complete **Multilevel Activities 5 Unit 8, Lesson 1.**

Lesson Notes

CORRELATIONS

CCRS: RI.6.7 Integrate information presented in different media or formats (e.g., in charts, graphs, photographs, videos, or maps) as well as in words to develop a coherent understanding of a topic or issue.

SL.8.1.a. Come to discussions prepared, having read or researched material under study; explicitly draw on that preparation by referring to evidence on the topic, text, or issue to probe and reflect on ideas under discussion.

SL.8.1.c. Pose questions that connect the ideas of several speakers and respond to others' questions and comments with relevant evidence, observations, and ideas.

SL.8.1.d. Acknowledge new information expressed by others, and, when warranted, qualify or justify their own views in light of the evidence presented.

L.6.4.c. Consult reference materials (e.g., dictionaries, glossaries, thesauruses), both print and digital, to find the pronunciation of a word or determine or clarify its precise meaning or its part of speech.

SL.8.4 Present claims and findings, emphasizing salient points in a focused, coherent manner with relevant evidence, sound valid reasoning, and well-chosen details; use appropriate eye contact, adequate volume, and clear pronunciation.

L.6.4.c. Consult reference materials (e.g., dictionaries, glossaries, thesauruses), both print and digital, to find the pronunciation of a word or determine or clarify its precise meaning or its part of speech.

L.8.6 Acquire and use accurately level-appropriate general academic and domain-specific words and phrases; gather vocabulary knowledge when considering a word or phrase important to comprehension or expression.

ELPS: ELP Standard 2

- participate in conversations, extended discussions, and written exchanges about a range of substantive topics, texts, and issues
- build on the ideas of others
- express his or her own ideas clearly and persuasively
- refer to specific and relevant evidence from texts or research to support his or her ideas
- ask and answer questions that probe reasoning and claim

ELP Standard 8

using context, questioning, and consistent knowledge of English morphology,

- determine the meaning of general academic and content-specific words and phrases, figurative and connotative language, and idiomatic expressions in spoken and written texts about a variety of topics, experiences, or events

Warm-up and Review
10–15 minutes (books closed)

Tell the class about a recent situation in which you experienced conflict, what caused it, how you felt, and if/how it was resolved. Have students share recent experiences of conflict in pairs. Ask: *Should you always avoid conflict?* Elicit situations in which some conflict might be positive.

Introduction
5 minutes

1. Say: *Conflict is universal and happens everywhere. It is not always something you should avoid.*

2. State the objective: *Today we're going to identify causes of workplace conflict.*

1 Discuss causes of conflict

Presentation I
20–25 minutes

 1. Read the directions aloud. Put students in teams to brainstorm. Assign roles: manager, fact checker, recorder, and reporter.

2. Elicit categories from the class (for example, at work: with co-workers, supervisors, the public; at home: with parents, spouses, children; at school: with classmates, teacher, other students/staff; in public places: with retail/office staff, agencies, service providers, strangers). Call on reporters to share their team's answers and write them on the board under the correct category.

B 1. Direct students to look at the definition. Ask: *What is the most important word in this definition?* [*opposing*]

2. Write *conflict* on the board, and elicit related words and phrases from the whole class. Write their ideas. Point out the connection between their ideas and their responses in 1A.

> **Possible Answers**
>
> to be in conflict, to avoid conflict, to resolve conflict, unresolved conflict
> synonyms: *battle, clash, compete/competition, disagreement, discord*
> forms: *conflict* (v), *conflicted, conflicting* (adj)

Explain or elicit that *conflict* is both a noun and a verb, but the syllable stress is different in each part of speech. In the noun, the stress is on the first syllable; in the verb, it is on the second. Provide other examples of nouns and verbs that look the same but have different stress (such as *conduct, record, increase/decrease, permit, contest, protest, contrast, detail*).

Guided Practice
10–20 minutes

C 1. Direct students to look at the picture. Ask: *What do you see?* [an office/cubicle, two workers with different styles, one messy and noisy, the other neat and bothered by her co-worker]

2. Direct students to look at the chart. Ask: *What does the chart show?* [different things that annoy people about their co-workers]

3. Point out any connections between the descriptions and students' ideas in 1A.

4. Direct students to look at the first question. Check comprehension of the collocation. Ask: *What does it mean to be* in conflict? [to not agree]

5. Set a time limit (five minutes). Direct students to work with their partners to complete the activity. Have a volunteer from each pair give their responses. Check answers as a class.

> **Possible Answers**
>
> 1. They are in conflict because one worker is messy and noisy, and the other doesn't like it.
> 2. The picture shows one worker who is noisy, is gossiping, and is messy.
> 3. It may be unresolved because it is hard to confront a co-worker. The second co-worker is obviously upset but trying to avoid conflict.
> 4. They could resolve the conflict if the second co-worker asks the first to use headphones and perhaps take personal phone calls outside.

Presentation II
20–25 minutes

 1. Read the directions aloud.

2. Have students work in their teams from 1A. Explain that students will work with their team to analyze the information. Verify students' understanding of the roles: the manager keeps the team on task and on time and asks the survey questions, the recorder takes notes, the fact checker checks numbers and definitions, and the reporter reports to the class.

3. Check comprehension of the task. Ask: *What will you analyze in this activity?* [the chart in 1C]

4. Set a time limit (five minutes) for students to complete the task.

5. Call time and have the reporters from each group take turns calling out their answers.

Answers
Answers will vary.

MULTILEVEL STRATEGIES

To adapt 1E:

• **On-level** Assign these students the roles of fact checker and reporter.

• **Pre-level** Assign these students the role of recorder.

• **Higher-level** Assign these students the role of manager.

EXTENSION ACTIVITY

Class Results

1. Write the annoying behaviors from the chart in 1C on the board.

2. Read each one and have students raise their hands if they find it annoying. Tally the results.

3. Direct students to make a bar graph of the results.

Evaluation
10–15 minutes

SELF-ASSESSMENT

1. Ask students to spend some time reflecting on what they have learned.

2. Set a time limit (three minutes). Ask for volunteers to share their thoughts.

3. Make a list of their questions to refer to at the end of the unit.

<table>
<tr><td colspan="2">

Lesson Overview

</td><td>

Lesson Notes

</td></tr>
</table>

MULTILEVEL OBJECTIVES

On-level and Pre-level: Read about anger and identify ways to resolve conflict

Higher-level: Read about anger and evaluate ways to resolve conflict

LANGUAGE FOCUS

Grammar: Modals

Vocabulary: *defuse, resolve*; expressions for highlighting important information

For vocabulary support, see these **Oxford Picture Dictionary** topics: Feelings, pages 42–43; Illnesses and Medical Conditions, pages 112–119; Taking Care of Your Health, pages 116–117; Soft Skills, page 178

STRATEGY FOCUS

Listen for how a speaker uses expressions to emphasize or highlight important information.

READINESS CONNECTION

In this lesson, students discuss ways to handle difficult conversations.

PACING

To compress this lesson: Assign 1C and 1D for homework.

To extend this lesson: Have students summarize an article (see page 172); Have students research workplace policies (see page 173).

And/or have students complete **Multilevel Activities 5 Unit 8, Lesson 2.**

CORRELATIONS

CCRS: RI/RL.7.1 Cite several pieces of textual evidence to support analysis of what the text says explicitly as well as inferences drawn from the text.

RI/RL.6.4 Determine the meaning of words and phrases as they are used in a text, including figurative, connotative, and technical meanings; analyze the impact of a specific word choice on meaning and tone.

SL.8.1.a. Come to discussions prepared, having read or researched material under study; explicitly draw on that preparation by referring to evidence on the topic, text, or issue to probe and reflect on ideas under discussion.

SL.8.1.c. Pose questions that connect the ideas of several speakers and respond to others' questions and comments with relevant evidence, observations, and ideas.

SL.8.1.d. Acknowledge new information expressed by others, and, when warranted, qualify or justify their own views in light of the evidence presented.

SL.8.2 Analyze the purpose of information presented in diverse media and formats (e.g., visually, quantitatively, orally) and evaluate the motives (e.g., social, commercial, political) behind its presentation.

SL.8.3 Delineate a speaker's argument and specific claims, evaluating the soundness of the reasoning and relevance and sufficiency of the evidence and identifying when irrelevant evidence is introduced.

SL.8.4 Present claims and findings, emphasizing salient points in a focused, coherent manner with relevant evidence, sound valid reasoning, and well-chosen details; use appropriate eye contact, adequate volume, and clear pronunciation.

L.6.3/7.3.c. Choose language that expresses ideas precisely and concisely, recognizing and eliminating wordiness and redundancy.

L.8.6 Acquire and use accurately level-appropriate general academic and domain-specific words and phrases; gather vocabulary knowledge when considering a word or phrase important to comprehension or expression

---

ELPS: ELP Standard 1

use a wide range of strategies to:

- determine central ideas or themes in oral presentations and spoken and written texts

- cite specific details and evidence from texts to support the analysis

<table>
<tr><td>

ELP Standard 2

- participate in conversations, extended discussions, and written exchanges about a range of substantive topics, texts, and issues
- build on the ideas of others
- express his or her own ideas clearly and persuasively
- refer to specific and relevant evidence from texts or research to support his or her ideas
- ask and answer questions that probe reasoning and claim
- summarize the key points and evidence discussed

</td><td>

ELP Standard 8

using context, questioning, and consistent knowledge of English morphology,

- determine the meaning of general academic and content-specific words and phrases, figurative and connotative language, and idiomatic expressions in spoken and written texts about a variety of topics, experiences, or events

</td></tr>
</table>

Warm-up and Review
10–15 minutes (books closed)

Write *Anger* on the board. Tell the class about a recent situation you were in where someone was angry and what happened. Have students share their own recent experiences in pairs.

Introduction
5 minutes

1. Say: *Anger is often a result of conflict.*

2. State the objective: *Today we will read about anger and identify ways to resolve conflict.*

1 Read about how people react to anger

Presentation I
10–15 minutes

A 1. Put students in pairs.

2. Read the directions aloud.

3. Assign a time limit (three minutes). Call on a volunteer from each pair to share their ideas. On the board, write the physical reactions.

Guided Practice I
15–20 minutes

B 1. Read the directions aloud. Check comprehension. Ask: *What are you going to do?* [scan the article] *What do you do when you scan?* [read quickly to find specific information] *What words will you scan for?* [*fight or flight*]

2. Set a time limit (three minutes). Direct students to underline the sentences when they find them.

3. Elicit the answer.

Answer
Underlined in text: *This primitive reaction triggers a need to either fight or run away from a threat. Stress hormones are released throughout the body, and heart rate and blood pressure increase.*

TIP

Direct students' attention to the article and photo. Ask: *What is the title?* [*What Exactly Is Anger?*] Ask: *What do you see in the photo?* [two people who look angry] *What makes you think they are angry?*

C 1. Read the directions aloud. Check comprehension. Ask: *What does* chronic *mean?* [long-term or recurring]

2. Set a time limit (five minutes). Direct students to independently answer the question.

3. Elicit ideas from the whole class.

Possible Answer
Chronic anger triggers the fight or flight response, which produces metabolic changes that could eventually contribute to health problems.

MULTILEVEL STRATEGIES
To adapt 1C: • **Pre-level** Read the article aloud, stopping after each paragraph to check comprehension.

Communicative Practice
10–20 minutes

 1. Read the questions aloud.

2. Ask students to think about and mark their answers in the text.

3. Set a time limit (five minutes) for students to discuss their answers with a partner.

4. Invite pairs to share their responses. Check answers as a class.

Possible Answers
1. Misdirected or badly managed anger can cause problems such as poor choices, damaged relationships, or even violence. 2. It is a way to warn aggressors to stop threatening behavior. 3. It can motivate people to try to change things, to fight injustice, and to solve problems. 4. The stress hormones released would help you either fight or run away in the face of real, physical danger. However, the stress hormones that are released with this reaction as a result of chronic anger could contribute to health problems. 5. A health practitioner would probably say that it isn't good for the person's health and would probably suggest ways to manage and deal with chronic anger.

MULTILEVEL STRATEGIES
To adapt 1D: • **Pre-level** Pair or group students to work together to find the answers in the text.

Presentation II
20–25 minutes

 1. Read the directions and question aloud.

2. Call on students to share their ideas.

EXTENSION ACTIVITY
Summarizing Practice 1. Tell students to write a summary of the article using their own words. Pre-level students can write a group summary. 2. Ask two or three volunteers to write their summaries on the board. Correct or revise with the class as needed.

2 Listen and take notes

Guided Practice II
20–25 minutes

 1. Say: *Now we're going to listen to a lecture about handling a difficult person at work.*

2. Read the directions aloud.

3. Brainstorm strategies with the class. Write their ideas on the board.

Answers
Answers will vary.

 2.09 1. Play the beginning of the audio. Direct students to listen without writing.

2. Replay the audio. Ask students to answer the question.

3. Elicit the answer.

Answer
an irritable customer, a friend or family member who is always upset about something, or a co-worker who got angry with you for no apparent reason

 2.10 1. Copy the chart on the board.

2. Play the whole audio. Direct students to write notes in the chart as they listen.

Answers
Dos: stay calm respond, don't just react breathe, assess situation listen! say, "Tell me more so I can understand better." keep space maintain safety!—ask for help or leave after—talk to manager or HR **Don'ts:** say, "I understand" argue, try to convince smile or make joke touch

Communicative Practice
10–20 minutes

 **D** ◀)) **2.10** 1. Set a time limit (five minutes) for students to discuss their answers with a partner.

2. Replay the audio. Ask students to confirm or add to their notes.

3. Ask volunteers to complete the chart on the board. Point out any connections between the answers and students' ideas in 2A.

Presentation II
20–25 minutes

 **E** ◀)) **2.10** 1. Read the directions aloud.

2. Call on students to read the expressions aloud.

3. Replay the audio so students can complete the task.

4. Elicit the answers.

Answers
Above all...
I want to emphasize...
Let me repeat that...
The next point is extremely important...

 **F** 1. Read the directions aloud. Point out the expressions from 2E that students can use to agree or disagree.

2. Have students rejoin their teams from 1A with the same roles.

3. Set a time limit (ten minutes). Remind students to use the expressions to highlight important information.

4. Call on reporters to share their team's ideas with the class.

Answers
Answers will vary.

Evaluation
10–15 minutes

SELF-ASSESSMENT

1. Read each item. Have students raise their hands if they have difficulty.

2. Pair students who have difficulty with those who do not to review ways to achieve each objective.

<table>
<tr><td>

Lesson Overview

MULTILEVEL OBJECTIVES

On-level and Higher-level: Identify and use synonyms to avoid repetition; use modals to soften statements

Pre-level: Learn synonyms to avoid repetition; recognize the use of modals to soften statements

LANGUAGE FOCUS

Grammar: Use modals to soften language

Vocabulary: *defuse, escalate, irritating, resolve; anxious, convince, essential, furious, heated, recommend*

For vocabulary support, see this **Oxford Picture Dictionary** topic: Feelings, pages 42–43

STRATEGY FOCUS

Use modals to soften statements.

READINESS CONNECTION

In this lesson, students work with a partner to offer advice on resolving conflict.

PACING

To compress this lesson: Assign 1B and/or 2C for homework.

To extend this lesson: Have students use synonyms to avoid repetition in their writing (see page 175); Have students do a team challenge to practice using modals (see page 177).

And/or have students complete **Multilevel Activities 5 Unit 8, Lesson 3.**

</td><td>

Lesson Notes

</td></tr>
</table>

CORRELATIONS

CCRS: SL.8.1.a. Come to discussions prepared, having read or researched material under study; explicitly draw on that preparation by referring to evidence on the topic, text, or issue to probe and reflect on ideas under discussion.

SL.8.1.c. Pose questions that connect the ideas of several speakers and respond to others' questions and comments with relevant evidence, observations, and ideas.

SL.8.1.d. Acknowledge new information expressed by others, and, when warranted, qualify or justify their own views in light of the evidence presented.

L.6.3/7.3.c. Choose language that expresses ideas precisely and concisely, recognizing and eliminating wordiness and redundancy.

L.6.4.c. Consult reference materials (e.g., dictionaries, glossaries, thesauruses), both print and digital, to find the pronunciation of a word or determine or clarify its precise meaning or its part of speech.

L.8.6 Acquire and use accurately level-appropriate general academic and domain-specific words and phrases; gather vocabulary knowledge when considering a word or phrase important to comprehension or expression.

ELPS: ELP Standard 2

- participate in conversations, extended discussions, and written exchanges about a range of substantive topics, texts, and issues
- build on the ideas of others
- express his or her own ideas clearly and persuasively

ELP Standard 8

using context, questioning, and consistent knowledge of English morphology,

- determine the meaning of general academic and content-specific words and phrases, figurative and connotative language, and idiomatic expressions in spoken and written texts about a variety of topics, experiences, or events

ELP Standard 10

- produce and expand simple, compound, and complex sentences

Warm-up and Review
10–15 minutes (books closed)

Ask: *In your culture, is it acceptable to show that you are angry?* Pair students to share their ideas. Elicit ideas from the class.

Introduction
5 minutes

1. Say: *It's important to avoid repeating the same words in writing or speaking. Using synonyms helps with this.*

2. State the objective: *Today we are going to identify and use synonyms to avoid repetition and use modals to soften statements.*

1 Vocabulary: Synonyms

Presentation and Guided Practice I
20–25 minutes

 1. Read the directions aloud. Say each word and have students repeat.

2. Call on students to read the sentences aloud.

3. Set a time limit (three minutes). Direct students to work individually to complete the task.

4. Go over the answers with the class.

Answers	
1. essential	3. increase
2. difficult, heated	4. de-escalate

MULTILEVEL STRATEGIES

To adapt 1A:
- **Pre-level** Allow students to use dictionaries.

Communicative Practice
15–20 minutes

 1. Read the directions aloud.

2. Direct students' attention to the Language Note.

3. Set a time limit (three minutes). Direct students to work in pairs to complete the task.

4. Call on students to provide synonyms.

Possible Answers
anxious: worried, apprehensive
convince: persuade, influence
furious: irate, enraged
irritate: annoy, bother
recommend: suggest, propose

TIP

Remind students that sometimes words are near synonyms but may vary in connotation or intensity. Write *furious* on the board. Elicit as many words with a similar meaning as you can (for example, *mad, angry, enraged, irate, livid, fuming*). Ask students to work in pairs to rank them by intensity. Elicit their ideas. If students disagree, have them use reference tools to refine their answers.

 1. Read the directions and the questions aloud.

2. Set a time limit (five minutes). Direct students to work individually to answer the questions.

MULTILEVEL STRATEGIES

To adapt 1C:
- **Pre-level** Work with students in a group to answer the questions.

D 1. Read the directions aloud. Review the expressions from Lesson 2.

2. Group students and check comprehension of the task. Ask: *How many questions will you discuss?* [one] *Who should talk?* [everyone]

3. Set a time limit (five minutes) for students to complete the activity in teams.

4. Call on reporters to tell the class about their teams' discussion. Call on someone from another team to follow up using an expression from Lesson 2.

EXTENSION ACTIVITY
Writing Practice

1. Tell students to choose one of the questions to answer in paragraph form.

2. Have students post their paragraphs on a discussion board.

2 Grammar: Using modals to soften statements

Presentation and Guided Practice II
20–25 minutes

A 1. Demonstrate how to read the chart. Read each sentence and have students repeat.

2. Check comprehension of the chart. Ask: *What structure do you see in the first column?* [imperatives] *What is the implied subject?* [*you*] *Is that the same subject in the middle column?* [yes] *Which sounds more polite of the two?* [the middle column] *Why?* [It is softer, not a command, uses modals.] Direct students' attention to the right column. Ask: *What is the subject?* [*I*] *Why does the speaker use* I? Point out or elicit that the implied condition is *If I were you / if I were in that situation, I would stop and take a few breaths.*

3. Have students complete the Language Connection paragraph about using modals to soften statements. Go over the answers with the class.

> **Answers**
>
> could, might, would, wouldn't
> You'd be better off not... , It'd be better if you (didn't)...

> **MULTILEVEL STRATEGIES**
>
> To adapt 2A:
> - **On-level** Have students work independently.
> - **Pre-level** Have higher-level classmates assist these students.
> - **Higher-level** Have these students work with pre-level classmates.

Guided Practice III
20–25 minutes

B 1. Read the directions aloud.

2. Ask students to work individually to complete the task and then compare answers with a partner.

3. Ask volunteers to write sentences on the board. Correct as necessary.

> **Possible Answer**
>
> First, remember to stay calm. It's natural to react. It'd be better if you didn't react immediately. I would take a few moments to assess the situation. Figure out the best way to respond. Listen to what the person says and focus on what they say. Don't just think about what you want to say next. I wouldn't use humor or make jokes because it may make the person angrier. If you don't feel safe, you need to act on that. Leave the situation or get help.

> **TIP**
>
> Write the first sentence on the board. Elicit other ways to say the same thing with softer language and write them on the board. Then ask students which version they think is best and why.

> **MULTILEVEL STRATEGIES**
>
> To adapt 2A:
> - **On-level** Have students work independently.
> - **Pre-level** Group pre-level students to complete the task together.
> - **Higher-level** Direct students to rewrite the paragraph in two different ways.

C 1. Read the directions aloud.

2. Set a time limit (five minutes). Direct students to work individually to write their sentences.

Answers
Answers will vary.

MULTILEVEL STRATEGIES

To adapt 2C:

• **Pre-level** Provide students with three sentences to rewrite.

• **Higher-level** Direct students to write six pairs of sentences.

• **On-level** Direct students to complete the activity as directed.

EXTENSION ACTIVITY

Team Challenge

1. Divide the class into two teams.

2. Have teams line up facing each other. Team members take turns making a recommendation using direct language. The person opposite them on the other team responds using modals to soften the statements. Each correct rephrasing earns the team a point.

3. Tally the points on the board. Award an extra point if the student also uses a synonym when rephrasing.

D 1. Set a time limit (five minutes) for students to share their sentences in 2C with a partner.

2. Ask volunteers to write sentences on the board.

3. If students disagree, ask them to look at the grammar charts and explain their answers.

Evaluation
10–15 minutes

SELF-ASSESSMENT

1. Have students complete the self-assessment.

2. Provide additional practice as needed.

Lesson Overview

MULTILEVEL OBJECTIVES

On-level and Pre-level: Read about potential benefits of conflict

Higher-level: Read about and analyze potential benefits of conflict

LANGUAGE FOCUS

Grammar: Modals

Vocabulary: *assumption, confront, constructive, grudge, intimidating, resolve*; synonyms of *imagine, awkward, disagreement, productive, possibilities, face up to*

For vocabulary support, see these **Oxford Picture Dictionary** topics: Feelings, pages 42–43; Taking Care of Your Health, pages 116–117; Soft Skills, page 178

STRATEGY FOCUS

Read for words and phrases that introduce opposing viewpoints.

READINESS CONNECTION

In this lesson, students assess consequences of different approaches to conflict.

PACING

To compress this lesson: Assign 2B and/or 2C for homework.

To extend this lesson: Have students practice giving feedback and response (see page 180); Have students role-play personal responses to situations involving conflict (see page 182).

And/or have students complete **Multilevel Activities 5 Unit 8, Lesson 4.**

Lesson Notes

CORRELATIONS

CCRS: RI/RL.7.1 Cite several pieces of textual evidence to support analysis of what the text says explicitly as well as inferences drawn from the text.

RI/RL.6.4 Determine the meaning of words and phrases as they are used in a text, including figurative, connotative, and technical meanings; analyze the impact of a specific word choice on meaning and tone.

RI.6.7 Integrate information presented in different media or formats (e.g., in charts, graphs, photographs, videos, or maps) as well as in words to develop a coherent understanding of a topic or issue.

SL.8.1.a. Come to discussions prepared, having read or researched material under study; explicitly draw on that preparation by referring to evidence on the topic, text, or issue to probe and reflect on ideas under discussion.

SL.8.1.c. Pose questions that connect the ideas of several speakers and respond to others' questions and comments with relevant evidence, observations, and ideas.

SL.8.1.d. Acknowledge new information expressed by others, and, when warranted, qualify or justify their own views in light of the evidence presented.

SL.8.4 Present claims and findings, emphasizing salient points in a focused, coherent manner with relevant evidence, sound valid reasoning, and well-chosen details; use appropriate eye contact, adequate volume, and clear pronunciation.

L.8.6 Acquire and use accurately level-appropriate general academic and domain-specific words and phrases; gather vocabulary knowledge when considering a word or phrase important to comprehension or expression.

ELPS: ELP Standard 1

use a wide range of strategies to:

• determine central ideas or themes in oral presentations and spoken and written texts

• cite specific details and evidence from texts to support the analysis

<table>
<tr><td>

ELP Standard 2

- participate in conversations, extended discussions, and written exchanges about a range of substantive topics, texts, and issues
- build on the ideas of others
- express his or her own ideas clearly and persuasively
- refer to specific and relevant evidence from texts or research to support his or her ideas
- ask and answer questions that probe reasoning and claims

ELP Standard 6

- analyze and evaluate the reasoning in persuasive spoken and written texts
- determine whether the evidence is sufficient to support the claim
- cite specific textual evidence to thoroughly support the analysis

</td><td>

ELP Standard 7

- adapt language choices and style according to purpose, task, and audience with ease in various social and academic contexts
- use a wide variety of complex general academic and content specific words and phrases
- employ both formal and more informal styles and tones effectively in spoken and written texts, as appropriate

ELP Standard 8

using context, questioning, and consistent knowledge of English morphology,

- determine the meaning of general academic and content-specific words and phrases, figurative and connotative language, and idiomatic expressions in spoken and written texts about a variety of topics, experiences, or events

</td></tr>
</table>

Warm-up and Review
10–15 minutes (books closed)

Brainstorm with the class a list of popular sports. Ask: *How is a sports competition similar to or different from a conflict?* Tell students to answer the question first thinking about sports in general and then identifying sports that may be more similar to a conflict. Have students share their ideas in pairs. Call on students to share their ideas with the class.

Introduction
5 minutes

1. Say: *Sports have some things in common with conflict. There are many benefits to playing sports.*

2. State the objective: *Today we will read about potential benefits of conflict.*

1 Get ready to read

Presentation I
20–25 minutes

 2.11 1. Say: *Now we're going to listen to a conversation.*

2. Play the audio. Direct students to answer the question.

Possible Answer
They're discussing Joan's behavior, or the way Joan interrupts, in meetings.

 2.11 1. Say the expressions and have students repeat. Point out that the expressions follow two patterns: *I (can) + verb + question word / noun clause* and *That's ______.*

2. Replay the audio. Ask students to check the expressions.

3. Check answers as a class.

Answers
I can see how that could be upsetting. That's fair.

> **TIP**
>
> Remind students about the Language Note in Lesson 3 on page 88. Suggest that students rank the expressions in order of formality. Write *Formal* on one side of the board and *Informal* on the other. Pair students to rank the expressions. Elicit their ideas and write them on the board in the correct place.

 1. Read the directions aloud.

2. Group students and assign roles: manager, fact checker, recorder, and reporter. Check comprehension of tasks: *Who keeps the team on task and on time?* [manager] *Who takes notes?* [recorder] *Who looks up information or unfamiliar words?* [fact checker] *Who reports to the class?* [reporter] Students will work in these teams for 1C, 2E, and 3C.

3. Set a time limit (five minutes) and have students work together to complete the task.

4. Call time and have the reporters from each group take turns calling out their ideas.

Answers
Answers will vary.

MULTILEVEL STRATEGIES

To adapt 1C:

• **On-level** Assign these students the roles of recorder and manager.

• **Pre-level** Assign these students the role of reporter.

• **Higher-level** Assign these students the role of fact checker.

EXTENSION ACTIVITY

Practice Responses

1. Model the activity. Draw a person's head on the board. Demonstrate how to tell the "person" a problem you have with his or her behavior in one sentence. Elicit a response from the list in 1B from the class.

2. Put students in pairs to take turns giving feedback on an imaginary problem and responding with one of the expressions.

3. Set a time limit (two minutes). Tell students to practice as many times as they can.

2 Preview and read

Guided Practice I
20–25 minutes

A 1. Read the directions aloud. Ask: *What words or phrases are you scanning for?* [*unproductive* and *productive conflict*]

2. Have students answer the question individually, and then check answers as a class.

Answers
Underlined in text: *With unproductive conflict, there are frequent disagreements and arguments where both parties feel frustrated and upset; productive conflict allows all parties to express differing ideas and opinions so that everyone feels heard and respected, with the goal of reaching a mutually acceptable solution*

TIP

Ask: *What is the title?* [*Conflict: It's Not Necessarily Bad*] *Do you think this is a good title? Why or why not?* Elicit that the title acknowledges the common idea that conflict is always negative. Tell students to look at the photo. Ask: *What do you see?* [two co-workers] *Do you think they are in agreement or disagreement?* Elicit answers and explanations.

B Ask students to read the article silently and answer the question and then compare answers with a partner. Check the answer with the class.

Answer
The author recommends managing and addressing conflict.

MULTILEVEL STRATEGIES

To adapt 2B:

• **Pre-level** Work with pre-level students to read the article aloud. Stop after each paragraph and check comprehension.

• **On-level** Have students complete the activity as directed.

• **Higher-level** Direct students to underline the main idea and/or write the main idea of the article in a statement using their own words.

Presentation II
20–25 minutes

C 1. Read the directions aloud. Call on students to read the questions aloud.

2. Set a time limit (five minutes) and have students work individually to complete the task.

3. Call time. Have students compare answers in pairs.

4. Go over the answers as a class. Call on students to cite the text to explain their answers.

MULTILEVEL STRATEGIES

To adapt 2B:

• **Pre-level and higher-level** Pair a pre-level student with a higher-level student to answer the questions. Tell higher-level students to help pre-level students find the place in the text that answers each question.

• **On-level** Have students complete the activity individually.

WORD STUDY

D 1. Read the directions and the prompts aloud.

2. Write the chart on the board.

3. Set a time limit (five minutes). Have students work in pairs to choose a column, or assign columns to pairs to make sure there is a balance. Then have students complete the task.

4. Have each pair join another pair to share synonyms and complete the chart.

5. Ask volunteers to write words in the chart.

6. Elicit synonyms. Then elicit discussion of differences in meaning, intensity, or formality.

Answers	
A	B
1. imagine—<u>envision</u> 2. awkward—<u>uncomfortable</u> 3. disagreements—<u>arguments</u>	1. productive—<u>constructive</u> 2. possibilities—<u>opportunities</u> 3. face up to—<u>confront, approach, deal with, address</u>

TIP

On the board, draw two continua, one with the headings *Less intense* and *More intense* and one with the headings *Informal* and *Formal*. With each pair of synonyms, elicit from students where they would position the words on the lines. For example, *imagine* is more common than *envision,* so it sounds less formal. Write it closer to the left and *envision* closer to the right. However, neither is particularly intense, so both might be more in the middle of the second continuum. Point out that phrasal verbs such as *face up to* are usually less formal than their single-word counterparts.

E 1. Read the directions aloud.

2. Have students work with their teams from 1C. Assign roles: manager (keeps team on time and on task), IT specialist (checks facts), recorder (takes notes), and reporter (reports to the class).

3. Set a time limit (five minutes). Have students discuss the question in their teams.

4. Call time. Ask reporters from each team to share their ideas.

3 Build on it

Presentation I
20–25 minutes

A 1. Direct students' attention to the chart. Check comprehension. Ask: *What is the survey about?* [handling difficult conversations] *How many behaviors does the survey ask about?* [six] *Are these behaviors positive or negative responses to conflict?* [positive/constructive]

2. Read the directions aloud.

3. Set a time limit (five minutes). Have students work in pairs to complete the activity.

4. Call on students to share their ideas with the class.

Possible Answers
People are more likely to prepare for the conversation, acknowledge that there are multiple ways to view the situation, and be direct and concise than they are to do the other behaviors.

 1. Have students rejoin their teams from 1C/1E with the same roles. The IT specialist checks numbers and creates bar charts.

2. Read the directions and prompts aloud.

3. Set a time limit (ten minutes). Have students work in teams to complete the task.

4. Call on each team's reporter to share their team's ideas while the IT specialist draws the chart on the board.

PROBLEM SOLVING

1. Ask students to stay in their teams but allow them to change roles.

2. Read the directions and prompt aloud.

3. Set a time limit (ten minutes) and have students work together to discuss advice and create a role play.

4. Call time. Ask teams to perform their role-plays for the class.

EXTENSION ACTIVITY
Personalized Role Play
1. Pair students to create role plays for a challenging situation they know about.
2. Set a time limit (five minutes). Remind pairs to use what they have learned from the article.
3. Call on volunteers to role-play for the class.

Evaluation
10–15 minutes

SELF-ASSESSMENT

1. Direct students to complete the self-assessment individually.

2. Have students choose the one objective they have the most difficulty with.

3. Group students according to their weakest skill. Provide each group with suggestions or feedback.

Lesson Overview

Lesson Notes

MULTILEVEL OBJECTIVES

On-level: Use the writing process to summarize an article
Pre-level: Work with others to summarize an article
Higher-level: Summarize an article and suggest ways to apply it

LANGUAGE FOCUS

Grammar: Use modals to soften statements
Vocabulary: Synonyms for advantages and disadvantages
For vocabulary support, see this **Oxford Picture Dictionary** topic: English Composition, pages 202–203

STRATEGY FOCUS

Use synonyms to avoid repetition.

PACING

To compress this lesson: Assign 1A for homework.
To extend this lesson: Have students write a paragraph about the best ways to deal with conflict (see page 185).
And/or have students complete **Multilevel Activities 5 Unit 8, Lesson 5.**

CORRELATIONS

CCRS: W/WHST.6-8.2.a. Introduce a topic clearly, previewing what is to follow; organize ideas, concepts, and information, using strategies such as definition, classification, comparison /contrast, and cause/effect; include formatting (e.g., headings), graphics (e.g., charts, tables), and multimedia when useful to aiding comprehension.

W/WHST.6-8.2.b. Develop the topic with relevant facts, definitions, concrete details, quotations, or other information and examples.

W/WHST.6-8.2.c. Use appropriate transitions to create cohesion and clarify the relationships among ideas and concepts.

W/WHST.6-8.2.d. Use precise language and domain-specific vocabulary to inform about or explain the topic.

W/WHST.6-8.2.f. Provide a concluding statement or section that follows from and supports the information or explanation presented.

W/WHST.6-8.4 Produce clear and coherent writing in which the development and organization and style are appropriate to task, purpose, and audience.

W/WHST.6-8.5 With some guidance and support from peers and others, develop and strengthen writing as needed by planning, revising, editing, rewriting, or trying a new approach, focusing on how well purpose and audience have been addressed.

L.6.3/7.3.c. Choose language that expresses ideas precisely and concisely, recognizing and eliminating wordiness and redundancy.

L.8.6 Acquire and use accurately level-appropriate general academic and domain-specific words and phrases; gather vocabulary knowledge when considering a word or phrase important to comprehension or expression.

ELPS: ELP Standard 7

- adapt language choices and style according to purpose, task, and audience with ease in various social and academic contexts
- use a wide variety of complex general academic and content specific words and phrases
- employ both formal and more informal styles and tones effectively in spoken and written texts, as appropriate

ELP Standard 9

- recount a complex and detailed sequence of events or steps in a process, with an effective sequential or chronological order
- introduce and effectively develop an informational topic with facts, details, and evidence
- use complex and varied transitions to link the major sections of speech and text and to clarify relationships among events and ideas
- provide a concluding section or statement

ELP Standard 10

- produce and expand simple, compound, and complex sentences

Warm-up and Review
10–15 minutes (books closed)

Look for articles in the news about various kinds of conflict (for example, business deals, war/peace agreements, protests/strikes, candidates for election, city council debates) Pair or group students. Assign each an article or topic. Tell students to brainstorm possible constructive responses to each conflict and possible positive outcomes. Call on students to share their ideas with the class.

Introduction
5 minutes

State the objective: *Today we will use the writing process to summarize an article.*

1 Write a summary

Presentation I
20–25 minutes

 1. Have students revisit the article on pages 90–91. Check comprehension. Ask: *What is the article about? What are the most important ideas?*

2. Elicit responses and jot them on the board.

Guided Practice I
15–20 minutes

B 1. Direct students to look at the chart. Ask about organization: *What do you see in the top row?* [things that are difficult and possible benefits of conflict] *How many benefits will you write in the chart?* [three]

2. Check comprehension of the activity. Ask: *Do you need to write complete sentences in the chart?* [no]

3. Have students work individually to complete their charts.

Answers	
"Conflict: It's Not Necessarily Bad"	
Difficult b/c: • uncertainty / uncomfortable • worst possible reactions • only "win" or "lose" • takes time & effort • intimidating	Possible benefits • can ↑ trust • stronger relationships • help us understand selves better

Answers (Continued)

Unproductive vs. productive conflict
Unproductive—frequent disagreements, arguments, feel upset and frustrated
Productive—allows all parties to express different ideas and opinions, so feel heard and respected. Goal = mutually acceptable outcome

Expert suggestions:
• takes practice
• have open mind
• possible to resolve in a way that both sides feel that they win

C 1. Read the directions aloud.

2. Have students work individually to write their statements. Encourage students to use the sentence frame. Then ask students to compare statements in pairs.

> **TIP**
>
> Remind students that the main idea can often be found in the introduction and in the conclusion. Suggest students reread those paragraphs and find ideas that are repeated in both.

D 1. Read the directions aloud.

2. Have students work individually to write their conclusions.

> **TIP**
>
> Suggest that students practice the strategy of using synonyms to write the conclusion in their own words.

E 1. Read the directions aloud. Check comprehension. Ask: *What will you include in your summary?* [introduction, notes from the chart, conclusion]

2. Draw students' attention to the Writer's Note. Ask: *What are some synonyms for* advantages? [*benefit, positive aspect of, upside, argument in favor of*] *Which is the least formal?* [*upside*]

3. Have students work individually to write their summaries.

> **MULTILEVEL STRATEGIES**
>
> To adapt 1E:
>
> • **On-level** Have students write summaries as directed.
>
> • **Pre-level** Work with students in a group to write the summary together.
>
> • **Higher-level** Have students write the summary in two different ways using synonyms.

2 Get feedback and revise

Guided Practice II
10–15 minutes

A Direct students to check their writing using the editing checklist. Tell them to read each item in the list and check their papers before moving on to the next item. Explain that students should not edit their writing at this stage. They should just use the checklist to check their work and mark any areas they want to revise.

Communicative Practice
10–15 minutes

B 1. Read the directions aloud. Emphasize to students that they are responding to their partners' work, not correcting it.

2. Direct students to exchange papers with a partner and follow the instructions.

C Allow students time to edit and revise their writing using the editing checklist and their partner's feedback. If necessary, students could complete this task as homework.

MULTILEVEL STRATEGIES

To adapt 2C:

• **Mixed-ability** Pair pre-level students with on- and higher-level students. Have all students point out ideas that are not clear. Instruct on- and higher-level partners to give feedback on spelling and grammar if helpful.

EXTENSION ACTIVITY

Paragraph Practice

1. Have students write a paragraph of at least five sentences explaining the best ways to deal with conflict.

2. Pair students to exchange and read their paragraphs.

Evaluation
10–15 minutes

SELF-ASSESSMENT

1. Call on students to read their completed sentences aloud.

2. Use the responses to the second statement to plan follow-up activities.

Lesson Overview

MULTILEVEL OBJECTIVES

On-level: Students research and conduct a role play about conflict

Pre-level: Students help research and conduct a role play about conflict

Higher-level: Students research, then edit and conduct a role play about conflict

LANGUAGE FOCUS

Grammar: Modals to soften statements

Vocabulary: *resolve*, other words related to conflict

For vocabulary support, see this **Oxford Picture Dictionary** topic: Internet Research, pages 212–213

STRATEGY FOCUS

Use natural speech and gestures.

READINESS CONNECTION

In this lesson, students write and perform a role play to exemplify how people might resolve a conflict.

PACING

To compress this lesson: Assign 1B for homework. Alternatively, assign students topics in 1A.

To extend this lesson: Have students debrief in pairs on ideas about dealing with conflict (see page 188). And/or have students complete **Multilevel Activities 5 Unit 8, Lesson 6.**

Lesson Notes

CORRELATIONS

CCRS: W.7.7 Conduct short research projects to answer a question, drawing on several sources and generating additional related, focused questions for further research and investigation.

W.7.8 Gather relevant information from multiple print and digital sources, using search terms effectively; assess the credibility and accuracy of each source; and quote or paraphrase the data and conclusions of others while avoiding plagiarism and following a standard format for citation.

SL.8.4 Present claims and findings, emphasizing salient points in a focused, coherent manner with relevant evidence, sound valid reasoning, and well-chosen details; use appropriate eye contact, adequate volume, and clear pronunciation.

SL.8.6 Adapt speech to a variety of contexts and tasks, demonstrating command of formal English when indicated or appropriate.

L.6.3/7.3.b. Maintain consistency in style and tone.

L.6.3/7.3.c. Choose language that expresses ideas precisely and concisely, recognizing and eliminating wordiness and redundancy.

L.8.6 Acquire and use accurately level-appropriate general academic and domain-specific words and phrases; gather vocabulary knowledge when considering a word or phrase important to comprehension or expression.

ELPS: ELP Standard 2

- participate in conversations, extended discussions, and written exchanges about a range of substantive topics, texts, and issues
- build on the ideas of others
- express his or her own ideas clearly and persuasively
- summarize the key points and evidence discussed

ELP Standard 3

- deliver oral presentations
- compose written informational texts
- fully develop the topic with relevant details, concepts, examples, and information
- integrate graphics or multimedia when useful about a variety of texts, topics, or events

<table>
<tr><td>

ELP Standard 5

- carry out both short and more sustained research projects to answer a question or solve a problem
- gather information from multiple print and digital sources
- use advanced search terms effectively
- synthesize information from multiple print and digital sources
- analyze and integrate information into clearly organized spoken and written texts
- include illustrations, diagrams, or other graphics as appropriate
- cite sources appropriately

</td><td>

ELP Standard 7

- adapt language choices and style according to purpose, task, and audience with ease in various social and academic contexts
- use a wide variety of complex general academic and content specific words and phrases
- employ both formal and more informal styles and tones effectively in spoken and written texts, as appropriate

</td></tr>
</table>

Warm-up and Review
10–15 minutes (books closed)

Brainstorm a list of movies, TV programs, or books about a conflict. Ask students to describe the conflict briefly.

Introduction
5 minutes

1. Say: *Conflict is such a big part of life that it drives the stories of most movies and books.*

2. State the objective: *Today we will research and conduct a role play about conflict.*

1 Research a conflict

Communicative Practice
40–45 minutes

A 1. Group students but do not assign roles yet. Explain that students will work with their team to narrow the topic.

2. Read the directions aloud.

3. Brainstorm a list of conflicts. Remind students of the conflicts in the warm-up for Lesson 5.

4. Direct students' attention to the Research Tip. Ask: *What is a case study?* [a specific example of something used to illustrate an idea]

5. Set a time limit (ten minutes) and have students work together to complete the task.

B 1. Read the directions aloud. Write: *Situation, Parties involved, Setting, Attempts at resolution/ outcome* on the board.

2. Tell teams to divide the aspects so that each member has one aspect to research.

3. Check comprehension of the task. Ask: *Should you copy information exactly?* [no, use own words] *What do you need to include?* [sources]

4. Set a time limit or assign research as an out-of-class task.

C 1. Have students share their research in their teams.

2. Read the directions and prompts.

3. Set a time limit (ten minutes) and have students work together to follow the steps.

2 Present the conflict and perform your role play

Presentation
40–45 minutes

A 1. Have students stay in their teams. Read the directions and steps.

2. Ask: *What do you do in the introduction?* [give a summary of the conflict and explain the roles of the parties involved] *When do the actors perform the role play?* [in the body] *What are you writing down?* [the conversation] *What grammar should you include?* [modals] *What kinds of expressions should you use in the conversation?* [for active listening and to acknowledge concerns] *When do you show how the conflict is resolved?* [in the conclusion]

3. Set a time limit (10 to 15 minutes) and have students work as a team to write the introduction, conversation, and conclusion.

B 🔊 **2.12** 🔊 **2.13** 🔊 **2.14** 1. Read the directions aloud.

2. Check comprehension of the activity. Ask: *Who will speak?* [everyone]

3. Draw students' attention to the Presentation Strategy. Read the sentences, and then play the audio.

4. Check comprehension. Ask: *How can you emphasize words?* [by saying them louder and slower] *Where should you pause?* [between thought groups] *What does it mean to enunciate?* [pronounce each word clearly]

5. Set a time limit (ten minutes) and have students work as a team to divide the roles— for example, director (keeps the team on task and on time, gives the conclusion), writer (writes down the role play the group creates, gives the introduction), and actors 1 and 2 (perform role play, make sure to include appropriate expressions and modals).

MULTILEVEL STRATEGIES

To adapt 2B:

• **On-level** Assign these students the roles of writer and actor.

• **Pre-level** Assign these students the role of actor.

• **Higher-level** Assign these students the role of director.

C 1. Read the directions and list aloud.

2. Check comprehension of the activity. Ask: *Should you rehearse the presentation exactly the way you will present it to the class?* [yes]

3. Set a time limit (ten minutes) and have students rehearse their presentations in teams.

D 1. Draw a chart on the board, listing the teams in the first column. In the other columns, list the note-taking prompts or shortened forms of them: *Introduction/narration, Actors' speech and gestures, Strengths, Advice.* Check comprehension of the activity. Ask: *What will you write under introduction/narration?* [whether those things were clear] Remind students to just use words and phrases in the chart.

2. Set a time limit (five minutes) for each presentation, and ask each team to present in turn.

E 1. Have each team discuss their feedback for the other teams.

2. Ask each team to nominate a reporter to give feedback on the other teams' presentations.

3. Beginning with the first team to present, collect feedback from the reporters. Write feedback in the table you drew on the board in 2D.

EXTENSION ACTIVITY

Pair Debrief

1. Pair students from different teams.

2. Have pairs talk about the ways that they used the ideas about dealing with conflict in the unit.

3. Call on students to share their ideas.

Evaluation
10–15 minutes

SELF-ASSESSMENT

1. Pair students to share their self-assessments.

2. Elicit suggestions from the class for developing more confidence in each of the three assessment areas.

Unit Overview

This unit explores leadership, ways to improve leadership skills, and the styles of famous leaders with a range of employability skills and contextualizes abstract nouns and unreal conditionals. By the end of this unit, you will be able to research and report on the life and work of an important leader.

KEY OBJECTIVES

Lesson 1	Identify and discuss leadership traits
Lesson 2	Read, listen, and take notes on ways to improve leadership skills
Lesson 3	Use suffixes to form abstract nouns to talk about leadership; use unreal conditionals to describe imaginary situations requiring leadership skills
Lesson 4	Read about leadership styles and discuss the styles of famous leaders
Lesson 5	Use the writing process to summarize an article
Lesson 6	Conduct and present research related to leadership

UNIT FEATURES

Academic Vocabulary	*apprenticeship, charismatic, competence, decisiveness, exclusive, judgment, overestimate, self-awareness, sensitivity, validate*
Employability Skills	• Relate leadership styles to leaders not mentioned in the text • Evaluate leadership traits and styles • Discuss how a store manager could become a more effective leader • Come to an informal consensus when planning a research project • Work in a team to assess primary and secondary sources for a group presentation • Develop a group presentation using effective visuals • Refer to visuals effectively while delivering a group presentation

Resources	**Class Audio** CD2, Tracks 15-20
	Teacher Resource Center
	    Multilevel Activities 5 Unit 9
	    Multilevel Grammar Activities 5 Unit 9
	    Unit 9 Test
	Oxford Picture Dictionary Feelings, Soft Skills, U.S. History, World History, English Composition, and Internet Research

Lesson Overview

MULTILEVEL OBJECTIVES

On-level and pre-level: Identify and discuss leadership traits

Higher-level: Identify, discuss, and analyze leadership traits

LANGUAGE FOCUS

Grammar: Simple present

Vocabulary: *competence*, *decisiveness*, *judgment*, synonyms and word forms related to leadership

For vocabulary support, see this **Oxford Picture Dictionary** topic: Soft Skills, page 178

READINESS CONNECTION

In this lesson, students identify and discuss leadership traits.

PACING

To compress this lesson: Do 1D as a class.

To extend this lesson: Have students interview each other in pairs (see page 192).

And/or have students complete **Multilevel Activities 5 Unit 9, Lesson 1**.

Lesson Notes

CORRELATIONS

CCRS: RI.6.7 Integrate information presented in different media or formats (e.g., in charts, graphs, photographs, videos, or maps) as well as in words to develop a coherent understanding of a topic or issue.

SL.8.1.a. Come to discussions prepared, having read or researched material under study; explicitly draw on that preparation by referring to evidence on the topic, text, or issue to probe and reflect on ideas under discussion.

SL.8.1.c. Pose questions that connect the ideas of several speakers and respond to others' questions and comments with relevant evidence, observations, and ideas.

SL.8.1.d. Acknowledge new information expressed by others, and, when warranted, qualify or justify their own views in light of the evidence presented.

L.6.4.c. Consult reference materials (e.g., dictionaries, glossaries, thesauruses), both print and digital, to find the pronunciation of a word or determine or clarify its precise meaning or its part of speech.

SL.8.4 Present claims and findings, emphasizing salient points in a focused, coherent manner with relevant evidence, sound valid reasoning, and well-chosen details; use appropriate eye contact, adequate volume, and clear pronunciation.

L.6.4.c. Consult reference materials (e.g., dictionaries, glossaries, thesauruses), both print and digital, to find the pronunciation of a word or determine or clarify its precise meaning or its part of speech.

L.8.6 Acquire and use accurately level-appropriate general academic and domain-specific words and phrases; gather vocabulary knowledge when considering a word or phrase important to comprehension or expression.

ELPS: ELP Standard 2

- participate in conversations, extended discussions, and written exchanges about a range of substantive topics, texts, and issues
- build on the ideas of others
- express his or her own ideas clearly and persuasively
- refer to specific and relevant evidence from texts or research to support his or her ideas
- ask and answer questions that probe reasoning and claim

ELP Standard 8

using context, questioning, and consistent knowledge of English morphology,

- determine the meaning of general academic and content-specific words and phrases, figurative and connotative language, and idiomatic expressions in spoken and written texts about a variety of topics, experiences, or events

Warm-up and Review
10–15 minutes (books closed)

Tell the class about people who lead in different aspects of your life (for example, a leader at your school). Pair students to tell each other about people who lead in their lives. Call on students to tell the class about their partners' examples.

Introduction
5 minutes

1. Say: *People lead in different ways and in different places in our lives.*

2. State the objective: *Today we're going to identify and discuss leadership traits.*

1 Discuss leadership traits

Presentation I
20–25 minutes

A 1. Read the directions aloud. Put students in teams to brainstorm. Assign roles: manager, fact checker, recorder, and reporter.

2. Elicit categories from the class (for example, political, business, entertainment, social, environmental). Call on reporters to share their team's answers and write them on the board under the correct category.

B 1. Direct students to look at the definition. Ask: *What is the suffix?* [*-ship*] *What part of speech does* -ship *usually indicate?* [a noun]

2. Write *leadership* on the board, and elicit related words and phrases from the whole class. Write students' ideas. Point out the connection between their ideas and their responses in 1A.

Possible Answers
synonyms: *guidance, direction, authority, control, management* other forms: *leader, lead*

TIP

Elicit the different shades of meaning in the synonyms. Ask: *Which seem softer, or more leading by suggestion or recommendation or model?* [*guidance, direction*] *Which are more forceful, or more leading by direction or command?* [*management, authority, control*]

Guided Practice
10–20 minutes

C 1. Read the directions aloud.

2. Direct students to look at the photo. Ask: *What do you see?* [a manager talking to employees at work]

3. Direct students to look at the chart. Ask: *What is the title of the chart?* [*Common traits of high-level supervisors*] Ask: *What is the first trait?* [intelligence and good judgment] *What does* good judgment *mean?* [the ability to make good decisions]

4. Pair students to discuss what they think each trait means. Allow them to use reference tools if needed.

5. Call on students to explain each trait and give examples.

D 1. Read the directions and the questions aloud.

2. Direct students to look at the first question. Check comprehension of the collocation. Ask: *What is an example of a* leadership skill? Point out that traits are qualities a person has and skills are things a person can do.

3. Set a time limit (five minutes). Direct students to work with their partners to complete the activity. Have a volunteer from each pair give their responses. Check answers as a class.

Answers
Answers will vary.

Presentation II
20–25 minutes

E 1. Read the directions aloud. Call on students to read the steps aloud.

2. Have students work in their teams from 1A. Explain that students will work with their team to analyze leadership traits. Verify students' understanding of the roles: the manager keeps the team on task and on time, the recorder takes notes, the fact checker checks numbers and definitions, and the reporter reports to the class.

3. Set a time limit (five minutes) for teams to complete the task. Remind students to follow the three steps.

4. Call time and have the reporters from each group take turns calling out their answers.

> **MULTILEVEL STRATEGIES**
>
> To adapt 1E:
>
> • **On-level** Assign these students the roles of fact checker and reporter.
>
> • **Pre-level** Assign these students the role of recorder.
>
> • **Higher-level** Assign these students the role of manager.

> **EXTENSION ACTIVITY**
>
> **Pair Interviews**
>
> 1. Model the activity with a higher-level student. Ask the student about each of the traits in the chart (for example, *Do you think you have intelligence and good judgment? What is an example? How would you rank yourself on a scale of 1 to 5 with 5 being the highest?*).
>
> 2. Put students in pairs to take turns asking and answering questions about the traits in the chart.
>
> 3. Call on students to tell the class about one of their partner's traits.

Evaluation
10–15 minutes

SELF-ASSESSMENT

1. Ask students to spend some time reflecting on what they have learned.

2. Set a time limit (three minutes). Ask for volunteers to share their thoughts.

3. Make a list of their questions to refer to at the end of the unit.

<table>
<tr><td colspan="2">

Lesson Overview

</td><td>

Lesson Notes

</td></tr>
<tr><td colspan="2">

MULTILEVEL OBJECTIVES

On-level and Pre-level: Read, listen, and take notes on ways to improve leadership skills

Higher-level: Read, listen, take notes, and interpret information on ways to improve leadership skills

LANGUAGE FOCUS

Grammar: Passive voice, modals

Vocabulary: *overestimate, self-awareness, sensitivity, validate, initial*

For vocabulary support, see these **Oxford Picture Dictionary** topics: Feelings, pages 42–43; Soft Skills, page 178

STRATEGY FOCUS

Predict content in a lecture.

READINESS CONNECTION

In this lesson, students discuss emotional intelligence with their classmates.

PACING

To compress this lesson: Assign 1C and 1D for homework.

To extend this lesson: Have students practice summarizing ways to improve leadership skills (see pages 195 and 196).

And/or have students complete **Multilevel Activities 5 Unit 9, Lesson 2**.

</td><td>

</td></tr>
</table>

CORRELATIONS

CCRS: RI/RL.7.1 Cite several pieces of textual evidence to support analysis of what the text says explicitly as well as inferences drawn from the text.

RI/RL.6.4 Determine the meaning of words and phrases as they are used in a text, including figurative, connotative, and technical meanings; analyze the impact of a specific word choice on meaning and tone.

RI.6.7 Integrate information presented in different media or formats (e.g., in charts, graphs, photographs, videos, or maps) as well as in words to develop a coherent understanding of a topic or issue.

SL.8.1.a. Come to discussions prepared, having read or researched material under study; explicitly draw on that preparation by referring to evidence on the topic, text, or issue to probe and reflect on ideas under discussion.

SL.8.1.c. Pose questions that connect the ideas of several speakers and respond to others' questions and comments with relevant evidence, observations, and ideas.

SL.8.1.d. Acknowledge new information expressed by others, and, when warranted, qualify or justify their own views in light of the evidence presented.

SL.8.2 Analyze the purpose of information presented in diverse media and formats (e.g., visually, quantitatively, orally) and evaluate the motives (e.g., social, commercial, political) behind its presentation.

L.6.3/7.3.c. Choose language that expresses ideas precisely and concisely, recognizing and eliminating wordiness and redundancy.

L.8.6 Acquire and use accurately level-appropriate general academic and domain-specific words and phrases; gather vocabulary knowledge when considering a word or phrase important to comprehension or expression.

ELPS: ELP Standard 1

use a wide range of strategies to:

- determine central ideas or themes in oral presentations and spoken and written texts
- cite specific details and evidence from texts to support the analysis

ELP Standard 2

- participate in conversations, extended discussions, and written exchanges about a range of substantive topics, texts, and issues
- build on the ideas of others
- express his or her own ideas clearly and persuasively
- refer to specific and relevant evidence from texts or research to support his or her ideas
- ask and answer questions that probe reasoning and claim

Warm-up and Review
10–15 minutes (books closed)

Suggest that students show photos of people they know, for example, on their phones. Encourage students to find photos with different facial expressions and explain the situation (for example, *This is my brother Sam. He's laughing really hard in this picture because my sister did something silly.*). After students share, ask: *What can you tell about people from their photos? Are facial expressions usually an accurate way to tell how people feel? Why or why not?*

Introduction
5 minutes

1. Say: *Most people rely on facial expressions to reveal something about how other people feel. Knowing how to "read people" is an important leadership skill.*

2. State the objective: *Today we will read, listen, and take notes on ways to improve leadership skills.*

1 Read about emotional intelligence

Presentation I
10–15 minutes

 1. Read the directions aloud.

2. Put students in pairs to discuss the question.

3. Assign a time limit (three minutes). Call on students to share their ideas with the class.

4. With the class, put the emotions/facial expressions in order from easiest to most difficult to read.

Answers
Answers should be based on the images.

Guided Practice I
15–20 minutes

 1. Read the directions aloud. Check comprehension. Ask: *What are you going to skim for?* [a definition of emotional intelligence]

2. Set a time limit (three minutes). Direct students to underline the sentence when they find it.

3. Elicit the answer.

Answer
Underlined in text: *Emotional intelligence is the ability to identify emotions in ourselves and others.*

TIP

Explain or elicit different ways to notice definitions in a text: the term followed by *is;* the words *means, is defined as,* or *the definition of;* or a definition set off by commas, dashes, or parentheses.

 1. Read the directions aloud. Check comprehension. Ask: *Are you looking for positive or negative things?* [positive]

2. Set a time limit (five minutes). Direct students to work independently to answer the question.

3. Elicit ideas from the whole class.

Possible Answer
Emotionally intelligent people are regarded by their colleagues as "more socially and politically skilled." They often have higher incomes and are more likely to be successful leaders.

MULTILEVEL STRATEGIES

To adapt 1C:

- **Pre-level** Read the article aloud, stopping after each paragraph to check comprehension.

Communicative Practice
10–20 minutes

D 1. Read the questions aloud.

2. Ask students to think about and mark their answers in the text.

3. Set a time limit (five minutes) for students to discuss their answers with a partner.

4. Invite pairs to share their responses. Check answers with the class.

Possible Answers
1. Underlined in text: *because most people overestimate their own abilities in this area* 2. the initial study = the first study, the results were validated = the results were shown to be correct 3. The results were not caused by things like gender, age, training, and position in the workplace. 4. Ruling out other factors allows a researcher to clearly identify causes.

MULTILEVEL STRATEGIES
To adapt 1D: • **Pre-level** Pair or group students to work together to find the answers in the text.

Presentation II
20–25 minutes

E 1. Read the directions and question.

2. Call on students to share their ideas.

EXTENSION ACTIVITY
Summarizing Practice 1. Tell students to write a summary of the article using their own words. Pre-level students can write a group summary. 2. Ask two or three volunteers to write their summaries on the board. Correct or revise with the class as needed.

2 Listen and take notes

Guided Practice II
20–25 minutes

A 1. Say: *Now we're going to listen to a lecture about developing leadership skills.*

2. Read the directions aloud.

3. Pair students to brainstorm predictions.

4. Elicit predictions from the class. Write their ideas on the board.

Answers
Answers will vary.

B  **2.15** 1. Play the beginning of the audio. Direct students to listen without writing.

2. Replay the audio. Ask students to complete the statement.

3. Elicit the answer.

Answer
be a leader, if your friends or family need help or advice / parenthood

C  **2.16** 1. Copy the chart on the board. Ask: *What will the lecture focus on in this section?* [a study by two psychologists]

2. Play the next section of the audio. Direct students to write notes in the chart as they listen.

Answers		
Employability Skills Lecture Series: Developing Leadership Skills		
Study by psychologists Kim Peters and S. Alexander Haslam	Research method: surveyed 218 recruits from British military	Findings: marines who described themselves as leaders were not seen as leaders by others
	asked: describe yourself as leader or follower	leaders who set themselves apart may lose followers
	tracked for 32 weeks	

Communicative Practice
10–20 minutes

 **2.17** 1. Copy the next chart on the board. Ask: *What will the lecture focus on in this section?* [the speaker's conclusions]

2. Play the final section of the audio. Direct students to write notes in the chart as they listen.

3. Set a time limit (five minutes) for students to discuss their answers with a partner.

Answers		
Speaker's conclusion	A leader needs:	Develop these traits by:
	self-awareness and sensitivity	focusing on understanding others
		reflecting on interactions with people

 **2.18** 1. Replay the entire audio. Ask students to confirm or add to their notes.

2. Ask volunteers to complete the charts on the board. Point out any connections between the answers and students' ideas in 2A.

Presentation II
20–25 minutes

 **2.19** 1. Read the directions aloud.

2. Read the first question. Have students discuss in pairs, and then elicit their answers.

3. Read the second question. Play the audio. Elicit the questions and write them on the board. [*What makes them respond negatively or positively to you? Is culture playing a part? Is gender? What can you learn from your interactions?*]

4. Direct students' attention to the sentence frames. Elicit answers.

Answers
Answers will vary.

TIP

Support students' discussion in response to question 2 in 2F. Give examples of your personal experiences: when someone reacted negatively to you, when culture or gender might have affected their reactions, and when you learned about leadership from your interactions. Suggest that students reflect on their own experiences as they answer the question.

Evaluation
10–15 minutes

SELF-ASSESSMENT

1. Read each item. Have students raise their hands if they have difficulty.

2. Pair students who have difficulty with those who do not to review ways to achieve each objective.

Lesson Overview

Lesson Notes

MULTILEVEL OBJECTIVES

On-level and Higher-level: Use suffixes to form abstract nouns to talk about leadership; use unreal conditions to describe imaginary situations requiring leadership skills

Pre-level: Learn about suffixes to form abstract nouns to talk about leadership; recognize the use of unreal conditionals to describe imaginary situations requiring leadership skills

LANGUAGE FOCUS

Grammar: Unreal conditionals

Vocabulary: *apprenticeship*, suffixes *-hood* and *-ship*

For vocabulary support, see this **Oxford Picture Dictionary** topic: Soft Skills, page 178

STRATEGY FOCUS

Use present and past unreal conditionals.

READINESS CONNECTION

In this lesson, students work with a partner to write responses to a lecture.

PACING

To compress this lesson: Assign 2C for homework.

To extend this lesson: Have students do research and write paragraphs (see page 198); Have students participate in a team challenge exploring conditionals (see page 200). And/or have students complete **Multilevel Activities 5 Unit 9, Lesson 3**.

CORRELATIONS

CCRS: SL.8.1.a. Come to discussions prepared, having read or researched material under study; explicitly draw on that preparation by referring to evidence on the topic, text, or issue to probe and reflect on ideas under discussion.

SL.8.1.c. Pose questions that connect the ideas of several speakers and respond to others' questions and comments with relevant evidence, observations, and ideas.

SL.8.1.d. Acknowledge new information expressed by others, and, when warranted, qualify or justify their own views in light of the evidence presented.

L.6.1/8.1.h. Form and use verbs in the indicative, imperative, interrogative, conditional, and subjunctive mood.

L.6.3/7.3.c. Choose language that expresses ideas precisely and concisely, recognizing and eliminating wordiness and redundancy.

L.6.4.b. Use common, grade-appropriate Greek or Latin affixes and roots as clues to the meaning of a word (e.g., *audience, auditory, audible*).

L.8.6 Acquire and use accurately level-appropriate general academic and domain-specific words and phrases; gather vocabulary knowledge when considering a word or phrase important to comprehension or expression.

ELPS: ELP Standard 2

- participate in conversations, extended discussions, and written exchanges about a range of substantive topics, texts, and issues
- build on the ideas of others
- express his or her own ideas clearly and persuasively

ELP Standard 8

using context, questioning, and consistent knowledge of English morphology,

- determine the meaning of general academic and content-specific words and phrases, figurative and connotative language, and idiomatic expressions in spoken and written texts about a variety of topics, experiences, or events

ELP Standard 10

- produce and expand simple, compound, and complex sentences

Warm-up and Review
10–15 minutes (books closed)

Dictate five of the words from 1A. Tell students to write a story using all five words. Set a time limit (three minutes). Call on volunteers to read their story aloud. Have the class vote on the most interesting story.

Introduction
5 minutes

1. Say: *When we write stories, we are usually writing about imaginary situations.*

2. State the objective: *Today we are going use suffixes to form abstract nouns to talk about leadership and use unreal conditionals to describe imaginary situations requiring leadership skills.*

1 Vocabulary: Suffixes *-hood* and *-ship*

Presentation and Guided Practice I
20–25 minutes

1. Read the directions aloud. Say each word and have students repeat. Ask: *What is an abstract noun?* [It represents an idea rather than an actual person, place, or thing.]

2. Point out or elicit that both *-hood* and *-ship* can refer to a condition, character, or skill. They can also refer to more than one person.

3. Set a time limit (three minutes). Direct students to work individually to complete the task and then discuss meanings with a partner.

4. Go over the answers as a class.

Answers
1. partnership, partner, leader
2. parenthood, adults, leadership

TIP

Point out that some of these nouns, especially those ending in *-ship,* have different meanings. For example, *leadership* can refer to a quality (*I'm grateful for her leadership on this.*) or to a specific group of people (*The company's leadership is divided on the new approach.*). Suggest that students use reference tools to look up various definitions and example sentences. Write sentences on the board and elicit the meanings.

MULTILEVEL STRATEGIES

To adapt 1A:

• **Pre-level** Have students work in pairs to complete the sentences and then join another pair to discuss.

Communicative Practice
15–20 minutes

1. Read the directions aloud.

2. Set a time limit (three minutes). Direct students to work in pairs to complete the task.

3. Call on students to write their sentences on the board. Correct with the class as needed.

Answers
Answers will vary.

MULTILEVEL STRATEGIES

To adapt 1B:

• **Higher-level** Have students write sentences using all the other words from the chart.

EXTENSION ACTIVITY

Writing Practice

1. Tell students to choose one of the words to research and write a paragraph describing it and giving examples.

2. Have students post their paragraphs on a discussion board.

2 Grammar: Unreal conditionals

Presentation and Guided Practice II
20–25 minutes

1. Demonstrate how to read the chart. Read each sentence and have students repeat.

2. Check comprehension of the chart. Ask: *What kind of clause do you see in the first column?* [an *if* clause] *What is in the column on the right?* [the main clause] *Do these sentences describe something real?* [no] Point out that you can talk about imaginary situations in the present, future, or past.

3. Have students complete the Language Connection about unreal conditionals. Go over the answers as a class.

Answers
not true, not possible, past tense, would, might, present not true, didn't happen, past perfect, present perfect, past

To adapt 2A:

• **On-level** Have students work independently.

• **Pre-level** Have higher-level classmates assist these students.

• **Higher-level** Have these students work with pre-level classmates.

TIP

To help students understand the Language Connection chart, copy an example of both present and past unreal conditional sentences on the board. Label the structure (for example, *if + subject + simple past verb, subject + might/ would/could + base form*). Direct students' attention to each sentence in the chart and ask comprehension questions—for example, *Is there an emergency?* No. *Do you need people to follow you?* No. *Did he listen to us?* No. *Was he a good leader?* No.

Guided Practice III
20–25 minutes

B 1. Read the directions aloud.

2. Ask students to work individually to complete the task and then compare answers with a partner.

3. Go over the answers as a class.

Answers
1. c 2. e 3. d 4. b 5. a 1. Sentences 2, 4, and 5 are about present time. Sentences 1 and 3 are about past time. 2. Sentence 4 is not an unreal conditional. It has a present verb form in the *if* clause and a future verb form in the main clause. It describes something that is possible.

MULTILEVEL STRATEGIES

To adapt 2B:

• **On-level** Have students work independently.

• **Pre-level** Group pre-level students to complete the task together.

• **Higher-level** Direct students to write an original sentence using unreal conditionals in both the present and the past tense.

C 1. Read the directions aloud. Write the first sentence on the board. Check comprehension. Ask: *Is the speaker talking about the present or the past?* [present] *So what form should we use in the* if *clause?* [simple past]

2. Set a time limit (three minutes). Direct students to work individually to complete the sentences.

3. Call on students to read their completed sentences aloud.

Answers
1. thought, wouldn't follow 2. listened, would be 3. had had, would have done

MULTILEVEL STRATEGIES

To adapt 2C:

• **Pre-level** Write real sentences on the board to scaffold the unreal sentences. For example, for item 1, write: *People think the leader is intelligent and honest. They follow that person.* With the group, demonstrate how to make unreal sentences. Check comprehension.

• **Higher-level** Direct students to write real sentences for each of the unreal sentences in 2C.

• **On-level** Direct students to complete the activity as directed.

D 1. Set a time limit (five minutes) for students to discuss their answers with a partner.

2. Elicit answers from the class.

EXTENSION ACTIVITY

Team Challenge

1. Divide the class into two teams.

2. Have teams write complex sentences, half real and half with unreal conditionals in both the present and the past.

3. Have members of each team take turns reading a sentence aloud. A member of the opposing team must say whether it describes a real or unreal situation. Each correct answer earns the team a point.

4. Tally the points on the board.

Evaluation

10–15 minutes

SELF-ASSESSMENT

1. Have students complete the self-assessment.

2. Provide additional practice as needed.

Lesson Overview	Lesson Notes

MULTILEVEL OBJECTIVES

On-level and Pre-level: Read about leadership styles and discuss the styles of famous leaders

Higher-level: Read about leadership styles; discuss and analyze the styles of famous leaders

LANGUAGE FOCUS

Grammar: Passive voice, subordinating clauses

Vocabulary: *charismatic, exclusive, quality/qualities, turning point, take a stand, mutually exclusive,* words to signal contrasts

For vocabulary support, see these **Oxford Picture Dictionary** topics: Soft Skills, page 178; U.S. History, page 208; World History, page 209

STRATEGY FOCUS

Compare and contrast leadership styles.

READINESS CONNECTION

In this lesson, students relate leadership styles to leaders.

PACING

To compress this lesson: Assign 2A and 2B for homework.

To extend this lesson: Have students role-play giving feedback in work situations (see page 205).

And/or have students complete **Multilevel Activities 5 Unit 9, Lesson 4**.

CORRELATIONS

CCRS: RI/RL.7.1 Cite several pieces of textual evidence to support analysis of what the text says explicitly as well as inferences drawn from the text.

RI.8.3 Analyze how a text makes connections among and distinctions between individuals, ideas, or events (e.g., through comparisons, analogies, or categories).

RI/RL.6.4 Determine the meaning of words and phrases as they are used in a text, including figurative, connotative, and technical meanings; analyze the impact of a specific word choice on meaning and tone.

RI.6.7 Integrate information presented in different media or formats (e.g., in charts, graphs, photographs, videos, or maps) as well as in words to develop a coherent understanding of a topic or issue.

W.7.7 Conduct short research projects to answer a question, drawing on several sources and generating additional related, focused questions for further research and investigation.

SL.8.1.a. Come to discussions prepared, having read or researched material under study; explicitly draw on that preparation by referring to evidence on the topic, text, or issue to probe and reflect on ideas under discussion.

SL.8.1.c. Pose questions that connect the ideas of several speakers and respond to others' questions and comments with relevant evidence, observations, and ideas.

SL.8.1.d. Acknowledge new information expressed by others, and, when warranted, qualify or justify their own views in light of the evidence presented.

SL.8.4 Present claims and findings, emphasizing salient points in a focused, coherent manner with relevant evidence, sound valid reasoning, and well-chosen details; use appropriate eye contact, adequate volume, and clear pronunciation.

L.6.4.a. Use context (e.g., the overall meaning of a sentence or paragraph; a word's position or function in a sentence) as a clue to the meaning of a word or phrase.

L.6.4.d. Verify the preliminary determination of the meaning of a word or phrase (e.g., by checking the inferred meaning in context or in a dictionary).

L.8.6 Acquire and use accurately level-appropriate general academic and domain-specific words and phrases; gather vocabulary knowledge when considering a word or phrase important to comprehension or expression.

Warm-up and Review
10–15 minutes (books closed)

Write the names of all the leaders mentioned in this lesson on slips of paper (*Bill Gates, Florence Nightingale, Dr. Martin Luther King, Jr., Rosa Parks, Cesar Chavez, Dolores Huerta, Eleanor Roosevelt, Abraham Lincoln, Mahatma Gandhi, Nelson Mandela, Albert Schweitzer, Mother Teresa*). Distribute a slip to each student. If helpful, allow students to use reference tools to check their knowledge of the leader on the slip. Call a student to the front of the room. Tell other students to ask a series of *yes/no* questions to try to identify the leader (for example, *Is this leader a man? Is this leader alive?*). The class has only 21 questions to determine the person's identity.

Introduction
5 minutes

1. Say: *There are many kinds of leaders, and they represent all aspects of human life.*

2. State the objective: *Today we will read about leadership styles and discuss the styles of famous leaders.*

1 Get ready to read

Presentation I
20–25 minutes

A  **2.20** 1. Say: *Now we're going to listen to students talk about leaders they admire.*

2. Play the audio. Direct students to answer the question.

3. Elicit the answer.

Possible Answer
Both Bill Gates and Florence Nightingale care(d) about humanity / worked to help people.

B  1. Read the directions aloud. Read each phrase aloud.

2. Replay the audio. Ask students to match the phrases.

3. Call on students to read the completed sentences aloud.

Answers
1. d
2. c
3. e
4. b
5. a

TIP

Ask students to underline the words in the activity that suggest similarities or differences. [*different, differences, both, in common, similarity*] Elicit other words and phrases and categorize them by the relationship. [similarities: *both, in common, similarity, similar, like*; differences: *different, differences, differ from, unlike, in contrast*] Write students' ideas on the board.

C 1. Read the directions aloud.

2. Group students and assign roles: manager, fact checker, recorder, and reporter. Check comprehension of tasks. Ask: *Who keeps the team on task and on time?* [manager] *Who takes notes?* [recorder] *Who looks up spelling of names or other biographical details?* [fact checker] *Who reports to the class?* [reporter] Students will work in these teams for 1C, 2C, 2E, 3B, and 3C.

3. Set a time limit (five minutes) and have students work together to complete the task.

4. Call time and have the reporters from each group take turns identifying a leader.

Answers
Answers will vary.

MULTILEVEL STRATEGIES

To adapt 1C:

• **On-level** Assign these students the roles of recorder and manager.

• **Pre-level** Assign these students the role of reporter.

• **Higher-level** Assign these students the role of fact checker.

2 Preview and read

Guided Practice I
20–25 minutes

A 1. Read the directions aloud. Ask: *What are you scanning for?* [names]

2. Have students circle the names individually, and then check answers as a class.

Answers
Dr. Martin Luther King, Jr., Rosa Parks, Cesar Chavez, Dolores Huerta

TIP

Help students preview the article. Ask: *What is the title?* [*Four Leaders, Three Leadership Styles*] *What are the three headings?* [*Charismatic Leadership, Quiet Leadership, Servant Leadership*] Elicit students' ideas on what each might mean.

B 1. Read the directions aloud.

2. Have the students read the article and answer the question.

3. Check the answer as a class.

Answer
They were all civil rights leaders.

MULTILEVEL STRATEGIES

To adapt 2B:

• **Pre-level** Work with pre-level students to read the article aloud. Stop after each paragraph and check comprehension.

• **On-level** Have students complete the activity as directed.

• **Higher-level** Direct students to underline the main idea and/or write the main idea of the article in a statement using their own words.

TIP

To reinforce passive voice from Unit 7, tell students to find and underline ten passive forms in the article. Ask: *Why do you think the writer used the passive voice?* Elicit ideas. Call on volunteers to write the passive forms on the board. For extra practice, have students rewrite the sentences using active forms.

Presentation II
20–25 minutes

 **C** 1. Read the directions aloud. Call on students to read the questions aloud.

2. Direct students' attention to the Reader's Note. Elicit other examples (such as *even though, on the other hand, in contrast*).

3. Set a time limit (five minutes) and have students work in their teams from 1C to complete the task.

4. Call time. Go over the answers as a class. Call on reporters for the answers and fact checkers to cite the text to explain their answers.

Possible Answers
1. excellent communication skills 2. He brought the largest crowd of protesters ever to Washington, D.C., and his "I Have a Dream" speech is considered to be one of the greatest speeches in U.S. history. 3. She wasn't a spokesperson for the civil rights movement, but she led by example. 4. Servant leaders focus "primarily on the growth and well-being of people and the communities to which they belong." 5. They lived among the people they were trying to help; they were poor. 6. From text: *While charismatic leaders are usually the ones whose voices we hear the most in many organizations, there are also quiet leaders; Although she wasn't the spokesperson for the movement, Parks is widely recognized as the "mother of the Civil Rights movement.";* *Instead of accumulating power for themselves, servant leaders, according to Robert Greenleaf, who coined the term in 1970, focus "primarily on the growth and well-being of people and the communities to which they belong."* 7. "became the trigger for the Montgomery Bus Boycott" means "caused the Montgomery Bus Boycott" 8. Possible answer: times of their lives

WORD STUDY

 **D** 1. Read the directions and prompts aloud.

2. Write the chart on the board.

3. Set a time limit (five minutes). Have students work in their teams to complete the task.

4. Have each pair join another pair to share synonyms and complete the chart.

5. Ask reporters to write words in the chart. Ask recorders to write sentences on the board.

Answers
Answers will vary. Possible answers for meanings: turning point: an event or time when a change came about take a stand: to protest or make one's opinion known mutually exclusive: other categories don't apply

 **E** 1. Read the directions aloud.

2. Set a time limit (three minutes). Have students stay with their teams to discuss the question.

3. Call time. Ask reporters from each team to share their teams' ideas.

Answers
Answers will vary.

3 Build on it

Presentation I
20–25 minutes

 **A** 1. Have students look at the infographic. Ask: *What kind of diagram is it?* [a Venn diagram] *What three things are being compared/contrasted?* [the three leadership styles] *What leaders does the infographic refer to?* [Eleanor Roosevelt, Abraham Lincoln, Albert Schweitzer, Nelson Mandela, Mahatma Gandhi, Mother Teresa]

2. Read the directions and questions aloud.

3. Elicit answers from the class.

Possible Answers
1. they represent two (or three) categories that apply to the same people 2. because he is considered to represent all three types of leader

 **B** 1. Have students rejoin their teams with the same roles.

2. Direct students' attention to the Speaking Note. Check comprehension. Ask: *Which words refer to similarities?* [*in common, both, similarities*] *Which talk about the way two things are different?* [*difference*]

3. Read the directions and prompts aloud.

4. Set a time limit (ten minutes). Have students work in their teams to complete the task.

5. Call on reporters to share their team's ideas.

Answers
Answers will vary.

PROBLEM SOLVING

C 1. Ask students to stay in their teams with the same roles.

2. Read the directions and prompts aloud.

3. Set a time limit (ten minutes) and have students work together to discuss the problem.

4. Call time. Ask reporters to share their team's ideas.

Possible Answer
Brett didn't try to fit in with the people he was going to lead—he set himself apart and announced his plans without talking to them. He was not a good communicator (lacked charisma), so the employees were not interested in listening to him. He doesn't have very high emotional intelligence because he didn't notice that the employees weren't happy.
He could improve his leadership skills by becoming more sensitive to his employees' needs, listening to what they need, and working on his speaking/communication skills.

APPLY YOUR KNOWLEDGE 

D 1. Read the directions aloud.

2. Set a time limit or assign as an out-of-class task and have students work individually to complete the task.

3. Pair or group students to share what they found out.

EXTENSION ACTIVITY
Role Play
1. Review positive ways to resolve conflict from Unit 8.
2. Pair students to create role plays in which either a supervisor or an employee gives Brett feedback on his performance.
3. Set a time limit (ten minutes). Remind pairs to use what they learned in Unit 8.
4. Call on volunteers to role-play for the class.

Evaluation
10–15 minutes

SELF-ASSESSMENT

1. Direct students to complete the self-assessment individually.

2. Have students choose the one objective they have the most difficulty with.

3. Group students according to their weakest skill. Provide each group with suggestions or feedback.

Lesson Overview

Lesson Notes

MULTILEVEL OBJECTIVES

On-level: Use the writing process to summarize an article

Pre-level: Work with others to summarize an article

Higher-level: Summarize an article and include at least one unreal conditional to make an inference or suggest an implication

LANGUAGE FOCUS

Grammar: Simple present, passive

Vocabulary: *charismatic*, synonyms and word forms for *conclusion*

For vocabulary support, see this **Oxford Picture Dictionary** topic: English Composition, pages 202–203

STRATEGY FOCUS

Use expressions to refer to a conclusion.

PACING

To compress this lesson: Assign Activity 1 (A–E) and/or 2C for homework.

To extend this lesson: Have students write a paragraph comparing and contrasting two leaders mentioned in the unit (see page 208).

And/or have students complete **Multilevel Activities 5 Unit 9, Lesson 5**.

CORRELATIONS

CCRS: W/WHST.6-8.2.a. Introduce a topic clearly, previewing what is to follow; organize ideas, concepts, and information, using strategies such as definition, classification, comparison /contrast, and cause/effect; include formatting (e.g., headings), graphics (e.g., charts, tables), and multimedia when useful to aiding comprehension.

W/WHST.6-8.2.b. Develop the topic with relevant facts, definitions, concrete details, quotations, or other information and examples.

W/WHST.6-8.2.c. Use appropriate transitions to create cohesion and clarify the relationships among ideas and concepts.

W/WHST.6-8.2.d. Use precise language and domain-specific vocabulary to inform about or explain the topic.

W/WHST.6-8.2.f. Provide a concluding statement or section that follows from and supports the information or explanation presented.

W/WHST.6-8.4 Produce clear and coherent writing in which the development and organization and style are appropriate to task, purpose, and audience.

W/WHST.6-8.5 With some guidance and support from peers and others, develop and strengthen writing as needed by planning, revising, editing, rewriting, or trying a new approach, focusing on how well purpose and audience have been addressed.

L.6.3/7.3.c. Choose language that expresses ideas precisely and concisely, recognizing and eliminating wordiness and redundancy.

L.8.6 Acquire and use accurately level-appropriate general academic and domain-specific words and phrases; gather vocabulary knowledge when considering a word or phrase important to comprehension or expression.

ELPS: ELP Standard 7

- adapt language choices and style according to purpose, task, and audience with ease in various social and academic contexts
- use a wide variety of complex general academic and content specific words and phrases
- employ both formal and more informal styles and tones effectively in spoken and written texts, as appropriate

ELP Standard 9

- recount a complex and detailed sequence of events or steps in a process, with an effective sequential or chronological order
- introduce and effectively develop an informational topic with facts, details, and evidence
- use complex and varied transitions to link the major sections of speech and text and to clarify relationships among events and ideas
- provide a concluding section or statement

ELP Standard 10

- produce and expand simple, compound, and complex sentences

Warm-up and Review
10–15 minutes (books closed)

Tell students to check for recent news articles that mention leaders. Elicit the names of the leaders and why they are in the news.

Introduction
5 minutes

State the objective: *Today we will use the writing process to summarize an article.*

1 Write a summary

Presentation I
20–25 minutes

A 1. Have students revisit the article on pages 102–103. Check comprehension. Ask: *What is the article about? What are the most important ideas?*

2. Elicit responses and jot them on the board.

Guided Practice I
15–20 minutes

B 1. Read the directions aloud.

2. Have students work individually to write their statements. Then ask students to compare statements in pairs.

C 1. Direct students to look at the chart. Ask about organization: *What will you write about each leadership style?* [a description and example]

2. Check comprehension of the activity. Ask: *Do you need to write complete sentences in the chart?* [no]

3. Have students work individually to complete their charts.

Answers		
Leadership style	**Description**	**Example**
charismatic	excellent communication skills	Dr. Martin Luther King, Jr.
quiet	people who show the way by example	Rosa Parks
servant	people who focus on others, not themselves	Cesar Chaves and Dolores Huerta

D 1. Read the directions aloud.

2. Direct students' attention to the Writer's Note. Ask: *What words are synonyms?* [conclude, sum up]

3. Have students work individually to write conclusions. Encourage students to use one of the sentence frames. Then ask students to compare statements in pairs.

E 1. Read the directions aloud. Check comprehension. Ask: *What will you include in your summary?* [introduction, notes from the chart, conclusion]

2. Have students work individually to write their summaries.

MULTILEVEL STRATEGIES

To adapt 1E:

• **On-level** Have students write summaries as directed.

• **Pre-level** Work with students in a group to write the summary together.

• **Higher-level** Have students write the summary in two different ways using synonyms.

---

2 Get feedback and revise

Guided Practice II
10–15 minutes

A Direct students to check their writing using the editing checklist. Tell them to read each item in the list and check their papers before moving onto the next item. Explain that students should not edit their writing at this stage. They should just use the checklist to check their work and mark any areas they want to revise.

Communicative Practice
10–15 minutes

B 1. Read the directions aloud. Emphasize to students that they are responding to their partners' work, not correcting it.

2. Direct students to exchange papers with a partner and follow the instructions.

C Allow students time to edit and revise their writing using the editing checklist and their partner's feedback. If necessary, students could complete this task as homework.

<table><tr><td>

MULTILEVEL STRATEGIES

To adapt 2C:

• **Mixed-ability** Pair pre-level students with on- and higher-level students. Have all students point out ideas that are not clear. Instruct on- and higher-level partners to give feedback on spelling and grammar if helpful.

</td></tr></table>

<table><tr><td>

EXTENSION ACTIVITY

Paragraph Practice

1. Have students write a paragraph comparing and contrasting two leaders in the unit.

2. Pair students to exchange and read their paragraphs.

</td></tr></table>

Evaluation
10–15 minutes

SELF-ASSESSMENT

1. Call on students to read their sentences aloud.

2. Use the responses to the second statement to plan follow-up activities.

Lesson Overview

Lesson Notes

MULTILEVEL OBJECTIVES

On-level and Higher-level: Students conduct and present research related to leadership

Pre-level: Students help conduct and present research related to leadership

LANGUAGE FOCUS

Grammar: Unreal conditionals

Vocabulary: Words related to leadership

For vocabulary support, see this **Oxford Picture Dictionary** topic: Internet Research, pages 212–213

STRATEGY FOCUS

Speak effectively about visuals.

READINESS CONNECTION

In this lesson, students develop a group presentation using effective visuals.

PACING

To compress this lesson: Assign 1B for homework. Alternatively, assign students topics in 1A.

To extend this lesson: Have students debrief in pairs on what they've learned about leadership (see page 211). And/or have students complete **Multilevel Activities 5 Unit 9, Lesson 6**.

CORRELATIONS

CCRS: W.7.7 Conduct short research projects to answer a question, drawing on several sources and generating additional related, focused questions for further research and investigation.

W.7.8 Gather relevant information from multiple print and digital sources, using search terms effectively; assess the credibility and accuracy of each source; and quote or paraphrase the data and conclusions of others while avoiding plagiarism and following a standard format for citation.

SL.8.4 Present claims and findings, emphasizing salient points in a focused, coherent manner with relevant evidence, sound valid reasoning, and well-chosen details; use appropriate eye contact, adequate volume, and clear pronunciation.

SL.8.5 Integrate multimedia and visual displays into presentations to clarify information, strengthen claims and evidence, and add interest.

SL.8.6 Adapt speech to a variety of contexts and tasks, demonstrating command of formal English when indicated or appropriate.

L.6.3/7.3.b. Maintain consistency in style and tone.

L.6.3/7.3.c. Choose language that expresses ideas precisely and concisely, recognizing and eliminating wordiness and redundancy.

L.8.6 Acquire and use accurately level-appropriate general academic and domain-specific words and phrases; gather vocabulary knowledge when considering a word or phrase important to comprehension or expression.

ELPS: ELP Standard 2

- participate in conversations, extended discussions, and written exchanges about a range of substantive topics, texts, and issues
- build on the ideas of others
- express his or her own ideas clearly and persuasively
- summarize the key points and evidence discussed

ELP Standard 3

- deliver oral presentations
- compose written informational texts
- fully develop the topic with relevant details, concepts, examples, and information
- integrate graphics or multimedia when useful about a variety of texts, topics, or events

<table>
<tr><td>

ELP Standard 5

- carry out both short and more sustained research projects to answer a question or solve a problem
- gather information from multiple print and digital sources
- use advanced search terms effectively
- synthesize information from multiple print and digital sources
- analyze and integrate information into clearly organized spoken and written texts
- include illustrations, diagrams, or other graphics as appropriate
- cite sources appropriately

</td><td>

ELP Standard 7

- adapt language choices and style according to purpose, task, and audience with ease in various social and academic contexts
- use a wide variety of complex general academic and content specific words and phrases
- employ both formal and more informal styles and tones effectively in spoken and written texts, as appropriate

</td></tr>
</table>

Warm-up and Review
10–15 minutes (books closed)

Write the names of ten leaders on the board but scramble the letters (for example, *kracab moaba* instead of *Barack Obama*). Set a time limit (three minutes) and have students work individually to unscramble the names. Call on students to write the correct names on the board.

Introduction
5 minutes

State the objective: *Today we will conduct and present research related to leadership.*

1 Research a leader

Communicative Practice
40–45 minutes

A 1. Group students but do not assign roles yet. Explain that students will work with their team to narrow the topic.

2. Read the directions aloud.

3. Brainstorm a list of conflicts. Remind students of the conflicts in the warm-up for Lesson 5.

4. Direct students' attention to the Research Tip. Ask: *What are some possible problems with Wikipedia?* [The information might be inaccurate or biased, and it is not always reliable.]

5. Set a time limit (ten minutes) and have students work together to complete the task.

TIP

Work with teams to help them choose one of the two options. Teams whose members are all on- or higher-level might prefer to choose different leaders to research, whereas teams with mixed ability might do better to focus on one leader and choose different aspects of that leader's life. Then higher-level students will be able to help pre-level students with the content.

B 1. Read the directions aloud. Check comprehension. Ask: *What are primary sources?* [quotations, speeches, autobiographies] *In primary sources, who is telling you about the leader?* [the leader himself or herself] *What are secondary sources?* [articles, biographies] *Who is telling you about the leader?* [other people]

2. Check comprehension of the task. Ask: *For your notes, should you copy information exactly?* [no, use own words] *What is an example of something you might want to copy exactly?* [quotes] *What do you need to include?* [sources and links]

3. Set a time limit or assign research as an out-of-class task for students to complete the task.

C 1. Have students share their research in their teams.

2. Read the directions and prompts aloud.

3. Set a time limit (ten minutes) and have students work together to follow the steps.

2 Present your research

Presentation
40–45 minutes

 1. Have students stay in their same teams. Read the directions and steps aloud.

2. Ask: *What do you do in the introduction?* [say who you are going to talk about] *What should you include in the body?* [when and where they lived, why they are considered leaders] *Where should you talk about your own opinion of the leader?* [in the conclusion]

3. Set a time limit (10 to 15 minutes) and have students work as a team to outline the oral report.

B 1. Read the directions aloud.

2. Check comprehension of the activity. Ask: *Who will speak?* [everyone]

3. Draw students' attention to the Presentation Strategy. Read the expressions.

4. Set a time limit (five minutes) and have students work as a team to divide the parts of the presentation—for example: 1. introduction, 2. when/where they lived, 3. traits, skills and styles, 4. conclusion or 1. introduction + leader A, 2. leader B, 3. leader C, 4. leader D and conclusion.

MULTILEVEL STRATEGIES

To adapt 2B:

- **On-level** Assign these students one of the body sections.
- **Pre-level** Assign these students the introduction.
- **Higher-level** Assign these students the conclusion.

C 1. Read the directions and list aloud.

2. Check comprehension of the activity. Ask: *Should you rehearse the presentation in exactly the way you will present to the class?* [yes] *How long should the presentation be?* [two to four minutes]

3. Set a time limit (ten minutes) and have students rehearse their presentations in teams.

D 1. Draw a chart on the board, listing the teams in the first column. In the other columns, list the note-taking prompts or shortened forms of them: *Visuals, Strengths, Conclusion, Advice.* Check comprehension of the activity. Ask: *What will you write under* Visuals? [effectiveness and relationship to the topic] Remind students to just use words and phrases in the chart.

2. Set a time limit (up to four minutes) for each presentation, and ask each team to present in turn.

E 1. Ask each team to nominate a reporter to give feedback on the other teams' presentations.

2. Beginning with the first team to present, collect feedback from the reporters. Write feedback in the table you drew on the board in 2D.

EXTENSION ACTIVITY

Pair Debrief

1. Pair students from different teams.

2. Have pairs talk about the ways that they used what they had learned about leadership in the unit.

3. Call on students to share their ideas.

Evaluation
10–15 minutes

SELF-ASSESSMENT

1. Pair students to share their self-assessments.

2. Elicit suggestions from the class for developing more confidence in each of the three assessment areas.

10 Change

Unit Overview

This unit explores change and attitudes toward innovation with a range of employability skills and contextualizes commonly confused words and multi-word verbs. By the end of this unit, you will be able to research and debate the use of artificial intelligence.

KEY OBJECTIVES

Lesson 1	Identify attitudes toward change
Lesson 2	Identify changes in the workplace and stages of change
Lesson 3	Recognize commonly confused words and use the correct words; identify and use multi-word verbs in informal speech
Lesson 4	Listen for phrases that signal opinions or express hedging; read and discuss attitudes toward innovation
Lesson 5	Use the writing process to summarize an article
Lesson 6	Prepare for and conduct a debate on artificial intelligence (AI)

UNIT FEATURES

Academic Vocabulary	*advice, advise, affect, alternate, corroborate, debate, denial, effect, exploration, resistance*
Employability Skills	• Relate historic quotations with concepts in an article • Predict future effectiveness of new technologies • Offer ways to foster acceptance of a new workplace technology • Collaborate to research opposing viewpoints • Collect quotes and visuals to use in a debate • Debate the use of artificial intelligence as a team • Prepare for and address questions following a debate
Resources	**Class Audio** CD2, Tracks 21-23 **Teacher Resource Center** 　Multilevel Activities 5 Unit 10 　Multilevel Grammar Activities 5 Unit 10 　Unit 10 Test **Oxford Picture Dictionary** Feelings, Office Work, Soft Skills, Office Work, Information Technology (IT), World History, English Composition, Internet Research, Energy and the Environment, Electronics and Photography

<table>
<tr><td colspan="2">

Lesson Overview

MULTILEVEL OBJECTIVES

On-level and Pre-level: Identify attitudes toward change

Higher-level: Identify and analyze attitudes toward change

LANGUAGE FOCUS

Grammar: Simple present

Vocabulary: Words and phrases related to change

For vocabulary support, see this **Oxford Picture Dictionary** topic: Soft Skills, page 178

READINESS CONNECTION

In this lesson, students identify attitudes toward change.

PACING

To compress this lesson: Do 1C as a class.

To extend this lesson: Have students graph their own results of a survey (see page 215).

And/or have students complete **Multilevel Activities 5 Unit 10, Lesson 1.**

</td><td>

Lesson Notes

</td></tr>
</table>

CORRELATIONS

CCRS: RI.6.7 Integrate information presented in different media or formats (e.g., in charts, graphs, photographs, videos, or maps) as well as in words to develop a coherent understanding of a topic or issue.

SL.8.1.a. Come to discussions prepared, having read or researched material under study; explicitly draw on that preparation by referring to evidence on the topic, text, or issue to probe and reflect on ideas under discussion.

SL.8.1.c. Pose questions that connect the ideas of several speakers and respond to others' questions and comments with relevant evidence, observations, and ideas.

SL.8.1.d. Acknowledge new information expressed by others, and, when warranted, qualify or justify their own views in light of the evidence presented.

L.6.4.c. Consult reference materials (e.g., dictionaries, glossaries, thesauruses), both print and digital, to find the pronunciation of a word or determine or clarify its precise meaning or its part of speech.

L.8.6 Acquire and use accurately level-appropriate general academic and domain-specific words and phrases; gather vocabulary knowledge when considering a word or phrase important to comprehension or expression.

ELPS: ELP Standard 2

- participate in conversations, extended discussions, and written exchanges about a range of substantive topics, texts, and issues
- build on the ideas of others
- express his or her own ideas clearly and persuasively
- refer to specific and relevant evidence from texts or research to support his or her ideas
- ask and answer questions that probe reasoning and claim

ELP Standard 8

using context, questioning, and consistent knowledge of English morphology,

- determine the meaning of general academic and content-specific words and phrases, figurative and connotative language, and idiomatic expressions in spoken and written texts about a variety of topics, experiences, or events

Lead students through a series of tasks. First, direct students to cross their arms. Ask them to notice which arm goes over the other. Direct students to re-cross their arms, this time placing the opposite arm on top. Ask: *How does it feel to do it a different way?* Repeat the process by having students switch seats so they are sitting in a new place in the classroom. Elicit their feelings about these small changes.

Introduction
5 minutes

1. Say: *Change often makes us feel uncomfortable.*

2. State the objective: *Today we're going to identify attitudes toward change.*

1 Discuss attitudes toward change

Presentation I
20–25 minutes

 1. Read the directions aloud. Put students in teams to brainstorm. Assign roles: manager, fact checker, recorder, and reporter.

2. Elicit examples of changes from the class and write them on the board. With the class, categorize the changes if possible (for example, environment, climate, population, development, politics, technology, housing, food).

3. Direct students to rank the changes from smallest to biggest. Call on reporters to share their team's rankings. Write the number of the ranking next to the category.

B 1. Direct students to look at the definition. Ask: *What is the most important word in this definition?* [*different*]

2. Write *change* on the board, and elicit related words and phrases from the whole class. Write their ideas on the board. Explain or elicit that *change* can be both a noun and a verb. Point out the connection between their ideas and their responses in 1A.

Possible Answers
to be open to change, to welcome change, to look forward to change to resist change, to be resistant to change minor / major / significant change

Point out that *change* has both positive and negative connotations. As students provide related words and phrases, ask if the word or phrase suggests something positive or negative. Add + and – signs next to the words and phrases on the board.

Presentation II
20–25 minutes

 1. Read the directions aloud.

2. Direct students' attention to the quiz. Check comprehension. Ask: *How many items are there?* [six] *If you give yourself a 4, what does that mean?* [You strongly agree with the statement.]

3. Call on students to read each statement aloud. Explain any unfamiliar words or phrases (for example, *move forward*).

4. Set a time limit (two minutes). Direct students to take the quiz individually.

5. Pair students to discuss Hassan's scores and their own.

Possible Answer
Hassan is not very open to change. Out of a possible 20 points, he has 9. He can change his mind and ideas easily, but he doesn't like the unexpected and can't move forward unless he is sure.

Guided Practice
10–20 minutes

 1. Read the directions aloud.

2. Read the first question aloud. Ask: *Would you be open to this change?* Elicit responses from the class.

3. Pair students to take turns asking and answering the questions.

4. Set a time limit (five minutes). Direct students to work with their partners to complete the activity. Have a volunteer from each pair give their responses. Check answers as a class.

Possible Answers
1. Two seem resistant to change, but one seems open to it. 2. It might be a major change because there is resistance. 3. One worker and the manager welcome the change. 4. A company might look forward to the change if it increases their profits.

E 1. Read the directions and the steps aloud.

2. Have students work in their teams from 1A. Explain that students will work with their team to analyze the information. Verify students' understanding of the roles: the manager keeps the team on task and on time, the recorder takes notes, the fact checker looks up words, and the reporter reports to the class.

3. Check comprehension of the task. Ask: *What will you analyze in this activity?* [attitudes toward change] *What will you compare?* [attitudes toward the change in class time and scores on the quiz] *What does it mean to reach a consensus?* [come to an agreement]

4. Set a time limit (ten minutes) for teams to complete the task.

5. Call time and have the reporters from each team take turns calling out their answers.

Answers
Answers will vary.

MULTILEVEL STRATEGIES

To adapt 1E:

• **On-level** Assign these students the roles of fact checker and reporter.

• **Pre-level** Assign these students the role of recorder.

• **Higher-level** Assign these students the role of manager.

EXTENSION ACTIVITY

Class Results

1. Write the quiz items on the board.

2. Read each one and have students raise their hands if they think it is one of the statements that best reflects their attitude toward change. Tally the results.

3. Direct students to make a bar graph of the results.

Evaluation
10–15 minutes

SELF-ASSESSMENT

1. Ask students to spend some time reflecting on what they have learned.

2. Set a time limit (three minutes). Ask for volunteers to share their thoughts.

3. Make a list of their questions to refer to at the end of the unit.

Lesson Overview

MULTILEVEL OBJECTIVES

On-level and Pre-level: Identify changes in the workplace and stages of change

Higher-level: Identify and explain changes in the workplace and stages of change

LANGUAGE FOCUS

Grammar: Parallel structure, subordinating clauses

Vocabulary: *affect*, *effect*, expressions for causes and effects, commonly confused words

For vocabulary support, see these **Oxford Picture Dictionary** topics: Office Work, pages 188–189; Information Technology (IT), pages 190–191; Internet Research, pages 212–213; Electronics and Photography, pages 240–241

STRATEGY FOCUS

Listen for how a speaker uses expressions to show cause and effect.

READINESS CONNECTION

In this lesson, students work in a team to discuss experiences with change.

PACING

To compress this lesson: Assign 1B and 1C as homework.

To extend this lesson: Have students practice summarizing an article (see page 218); Have students create a role play on stages of change (see page 219). And/or have students complete **Multilevel Activities 5 Unit 10, Lesson 2.**

Lesson Notes

CORRELATIONS

CCRS: RI/RL.7.1 Cite several pieces of textual evidence to support analysis of what the text says explicitly as well as inferences drawn from the text.

RI.8.3 Analyze how a text makes connections among and distinctions between individuals, ideas, or events (e.g., through comparisons, analogies, or categories).

RI/RL.6.4 Determine the meaning of words and phrases as they are used in a text, including figurative, connotative, and technical meanings; analyze the impact of a specific word choice on meaning and tone.

RI.7.5 Analyze the structure an author uses to organize a text, including how the major sections contribute to the whole and to the development of the ideas.

SL.8.1.a. Come to discussions prepared, having read or researched material under study; explicitly draw on that preparation by referring to evidence on the topic, text, or issue to probe and reflect on ideas under discussion.

SL.8.1.c. Pose questions that connect the ideas of several speakers and respond to others' questions and comments with relevant evidence, observations, and ideas.

SL.8.1.d. Acknowledge new information expressed by others, and, when warranted, qualify or justify their own views in light of the evidence presented.

SL.8.2 Analyze the purpose of information presented in diverse media and formats (e.g., visually, quantitatively, orally) and evaluate the motives (e.g., social, commercial, political) behind its presentation.

SL.8.3 Delineate a speaker's argument and specific claims, evaluating the soundness of the reasoning and relevance and sufficiency of the evidence and identifying when irrelevant evidence is introduced.

L.6.3/7.3.c. Choose language that expresses ideas precisely and concisely, recognizing and eliminating wordiness and redundancy.

L.8.6 Acquire and use accurately level-appropriate general academic and domain-specific words and phrases; gather vocabulary knowledge when considering a word or phrase important to comprehension or expression.

ELPS: ELP Standard 1

use a wide range of strategies to:

- determine central ideas or themes in oral presentations and spoken and written texts
- cite specific details and evidence from texts to support the analysis

<table>
<tr>
<td>

ELP Standard 2

- participate in conversations, extended discussions, and written exchanges about a range of substantive topics, texts, and issues
- build on the ideas of others
- express his or her own ideas clearly and persuasively
- refer to specific and relevant evidence from texts or research to support his or her ideas
- ask and answer questions that probe reasoning and claim

</td>
<td>

ELP Standard 8

using context, questioning, and consistent knowledge of English morphology,

- determine the meaning of general academic and content-specific words and phrases, figurative and connotative language, and idiomatic expressions in spoken and written texts about a variety of topics, experiences, or events

</td>
</tr>
</table>

Warm-up and Review
10–15 minutes (books closed)

Write *My first job* on the board. Describe your first job to the class. Give enough details to show how things have changed since then (for example, *In my first teaching job, I used a chalkboard and ditto sheets, which was a way of making copies.*). Ask: *What was the first paid or volunteer job you had? What did you do? How is that job different now?* Pair students to share their experiences.

Introduction
5 minutes

1. Say: *Jobs have changed a lot in recent years.*

2. State the objective: *Today we will identify changes in the workplace and stages of change.*

1 Read about technological changes in the workplace

Presentation I
10–15 minutes

 1. Read the directions aloud.

2. Assign a time limit (five minutes). Have pairs work together to complete the activity.

3. Call on students to share their ideas. Write the ways technology has changed workplaces on the board.

Guided Practice I
15–20 minutes

B 1. Read the directions aloud. Check comprehension. Ask: *What are you going to do?* [skim the article] *What are you looking for?* [two benefits of technology in the workplace]

2. Set a time limit (three minutes). Direct students to underline two benefits when they find them.

3. Elicit the answers.

> **Possible Answers**
>
> easier and more efficient communication with online tools and video conferencing; more opportunities for meeting, working remotely; software that helps efficiency and productivity; automation and AI can help wide range of functions

TIP

Direct students' attention to the article and photo. Ask: *What is the title?* [*Technology and Change in the Workplace*] Ask: *What do you see in the photo?* [two people on a video call]

MULTILEVEL STRATEGIES

To adapt 1B:

- **Pre-level** Read the article aloud, stopping after each paragraph to check comprehension.

Communicative Practice
10–20 minutes

 1. Read the questions aloud.

2. Ask students to think about and mark their answers in the text.

3. Set a time limit (five minutes) for students to discuss their answers with a partner.

4. Invite pairs to share their responses. Check answers as a class.

MULTILEVEL STRATEGIES

To adapt 1C:

• **Pre-level** Pair or group students to work together to find the answers in the text.

Presentation II
20–25 minutes

1. Read the directions aloud.

2. Write a T-chart on the board with the headings *Benefits* and *Negative impacts*.

3. Pair students to discuss the questions.

4. Call on volunteers to share their ideas. Write the ideas in the correct place in the T-chart on the board.

2 Listen and take notes

Guided Practice II
20–25 minutes

1. Say: *Now we're going to listen to a lecture on change in the workplace.*

2. Read the directions aloud.

3. Brainstorm the four possible stages with the class.

Answers
Answers will vary.

 **2.21** 1. Play the beginning of the audio. Direct students to listen without writing.

2. Replay the audio. Ask students to answer the question.

3. Elicit the answer.

Answer
We can't avoid it, but it's happening faster and faster in today's world.

 **2.22** 1. Copy the chart on the board.

2. Play the whole audio. Direct students to write notes in the chart as they listen.

Answers

1. Denial
   • deny change isn't happening, not conscious
   • pretend it's not happening, everything same
2. Resistance
   • acknowledge, but don't want to accept change
   • open (e.g., complain or criticize) or hidden (e.g., whisper w/ co-workers)
   • morale ↓
   • address issues, don't ignore
   • communication!
     employees' fears, concerns → managers acknowledge → find strategies
3. Exploration
   • can go between resistance & exploration
   • give positive f/back on changes
   • some workers give up and look for other job
4. Acceptance
   • accept & commit to change
   • may not agree completely, but integrate into org

To adapt 2C:

- **On-level** Have students complete the activity as described.

- **Pre-level** Allow students to read the script as they listen. Pre-teach unfamiliar vocabulary (for example, *inevitable, engage, alternate, downright, morale, integrate, reluctance*).

- **Higher-level** Tell students to take notes on additional examples or explanations.

Communicative Practice
10–20 minutes

 **2.22** 1. Set a time limit (five minutes) for students to discuss their answers with a partner.

2. Replay the audio. Ask students to confirm or add to their notes.

3. Ask volunteers to complete the chart on the board. Point out any connections between the answers and students' ideas in 2A.

Presentation II
20–25 minutes

 **2.22** 1. Read the directions aloud.

2. Direct students' attention to the expressions. Call on students to read the expressions aloud.

3. Replay the audio so students can complete the task.

4. Elicit the answers.

Answers
The main causes of...are... The main effect is... Consequently, ... Therefore...

 1. Read the directions aloud.

2. Put students in teams and assign roles: manager, fact checker, recorder, and reporter.

3. Set a time limit (ten minutes). Remind students to use the expressions for cause and effect.

4. Call on reporters to share their team's ideas with the class.

Answers
Answers will vary.

EXTENSION ACTIVITY

Role Play

1. Pair students to role-play one or more of the stages of change. They can use the situation in 1E of this lesson or write about a workplace change that they have experience with.

2. Call on volunteers to perform their role plays for the class. Elicit the stage(s).

Evaluation
10–15 minutes

SELF-ASSESSMENT

1. Read each item. Have students raise their hands if they have difficulty.

2. Pair students who have difficulty with those who do not to review ways to achieve each objective.

<table>
<tr><td>

Lesson Overview

MULTILEVEL OBJECTIVES

On-level and Higher-level: Recognize commonly confused words and use the correct words; identify and use multi-word verbs in informal speech

Pre-level: Recognize commonly confused words and use the correct words; learn multi-word verbs for informal speech

LANGUAGE FOCUS

Grammar: Multi-word verbs

Vocabulary: *advice, advise, affect, alternate, corroborate, effect, exploration, resistance*

For vocabulary support, see these **Oxford Picture Dictionary** topics: Feelings, pages 42–43; Soft Skills, page 178

STRATEGY FOCUS

Use multi-word verbs.

READINESS CONNECTION

In this lesson, students work in a team to distinguish commonly confused words.

PACING

To compress this lesson: Assign 2B and 2C for homework.

To extend this lesson: Have students create a conversation with target vocabulary (see page 221); Have students participate in a challenge with multi-word verbs (see page 222).

And/or have students complete **Multilevel Activities 5 Unit 10, Lesson 3.**

</td><td>

Lesson Notes

</td></tr>
</table>

CORRELATIONS

CCRS: SL.8.1.a. Come to discussions prepared, having read or researched material under study; explicitly draw on that preparation by referring to evidence on the topic, text, or issue to probe and reflect on ideas under discussion.

SL.8.1.c. Pose questions that connect the ideas of several speakers and respond to others' questions and comments with relevant evidence, observations, and ideas.

SL.8.1.d. Acknowledge new information expressed by others, and, when warranted, qualify or justify their own views in light of the evidence presented.

L.6.3/7.3.c. Choose language that expresses ideas precisely and concisely, recognizing and eliminating wordiness and redundancy.

L.6.4.c. Consult reference materials (e.g., dictionaries, glossaries, thesauruses), both print and digital, to find the pronunciation of a word or determine or clarify its precise meaning or its part of speech.

L.8.6 Acquire and use accurately level-appropriate general academic and domain-specific words and phrases; gather vocabulary knowledge when considering a word or phrase important to comprehension or expression.

ELPS: ELP Standard 2

• participate in conversations, extended discussions, and written exchanges about a range of substantive topics, texts, and issues

• build on the ideas of others

• express his or her own ideas clearly and persuasively

ELP Standard 8

using context, questioning, and consistent knowledge of English morphology,

• determine the meaning of general academic and content-specific words and phrases, figurative and connotative language, and idiomatic expressions in spoken and written texts about a variety of topics, experiences, or events.

ELP Standard 10

• produce and expand simple, compound, and complex sentences

Warm-up and Review
10–15 minutes (books closed)

Dictate commonly confused words and multi-word verbs (for example, *affect, effect, personal, except, end up, call off, run away from*) and use them in example sentences. Pair students to write a story using as many of the words and phrases as they can. Call on students to read the stories aloud. Have the class vote on the best one. Then ask the writers to copy it on the board. Circle the targeted words and correct as needed.

Introduction
5 minutes

1. Say: *We often use commonly confused words and multi-word verbs in everyday speech.*

2. State the objective: *Today we are going to recognize commonly confused words and use the correct words and identify and use multi-word verbs in informal speech.*

1 Vocabulary: Commonly confused words

Presentation and Guided Practice I
20–25 minutes

1. Read the directions aloud. Say each underlined word in the chart and have students repeat.

2. Call on students to read the sentences aloud.

3. Set a time limit (three minutes). Direct students to work individually to complete the task.

4. Pair students to discuss differences in meaning.

5. Go over the answers with the class.

Answers

1. verb
   noun
2. verb
   preposition
3. adjective
   noun
4. verb
   noun

MULTILEVEL STRATEGIES

To adapt 1A:

- **Mixed-ability** Ask higher-level students to provide other examples of sentences for each word in 1A.

Communicative Practice
15–20 minutes

1. Read the directions aloud.

2. Set a time limit (three minutes). Direct students to work individually to complete the task.

3. Call on students to read the completed sentences aloud.

Answers
accept, personnel, effect, alternate, alternative, affect

1. Read the directions aloud. Say each word and have students repeat.

2. Put students in teams and assign roles: manager, fact checker, recorder, and reporter.

3. Set a time limit (three minutes). Direct students to work in teams to write sentences.

4. Call on reporters to read their sentences aloud.

TIP

Remind students to use suffixes as a way to identify parts of speech, which may help them distinguish between confusing words—for example, *conscience* has a noun ending, whereas *conscious* has an adjective ending.

EXTENSION ACTIVITY

Role Play

1. Pair students to create a conversation. Instruct students to use at least four words from Activity 1 in the conversation.

2. Call on students to perform their conversations for the class. Elicit the words each pair used and confirm that the usage was correct.

2 Grammar: Multi-word verbs

Presentation and Guided Practice II
20–25 minutes

1. Demonstrate how to read the chart. Read each sentence and have students repeat.

2. Check comprehension of the chart. Ask: *What follows each verb?* [one or more particles] Point out that particles look like prepositions or adverbs but function in a different way—they change the meaning of the verb.

3. Have students complete the paragraph in the Language Connection box about multi-word verbs. Go over the answers with the class.

Answers
is not, transitive, intransitive, cannot be, noun, pronoun

MULTILEVEL STRATEGIES

To adapt 2A:

• **On-level** Have students work independently.

• **Pre-level** Have higher-level classmates assist these students.

• **Higher-level** Have these students work with pre-level classmates.

TIP

To help students understand the function of a particle versus a preposition, write example sentences on the board: *1. Morale may go down quickly at this stage. 2. I often go down the stairs too fast. 3. Did you come up the stairs or the elevator? 4. Did you come up with a plan?* Elicit the difference in meaning between the multi-word verbs and the verbs + prepositions.

Guided Practice III
20–25 minutes

 1. Read the directions aloud.

2. Ask students to work individually to complete the task and then compare answers with a partner.

3. Call on students to give the answers.

Answers	
1. f	5. d
2. c	6. g
3. b	7. e
4. a	

TIP

Write the first sentence on the board. Elicit other ways to say the same thing with softer language and write them. Then ask students which version they think is best and why.

 1. Read the directions aloud.

2. Set a time limit (five minutes). Direct students to work individually to complete the task.

3. Go over the answers as a class.

Answers
1. call off
2. come up with
3. turn down
4. go back
5. let go of

MULTILEVEL STRATEGIES

To adapt 2C:

• **On-level** Have students work independently.

• **Pre-level** Group pre-level students to complete the task together.

• **Higher-level** Direct students to write one additional sentence for each multi-word verb.

D 1. Read the directions aloud.

2. Set a time limit (five minutes) for students to complete the task.

3. Call on volunteers to read their conversations to the class. Correct as needed.

MULTILEVEL STRATEGIES

To adapt 2C:

• **On-level** Tell students to use three to five multi-word verbs.

• **Pre-level** Tell students to use at least two multi-word verbs.

• **Higher-level** Tell students to use at least five multi-word verbs.

EXTENSION ACTIVITY

Challenge

Have students close their books. Call on students to challenge classmates. The first student says a sentence with a multi-word verb and calls on a classmate. The second student repeats the sentence with a formal synonym. For extra challenge, encourage students to use commonly confused words.

Evaluation
10–15 minutes

SELF-ASSESSMENT

1. Have students complete the self-assessment.

2. Provide additional practice as needed.

Lesson Overview

MULTILEVEL OBJECTIVES

On-level and Pre-level: Listen for phrases that signal opinions or express hedging; read and discuss attitudes toward innovation

Higher-level: Listen for phrases that signal opinions or express hedging; read, discuss and synthesize information about attitudes toward innovation

LANGUAGE FOCUS

Grammar: Passive

Vocabulary: *advise, debate, resistance, accelerate, bolster, backlash, shortcomings, novelty, fad, flop, catastrophically collapse*

For vocabulary support, see these **Oxford Picture Dictionary** topics: Feelings, pages 42–43; World History, page 209

STRATEGY FOCUS

Recognize connectors used to introduce differing opinions.

READINESS CONNECTION

In this lesson, students work together to offer ways to foster acceptance of a new workplace technology.

PACING

To compress this lesson: Assign 2B and/or 2C for homework.

To extend this lesson: Have students role-play a work situation involving change (see page 228).

And/or have students complete **Multilevel Activities 5 Unit 10, Lesson 4.**

Lesson Notes

CORRELATIONS

CCRS: RI/RL.7.1 Cite several pieces of textual evidence to support analysis of what the text says explicitly as well as inferences drawn from the text.

RI/RL.6.4 Determine the meaning of words and phrases as they are used in a text, including figurative, connotative, and technical meanings; analyze the impact of a specific word choice on meaning and tone.

RI.6.7 Integrate information presented in different media or formats (e.g., in charts, graphs, photographs, videos, or maps) as well as in words to develop a coherent understanding of a topic or issue.

RI.8.8 Delineate and evaluate the argument and specific claims in a text, assessing whether the reasoning is sound and the evidence is relevant and sufficient; recognize when irrelevant evidence is introduced.

W.7.7 Conduct short research projects to answer a question, drawing on several sources and generating additional related, focused questions for further research and investigation.

SL.8.1.a. Come to discussions prepared, having read or researched material under study; explicitly draw on that preparation by referring to evidence on the topic, text, or issue to probe and reflect on ideas under discussion.

SL.8.1.c. Pose questions that connect the ideas of several speakers and respond to others' questions and comments with relevant evidence, observations, and ideas.

SL.8.1.d. Acknowledge new information expressed by others, and, when warranted, qualify or justify their own views in light of the evidence presented.

SL.8.4 Present claims and findings, emphasizing salient points in a focused, coherent manner with relevant evidence, sound valid reasoning, and well-chosen details; use appropriate eye contact, adequate volume, and clear pronunciation.

L.6.4.a. Use context (e.g., the overall meaning of a sentence or paragraph; a word's position or function in a sentence) as a clue to the meaning of a word or phrase.

L.6.4.c. Consult reference materials (e.g., dictionaries, glossaries, thesauruses), both print and digital, to find the pronunciation of a word or determine or clarify its precise meaning or its part of speech.

L.6.4.d. Verify the preliminary determination of the meaning of a word or phrase (e.g., by checking the inferred meaning in context or in a dictionary).

L.8.6 Acquire and use accurately level-appropriate general academic and domain-specific words and phrases; gather vocabulary knowledge when considering a word or phrase important to comprehension or expression.

ELPS: ELP Standard 1

use a wide range of strategies to:

- determine central ideas or themes in oral presentations and spoken and written texts
- cite specific details and evidence from texts to support the analysis

ELP Standard 2

- participate in conversations, extended discussions, and written exchanges about a range of substantive topics, texts, and issues
- build on the ideas of others
- express his or her own ideas clearly and persuasively
- refer to specific and relevant evidence from texts or research to support his or her ideas
- ask and answer questions that probe reasoning and claims

ELP Standard 5

- carry out both short and more sustained research projects to answer a question or solve a problem

ELP Standard 6

- analyze and evaluate the reasoning in persuasive spoken and written texts
- determine whether the evidence is sufficient to support the claim
- cite specific textual evidence to thoroughly support the analysis

ELP Standard 7

- adapt language choices and style according to purpose, task, and audience with ease in various social and academic contexts
- use a wide variety of complex general academic and content specific words and phrases
- employ both formal and more informal styles and tones effectively in spoken and written texts, as appropriate

ELP Standard 8

using context, questioning, and consistent knowledge of English morphology,

- determine the meaning of general academic and content-specific words and phrases, figurative and connotative language, and idiomatic expressions in spoken and written texts about a variety of topics, experiences, or events

Warm-up and Review
10–15 minutes (books closed)

Write *Innovations* on the board. Explain or elicit that an innovation is a new method, idea, or product. It also refers to the process of creating something new. Pair students to brainstorm innovations throughout history. Encourage students to think back to prehistoric times and list innovations over the time since then. Set a time limit (five minutes). Elicit ideas and write them on the board.

Introduction
5 minutes

1. Say: *People have been innovating since the dawn of time. Think about cooking over fire or the invention of the wheel. Innovation changes our lives, but it isn't always easy or comfortable.*

2. State the objective: *Today we will listen for phrases that signal opinions or express hedging and read and discuss attitudes toward innovation.*

1 Get ready to read

Presentation I
20–25 minutes

A  1. Say: *Now we're going to listen to a conversation.* Read the directions aloud.

2. Play the audio. Direct students to answer the question.

Possible Answer
They're discussing drones creating problems for firefighting and then, in general, possible problems of new technologies.

B  1. Say the expressions and have students repeat.

2. Replay the audio. Ask students to check the expressions.

3. Check answers with the class.

Answers
My impression is that... From my perspective... As far as I'm concerned... I guess you're right. That's one way of looking at it.

Help students understand the differences between the phrases. Tell students to reread the expressions for giving opinions. Ask: *Which is the most direct?* [*In my view...*] *Which is the least direct, or the most polite?* [*I see your point, but the way I see it...*] *Which do you think is the softest,* impression, perspective, or point? [probably *impression*] Direct students to reread the expressions for hedging and rank them in terms of politeness or formality. [*If you say so* is the least polite. *You could be right* is probably the most polite.]

C 1. Read the directions aloud.

2. Group students and assign roles: manager, fact checker, recorder, and reporter. Check comprehension of tasks. Ask: *Who keeps the team on task and on time?* [manager] *Who takes notes?* [recorder] *Who looks up information or unfamiliar words?* [fact checker] *Who reports to the class?* [reporter] Students will work in these teams for 1C, 2D, 3B, and 3C.

3. Set a time limit (three minutes) and have students work together to complete the task.

4. Call time and have the reporters from each group take turns calling out their ideas.

Answers
Answers will vary.

MULTILEVEL STRATEGIES

To adapt 1C:

• **On-level** Assign these students the roles of recorder and manager.

• **Pre-level** Assign these students the role of reporter.

• **Higher-level** Assign these students the role of fact checker.

2 Preview and read

Guided Practice I
20–25 minutes

A 1. Read the directions aloud. Ask: *What information are you scanning for?* [the source for ideas and arguments]

2. Have students answer the question individually, and then check answers as a class.

Answers
a book titled *Innovation and Its Enemies: Why People Resist New Technologies* by Calestous Juma and reasons for human opposition to innovation

Ask: *What is the title?* [*Why Do People Resist Innovation?*] *What will the article focus on?* [reasons] *Do you think the title is interesting? Why or why not?* Tell students to look at the photo. Ask: *What do you see?* [a farmer plowing a field with horses] *What innovation is being resisted in the photo?* [using mechanical plows instead of horses with a plow to plant crops] *Why might people prefer to use the horse and plow rather than the new mechanical plow?* [the expense, lack of knowledge/experience, some people might lose jobs]

B 1. Ask students to read the article silently and answer the questions and then compare answers with a partner.

2. Check the answers as a class.

Possible Answers
because they fear loss; It's important to understand resistance because new technologies may benefit society.

MULTILEVEL STRATEGIES

To adapt 2B:

• **Pre-level** Work with pre-level students to read the article aloud. Stop after each paragraph and check comprehension.

• **On-level** Have students complete the activity as directed.

• **Higher-level** Direct students to underline the main idea and/or write the main idea of the article in a statement using their own words.

Presentation II
20–25 minutes

C 1. Read the directions aloud. Call on students to read the questions aloud.

2. Set a time limit (five minutes) and have students work individually to complete the task.

3. Call time. Have students compare answers
in pairs.

4. Go over the answers with the class. Call
on students to cite the text to explain their
answers.

> **Possible Answers**
>
> 1. People have resisted new technology even
> when it could benefit them.
> 2. They resist because of fear of loss of identity,
> income, power or traditional way of life.
> 3. People who depended on the land for food
> and money resisted farm machinery because
> they knew it would change their way of life.
> 4. It was banned at different times in different
> places based on emotion rather than actual
> evidence.
> 5. If people feel that benefits will only be felt
> by a small part of society, but risks could have
> an impact on a larger part of society, they are
> more likely to resist.
> 6. If people feel risks will be felt in short term,
> but benefits will only come later, they will resist
> more. If the underlying loss isn't addressed,
> people are more likely to resist.
> 7. The article states that he recognizes the need
> for adequate research, so he probably supports
> extensive testing of new technologies.
> 8. First, make sure that safety and security are
> addressed, and then consider the potential loss
> that people will experience with the innovation
> and address that.

> **MULTILEVEL STRATEGIES**
>
> To adapt 2B:
>
> • **Pre-level and higher-level** Pair a pre-level
> student with a higher-level student to answer
> the questions. Tell higher-level students to help
> pre-level students find the place in the text that
> answers each question.
>
> • **On-level** Have students complete the activity
> individually.

WORD STUDY

D 1. Read the directions and prompts aloud.

2. Set a time limit (five minutes). Have
students work in their teams to follow the
steps.

3. Elicit the definitions. Ask volunteers to write
sentences on the board.

> **Answers**
>
> Answers may vary.
> *Accelerate* means "to happen or to make
> something happen faster or earlier than
> expected."
> *Bolster* means "to improve something or make
> it stronger."
> A *backlash* is a strong negative reaction by
> a large number of people—for example, to
> something that has recently changed in society.

3 Build on it

Presentation I
20–25 minutes

A 1. Have students look at the photos. Ask: *What
do you see?* [cars in traffic, people watching
sports on a big-screen TV, people texting]

2. Direct students' attention to the quotes. Call
on students to read them aloud.

3. Read the directions and questions aloud.

4. Set a time limit (five minutes). Have
students work in pairs to complete the activity.

5. Call on students to share their ideas with
the class.

> **Answers**
>
> 1. Shortcomings are faults or things that are
> wrong with something.
> A novelty is something that is interesting only
> because it is new.
> A fad is something that is temporarily popular.
> If something flops, it fails.
> If something catastrophically collapses, it fails
> terribly.
> 2. All of these terms were used to suggest that
> new technologies would fail even if they were
> popular initially.

B 1. Have students rejoin their teams with the
same roles.

2. Read the directions and the prompts.

3. Set a time limit (ten minutes). Students
work in teams to complete the task.

4. Call on reporters to share their team's ideas.

> **Answers**
>
> Answers will vary.

C 1. Ask students to stay in their teams with the same roles.

2. Read the directions aloud.

3. Tell students to read the email. Check comprehension. Ask: *What is the problem?* [employees won't use a software program] *Why is Zach writing to Sheila?* [he wants advice]

4. Set a time limit (ten minutes) and have students work together to discuss solutions and their possible consequences.

5. Call time. Ask each team to join another and share ideas.

6. Call on reporters to share their ideas with the class.

Answers
Answers will vary.

D 1. Set a time limit (five minutes) for students to write their conversation with a partner.

2. Ask volunteers to read out their conversation.

EXTENSION ACTIVITY
Role Play
1. Pair students to create role plays for this work situation or another one that involves change.
2. Set a time limit (five minutes). Remind pairs to use what they have learned from the article.
3. Call on volunteers to role-play for the class.

Evaluation
10–15 minutes

SELF-ASSESSMENT

1. Direct students to complete the self-assessment individually.

2. Have students choose the one objective they have the most difficulty with.

3. Group students according to their weakest skill. Provide each group with suggestions or feedback.

Lesson Overview

| Lesson Notes |

MULTILEVEL OBJECTIVES

On-level: Use the writing process to summarize an article

Pre-level: Work with others to summarize an article

Higher-level: Summarize an article using examples of commonly confused words

LANGUAGE FOCUS

Grammar: Multi-word verbs

Vocabulary: *proponent, opponent, premise, resistance, intensify,* expressions for cause and effect

For vocabulary support, see this **Oxford Picture Dictionary** topic: English Composition, pages 202–203

STRATEGY FOCUS

Use expressions for cause and effect.

PACING

To compress this lesson: Assign Activity 1 (A–E) for homework.

To extend this lesson: Have students write a paragraph about the best ways to deal with change (see page 231). And/or have students complete **Multilevel Activities 5 Unit 10, Lesson 5.**

CORRELATIONS

CCRS: W/WHST.6-8.2.a. Introduce a topic clearly, previewing what is to follow; organize ideas, concepts, and information, using strategies such as definition, classification, comparison /contrast, and cause/effect; include formatting (e.g., headings), graphics (e.g., charts, tables), and multimedia when useful to aiding comprehension.

W/WHST.6-8.2.b. Develop the topic with relevant facts, definitions, concrete details, quotations, or other information and examples.

W/WHST.6-8.2.c. Use appropriate transitions to create cohesion and clarify the relationships among ideas and concepts.

W/WHST.6-8.2.d. Use precise language and domain-specific vocabulary to inform about or explain the topic.

W/WHST.6-8.2.f. Provide a concluding statement or section that follows from and supports the information or explanation presented.

W/WHST.6-8.4 Produce clear and coherent writing in which the development and organization and style are appropriate to task, purpose, and audience.

W/WHST.6-8.5 With some guidance and support from peers and others, develop and strengthen writing as needed by planning, revising, editing, rewriting, or trying a new approach, focusing on how well purpose and audience have been addressed.

L.6.3/7.3.c. Choose language that expresses ideas precisely and concisely, recognizing and eliminating wordiness and redundancy.

L.8.6 Acquire and use accurately level-appropriate general academic and domain-specific words and phrases; gather vocabulary knowledge when considering a word or phrase important to comprehension or expression.

ELPS: ELP Standard 7

- adapt language choices and style according to purpose, task, and audience with ease in various social and academic contexts
- use a wide variety of complex general academic and content specific words and phrases
- employ both formal and more informal styles and tones effectively in spoken and written texts, as appropriate.

ELP Standard 9

- recount a complex and detailed sequence of events or steps in a process, with an effective sequential or chronological order
- introduce and effectively develop an informational topic with facts, details, and evidence
- use complex and varied transitions to link the major sections of speech and text and to clarify relationships among events and ideas
- provide a concluding section or statement.

ELP Standard 10

- produce and expand simple, compound, and complex sentences

Warm-up and Review
10–15 minutes (books closed)

Look for articles in the news about changes in your community, your country, or the world. Pair students to brainstorm positive and negative results of those changes. Call on students to share their ideas with the class.

Introduction
5 minutes

State the objective: *Today we will use the writing process to summarize an article.*

1 Write a summary

Presentation I
20–25 minutes

 1. Have students revisit the article on pages 114–115. Check comprehension. Ask: *What is the article about? What are the most important ideas?*

2. Elicit responses and jot them on the board.

TIP

Remind students that the main idea can often be found in the introduction and in the conclusion. Suggest students reread those paragraphs and find ideas that are repeated in both.

Guided Practice I
15–20 minutes

B 1. Direct students to look at the chart. Ask about organization: *How many rows do you see?* [six] Direct students' attention to the article. Ask: *How many paragraphs are there?* [five] Point out that the last paragraph provides information for the last two rows.

2. Check comprehension of the activity. Ask: *Do you need to write complete sentences in the chart?* [no]

3. Have students work individually to complete their charts.

Answers

Book title and author: *Innovation and Its Enemies: Why People Resist New Technologies* by Calestous Juma	What the book is about: chronicles history of human opposition to innovation over 600 years and considers reasons for that
Reasons for resistance: fear loss (identity, income, power, or way of life)	Example: mechanical farm equipment—people who grew food to live or for money resisted it b/c they knew would change way of life
Proponent and opponent claims: both make claims to support their arguments but not always based on fact, actual evidence. Based on emotion, e.g., fear	Example: coffee—banned different times, places for different reasons, e.g., "caused hysteria"

Reactions intensify if:
• public believes only small part of society benefits, but risk for larger part (e.g., large corporations pushing innovation) • public feels risks will be felt in short term, but benefits only come later • giving scientific evidence w/out addressing underlying loss—less likely successful
Important to understand because: • resistance could mean society doesn't benefit from new tech that could help environmental, economic, health challenges
Safety & security: • Need this, esp with speed of innovation and new tech, e.g., robotics, AI, gene editing

C 1. Read the directions aloud.

2. Have students work individually to write their statements. Then ask students to compare statements in pairs.

D 1. Read the directions aloud.

2. Have students work individually to write their conclusions.

TIP

Suggest that students practice the strategy of using synonyms to write the conclusion in their own words.

1. Read the directions aloud. Check comprehension. Ask: *What will you include in your summary?* [introduction, notes from the chart, conclusion]

2. Draw students' attention to the Writer's Note. Ask: *Which expressions introduce causes?* [*The reason X happened was…, One cause of this was…, The main cause was…*] *Which introduce effects?* [*This explains why…, If X hadn't happened…, One effect was…, Another result was…*]

3. Have students work individually to write their summaries.

> **MULTILEVEL STRATEGIES**
>
> To adapt 1E:
>
> • **On-level** Have students write summaries as directed.
>
> • **Pre-level** Work with students in a group to write the summary together.
>
> • **Higher-level** Have students write the summary in two different ways using synonyms.

2 Get feedback and revise

Guided Practice II
10–15 minutes

A Direct students to check their writing using the editing checklist. Tell them to read each item in the list and check their papers before moving on to the next item. Explain that students should not edit their writing at this stage. They should just use the checklist to check their work and mark any areas they want to revise.

Communicative Practice
10–15 minutes

B 1. Read the directions aloud. Emphasize to students that they are responding to their partners' work, not correcting it.

2. Direct students to exchange papers with a partner and follow the instructions.

C Allow students time to edit and revise their writing using the editing checklist and their partner's feedback. If necessary, students could complete this task as homework.

> **MULTILEVEL STRATEGIES**
>
> To adapt 2C:
>
> • **Mixed-ability** Pair pre-level students with on- and higher-level students. Have all students point out ideas that are not clear. Instruct on- and higher-level partners to give feedback on spelling and grammar if helpful.

> **EXTENSION ACTIVITY**
>
> **Paragraph Practice**
>
> 1. Have students write a paragraph about a change, how people responded, and any positive or negative effects.
>
> 2. Pair students to exchange and read their paragraphs.

Evaluation
10–15 minutes

SELF-ASSESSMENT

1. Call on students to read their sentences aloud.

2. Use the responses to the second statement to plan follow-up activities.

<table>
<tr><td>

Lesson Overview

MULTILEVEL OBJECTIVES

On-level and Higher-level: Students prepare for and conduct a debate on artificial intelligence (AI)

Pre-level: Students help prepare for and conduct a debate on artificial intelligence (AI)

LANGUAGE FOCUS

Grammar: Multi-word verbs

Vocabulary: Words related to change, causes and effects, advantages and disadvantages

For vocabulary support, see this **Oxford Picture Dictionary** topic: Internet Research, pages 212–213

STRATEGY FOCUS

Open the floor to questions.

READINESS CONNECTION

In this lesson, students work in teams to debate the use of artificial intelligence.

PACING

To compress this lesson: Assign 1B for homework.

To extend this lesson: Have students debrief in pairs on the ways they have changed (see page 234).

And/or have students complete **Multilevel Activities 5 Unit 10, Lesson 6.**

</td><td>

Lesson Notes

</td></tr>
</table>

CORRELATIONS

CCRS: W.7.7 Conduct short research projects to answer a question, drawing on several sources and generating additional related, focused questions for further research and investigation.

W.7.8 Gather relevant information from multiple print and digital sources, using search terms effectively; assess the credibility and accuracy of each source; and quote or paraphrase the data and conclusions of others while avoiding plagiarism and following a standard format for citation.

SL.8.4 Present claims and findings, emphasizing salient points in a focused, coherent manner with relevant evidence, sound valid reasoning, and well-chosen details; use appropriate eye contact, adequate volume, and clear pronunciation.

SL.8.6 Adapt speech to a variety of contexts and tasks, demonstrating command of formal English when indicated or appropriate.

L.6.3/7.3.b. Maintain consistency in style and tone.

L.6.3/7.3.c. Choose language that expresses ideas precisely and concisely, recognizing and eliminating wordiness and redundancy.

L.8.6 Acquire and use accurately level-appropriate general academic and domain-specific words and phrases; gather vocabulary knowledge when considering a word or phrase important to comprehension or expression.

ELPS: ELP Standard 2

- participate in conversations, extended discussions, and written exchanges about a range of substantive topics, texts, and issues
- build on the ideas of others
- express his or her own ideas clearly and persuasively
- summarize the key points and evidence discussed

ELP Standard 3

- deliver oral presentations
- compose written informational texts
- fully develop the topic with relevant details, concepts, examples, and information
- integrate graphics or multimedia when useful about a variety of texts, topics, or events

<table>
<tr>
<td>

ELP Standard 5

- carry out both short and more sustained research projects to answer a question or solve a problem
- gather information from multiple print and digital sources
- use advanced search terms effectively
- synthesize information from multiple print and digital sources
- analyze and integrate information into clearly organized spoken and written texts
- include illustrations, diagrams, or other graphics as appropriate
- cite sources appropriately

</td>
<td>

ELP Standard 6

- analyze and evaluate the reasoning in persuasive spoken and written texts
- determine whether the evidence is sufficient to support the claim
- cite specific textual evidence to thoroughly support the analysis

ELP Standard 7

- adapt language choices and style according to purpose, task, and audience with ease in various social and academic contexts
- use a wide variety of complex general academic and content specific words and phrases
- employ both formal and more informal styles and tones effectively in spoken and written texts, as appropriate

</td>
</tr>
</table>

Warm-up and Review
10–15 minutes (books closed)

Write *Artificial intelligence* on the board. Brainstorm a list of all the applications of artificial intelligence that students know about and write them on the board. Categorize the various applications (for example, manufacturing, navigation, personal assistance, entertainment).

Introduction
5 minutes

1. Say: *Artificial intelligence is being used in many ways in our everyday lives.*

2. State the objective: *Today we will prepare for and conduct a debate on artificial intelligence (AI).*

1 Research artificial intelligence (AI)

Communicative Practice
40–45 minutes

1. Group students. Tell students that they will work with members of their team to divide into sides.

2. Read the directions aloud.

3. Direct students' attention to the Research Tip. Ask: *What are* pros? [arguments for something or positive points] *What are* cons? [arguments against something or negative points]

4. Set a time limit (three minutes) and have students decide which members will argue for artificial intelligence and which will argue against it.

To adapt 1A:

- **Mixed-ability** Make sure a higher-level or on-level student is on each side to work with any pre-level students.

B 1. Read the directions aloud.

2. Check comprehension of the task. Ask: *Can you quote someone in your debate?* [yes] *What do you need to do if you want to quote?* [use the exact words and give a source]

3. Set a time limit or assign research as an out-of-class task.

C 1. Have students share their research with team members who are arguing the same side.

2. Read the directions and prompts.

3. Set a time limit (15 minutes) and have students work together to follow the steps.

2 Present your research

Presentation
40–45 minutes

A

1. Have students stay with other team members on their side. Read the directions and steps.

2. Ask: *What do you do in the introduction?* [give an overview of your argument] *When do you give examples or quotes?* [in the body to support specific arguments] *What two things should you do in your conclusion?* [summarize arguments and restate your side's overall opinion]

3. Set a time limit (10 to 15 minutes) and have students work with their sides to plan their debate.

B

1. Read the directions aloud.

2. Set a time limit (two minutes). Elicit who will do which part.

C

1. Read the directions and list aloud.

2. Check comprehension of the activity. Ask: *How can you convey confidence?* [stand tall and project your voice] *What kind of language do you think is persuasive?* Elicit examples.

3. Direct students' attention to the Presentation Strategy. Ask: *What does it mean to* open the floor? [invite/allow the audience to speak] *What are some ways to open the floor?* [Do you have any questions? Is there anything you'd like to know more about? Do you understand our arguments? What do you think?]

4. Set a time limit (ten minutes) and have students rehearse their side of the debate.

D

1. Draw a chart on the board, listing the teams in the first column. In the other columns, list the note-taking prompts, or shortened forms of them: *Strengths/weaknesses, Persuasive, Questions/clarification, Final opinion, Advice.* Remind students to just use words and phrases in the chart.

2. Set a time limit (five minutes) for each debate, and ask each team to present in turn.

E

1. Have each team discuss their feedback for the other teams. Ask each team to nominate a reporter to give feedback on the other teams' debates.

2. Beginning with the first team to present, collect feedback from the reporters. Write feedback in the table you drew on the board in 2D.

Evaluation
10–15 minutes

SELF-ASSESSMENT

1. Pair students to share their self-assessments.

2. Elicit suggestions from the class for developing more confidence in each of the three assessment areas.